# kitchen

# acknowledgments

A heartfelt thanks to Kay Scarlett and Juliet Rogers for being brave enough to tackle another book with me, especially when a simple book grew to enormous proportions. Thanks also to Jackie Frank for giving me the opportunity to see the project through. A huge thank you also to Marylouise Brammer for all her hard work with the design. Margaret Malone probably deserves a sainthood for her tireless work and enthusiasm in editing such a monster. I owe you several stiff drinks when we finally say farewell to the words which have bounced between us for months. Indeed, a big thank you to the whole team at Murdoch Books.

The studio was once again a time for friends to get together and work on a project for what always seems like an endless number of days. A big hug to Jo Glynn for all her hard work in the kitchen, and to Ross Dobson for making a star appearance at the end of the shoot. To Petrina Hicks for her attention to detail in the studio, raising the bar for photography assistants to an impossible height. A big thank you to Margot Braddon for all your running around in search of interesting kitchen paraphernalia, and to Marcus Hay for some beautiful rooms.

As always, this book would not have been possible without Petrina Tinslay. This is our fourth book together, so I'm fast running out of superlatives that encompass the debt I owe. However, thank you for your beautiful images, your friendship and your calm patience in the face of a huge workload, miles of film and the occasional crying baby. For a while your studio felt like our second home.

Another unpayable debt of gratitude goes to Warwick who provides love, laughter and, for the last six months, distracting and comforting arms for Sam, whose mother was often too busy by the stove or at the computer. I couldn't have done it without you. Thanks also to Warwick's family, especially sister Kate and Grandpa and Nanny Orme who, in Virginia Woolf's immortal words, helped me on many an occasion to have a room of my own when the deadline panic set in. Thanks to Ben and Sam for forgiving me my absences and to Mum and Dad for a lifetime's friendship and for always being there.

A book full of bowls and bits necessitates a heady list of thank yous. So thank you to Mark Conway for lovely enamelled pieces and Bison for their multi-coloured kitchenware. Thank you to Mud Australia and Dinosaur Designs for their delicate bowls and plates and Orson & Blake, The Bay Tree, Design Mode International and The Sydney Antique Centre for bits and pieces. A big hug to David Edmonds for his generosity with his smoothly sublime ceramics. Thanks also to Smeg and Wheel & Barrow for the kitchen appliances and Marblo, Major and Tom, Sydney Countertop Fabrications, Thonet Australia and Worling Saunders for their help with benchtops, furniture and clothing.

This edition first published in Canada in 2004 by Whitecap Books, 351 Lynn Ave., North Vancouver, British Columbia, Canada, V7J 2C4.

www.whitecap.ca

First published by Murdoch Books®, a division of Murdoch Magazines Pty Ltd.

Author and stylist: Michele Cranston
Photographer: Petrina Tinslay
Creative director: Marylouise Brammer
Project manager: Margaret Malone
Designer: Jacqueline Duncan
Editor: Susin Chow
Food preparation: Jo Glynn and Ross Dobson
Extra styling: Marcus Hay (cover and pages 6–7, 182–3 and 208)

Chief executive: Juliet Rogers
Publisher: Kay Scarlett
Editorial director: Diana Hill
Production: Monika Vidovic

Printed by Toppan Printing Hong Kong Co. Ltd. PRINTED IN CHINA.

ISBN 1 55285 629 1

Note: We have used 20 ml tablespoon measures. If you are using a 15 ml tablespoon, for most recipes the difference will not be noticeable. However, for recipes using small amounts of flour and cornflour, add an extra teaspoon for each tablespoon specified.

Important: Those at risk from the effects of salmonella food poisoning (including the elderly, pregnant women and children) should consult their GP with any concerns about eating raw eggs.

# kitchen

the best of the best

michele cranston

photography by
petrina tinslay

whitecap

# contents

# keeping things simple

One of the great joys of life is eating, and for those who feel comfortable in the kitchen there is nothing more calming or satisfying than having a recipe book open, a shopping basket full of fresh ingredients and a sharp knife at the ready.

Peeling, slicing and dicing while whistling away to a favourite song may be an idyllic afternoon for some, but not all of us have our Doris Day moments over a bowl of ripe tomatoes. For many, the kitchen can be a battleground of rushed minutes and growing exasperation. It needn't be this way, of course. Keeping things simple, fresh and easy has always been the way I like to work and eat, and for most home cooks, *simplicity* is the best advice I can give. The key is to master a few classic techniques, buy good-quality food and invest in the occasional luxury cupboard item that will give an extra flavoursome twist to your food. Keep things simple during the week and if you want to spread your culinary wings, then do it with all the luxury that a weekend brings.

This book started its life as an essential guide to the kitchen. A work manual, if you like, to help you enjoy cooking for friends, family and, of course, yourself. But as I started thinking about the basics I started remembering some of our most popular recipes from the past. So, the book has become a double whammy — an essentials guide plus a greatest hits.

There are eight chapters: breakfast, kitchen bench, salads, summertime, afternoon tea, cocktails, dinner and desserts. Each chapter contains an 'inspiration' section, which is just that. It features basic step-by-step directions to everything from scrambled eggs to a golden roasted chicken or a rich vanilla ice cream; classic recipes that sum up a technique or method; and lots of great essential advice including hints and tips on how to extend or adapt recipes, how to play with ingredients or just plain cheat when time is not available or your spirit is flagging. Finally, each chapter ends with its recipes — the 'best of the best'. These are simply my favourites from the growing collection and all reflect my belief in fresh, fast and simple cooking. I've enjoyed putting this book together, and I hope it will bring an air of calm assurance to your kitchen and yummy flavours to your table.

# breakfast

Weekends are undoubtedly the best time to indulge in a good breakfast. The luxury of being in pyjamas at 9 a.m. is a thing to be celebrated. And what better way than with crunchy toast, the aroma of fresh coffee and mouth-watering options to tempt sleepy-heads?

# breakfast inspiration
gather the essentials around you:
## eggs and sides and
## fruit and coffee
then whisk, fry, bake,
scramble and slurp your way to
## breakfast heaven

Don't skimp on quality here — use
wonderful taste really does make

## scrambled egg basics

1 Put 2 eggs and 4 tablespoons cream into a bowl. Add a pinch of sea salt and whisk together.

2 Heat a nonstick pan over medium to high heat. Add 2 teaspoons butter and allow the butter to just melt over the surface of the pan. Add the egg mixture and let it cook until the egg is just beginning to set around the edges. Then, using a wooden spoon, fold the edges into the centre. If the egg is cooking too quickly, lower the heat slightly.

3 Continue cooking the egg in this way, gently folding in the egg as it begins to set. As soon as all the egg is set, remove the pan from the heat and spoon the egg onto a plate. Serve with hot toast and sides. Serves 1

### hints & tips

● The secret to great scrambled eggs is a good pan. If you are going to be cooking eggs often it is worth investing in a heavy-based nonstick pan. The egg will cook at a more even temperature and because it doesn't stick to the base of the pan, it is easier to fold.

● If cooking more than two serves of scrambled eggs, cook them in batches since too much mixture in the pan will cause the egg to overcook.

● Keep an eye on the 'best before' date of eggs when buying them to ensure that they are the freshest possible, and always use good-quality eggs such as free-range ones. If you can find them, organic or bio-dynamic eggs will remind you of how eggs should taste.

fresh organic or bio-dynamic eggs if you can. Their all the difference with such a simple dish

# classic eggs

## poached

For great poached eggs, really fresh eggs are essential. Fill a deep frying pan with about 5 cm (2 in) cold water. Add 1 teaspoon white wine vinegar and bring to a simmering boil. Crack an egg into a saucer and gently lower the egg into the water. Lower the heat and cook for 5 minutes. Remove the egg with a slotted spoon and drain on paper towels. Serve with wholemeal toast. Serves 1

## boiled

Take 2 eggs from the refrigerator and allow to come to room temperature. Fill a small saucepan with enough cold water to cover the eggs and bring it to the boil over high heat. When it has reached boiling point, reduce the heat to a rolling boil. Using a spoon, lower the eggs, one at a time, into the water. Boil for 5 minutes, then remove. If you prefer your eggs set firmly, then cook for a further 1 minute. Perch each egg in an egg cup and, with a sharp knife, crack off the top. Serve with sea salt, pepper and buttered toast soldiers. Serves 2

The key to great egg dishes is simplicity: just add

## fried

Put 2 tablespoons vegetable oil and 1 tablespoon butter in a heavy-based nonstick pan. Put the pan over medium to high heat and when the butter begins to sizzle, crack an egg and carefully break it into the pan. Reduce the heat to medium and cook for 1 minute, spooning some of the butter and oil over the yolk so that it cooks. Remove the pan from the heat and butter your toast. Using a spatula, remove the egg and serve with the toast. Season with sea salt and freshly ground black pepper. Serves 1

## baked

Preheat the oven to 180°C (350°F/Gas 4). Generously grease two 8 cm (3¹/₄ in) ramekins and put them in a roasting tin half-filled with water. Put 4 eggs into a small bowl and add 1 tablespoon finely chopped chives and 2 tablespoons finely grated Parmesan cheese. Whisk together and season with sea salt and ground white pepper. Divide the egg mixture between the two ramekins and bake for 15 minutes, or until the egg is cooked through. Serves 2

salt, pepper, creamy butter and crunchy bread.

# omelette basics

1 Separate 3 eggs. Whisk the egg whites until they form soft peaks, then lightly fold the egg yolks and whites together.

2 Heat a 25 cm (10 in) nonstick pan over medium heat and add 1 tablespoon butter. When the butter has melted and begins to sizzle, pour in the egg mixture. Using a spatula, fold the edges of the egg into the centre as it cooks.

3 When the egg is nearly cooked, flip one side of the omelette over the other and remove the pan from the heat. Gently slide the cooked omelette onto a plate and serve. Garnish with a salad of baby English spinach leaves and a sprinkling of fresh chives. Serves 1–2

## hints & tips

● If you wish to make a filled omelette, add some grated cheese, chopped herbs or sautéed mushrooms to the centre of the omelette just prior to folding the omelette in half.

● Depending on hunger levels, this omelette will feed one to two people. If you wish to feed more, cook the omelettes separately as a larger quantity in a single pan can be quite difficult to manage.

● Another easy kind of omelette is the 'in-the-pan' style. Whisk 3 eggs and pour the mixture into a warmed pan coated with melted butter. Cook over low heat until the egg is beginning to firm on the base, then sprinkle with some grated cheese and herbs. Cook under a hot grill (broiler) until the cheese is golden and the egg is cooked through. For a heartier version, add other ingredients such as crisp bacon or cooked mushrooms and baby English spinach leaves when you add the cheese.

# classic sides

## sautéed mushrooms

Slice 400 g (14 oz) Swiss brown mushrooms and put them in a pan with 2 tablespoons butter, 1 finely chopped garlic clove and a little sea salt. Heat over medium heat and when the butter begins to sizzle, cover with a lid and reduce the heat to low. Cook for 10 minutes, then remove from the heat. Season with freshly ground black pepper before serving. Serves 4 as a side dish

## baked beans

Soak 500 g (1 lb 2 oz/2$^1$/2 cups) haricot beans in water overnight. Preheat the oven to 180°C (350°F/Gas 4). Combine a 400 g (14 oz) tin crushed tomatoes, 3 tablespoons molasses, 3 tablespoons soft brown sugar, 1 teaspoon mustard powder, 750 ml (26 fl oz/3 cups) water, 1 tablespoon sea salt and a generous grind of black pepper in a medium saucepan. Bring to the boil and stir until the sugar has dissolved. Remove from the heat and set aside. Finely slice 3 rashers of bacon and put them into a large casserole dish. Drain the beans and add them to the dish. Add the tomato mixture, stir to combine and then cover. Bake for 6 hours. Check every hour to ensure there is enough liquid around the beans and add water if necessary. Serves 8–10 as a side dish

## sautéed spinach

Rinse 500 g (1 lb 2 oz/1 bunch) English spinach under running water. Remove the stalks and roots and roughly chop the leaves. Heat 1 tablespoon butter in a large pan over medium heat and add the chopped spinach. Cover with a lid and cook for 2 minutes. Remove from the heat. Season with sea salt and freshly ground black pepper before serving. Serves 4 as a side dish

## oven-roasted tomatoes

Preheat the oven to 180°C (350°F/Gas 4). Slice 2 Roma (plum) tomatoes in half lengthways and put them on a baking tray lined with baking paper. Scatter with thyme sprigs and season liberally with sea salt and freshly ground black pepper. Drizzle with a little extra virgin olive oil, then bake for 40 minutes. Serves 2 as a side dish

# toasted essentials

Sometimes the simplest things in life really are the most satisfying. How else to explain that after years of cooking with varied ingredients I still gain great pleasure from that simplest of dishes — crisp, warm, buttery toast. Throw in a few sides — succulent mushrooms, rich oven-roasted tomatoes or juicy ham — and you've got breakfast to tempt even the sleepiest of tastebuds.

But with the range of breads available these days, even this simple meal is complicated by choice. There is fruit loaf, wholemeal, sourdough and grainy bread, focaccia, brioche, Turkish bread and all the gluten-free forms — the selection is as varied as the toppings available.

## more than just toast

Everyone has their preferred method of ensuring their toast is just right — here are some other ideas for a fast and flavoursome breakfast:

- Toast Turkish bread and top it with fresh ricotta cheese drizzled with honey and sprinkled with a little cinnamon. Serve sliced banana or fresh peaches on the side.

- Toast a thick slice of brioche and top it with a dollop of Greek-style yoghurt and stewed fruit. Sprinkle with a little icing (confectioners') sugar.

- Serve toasted grain bread with hot baked beans, grated Cheddar cheese and some rocket (arugula) leaves.

- Serve toasted fruit bread with a dollop of Greek-style yoghurt and stewed rhubarb (page 27).

- Mash avocado onto wholemeal bread with a squeeze of lemon juice and lots of freshly ground black pepper — this is an all-time classic.

- For a taste that is fresh and savoury, put thin slices of tomato on sourdough bread, add a drizzle of extra virgin olive oil, season with sea salt and pepper and scatter over torn basil leaves. For a slightly more substantial meal, add slices of avocado or thick slices of cheese.

- Top toasted grain bread with slices of banana, squeeze over a little lemon juice and sprinkle with soft brown sugar.

- Blend a little ground cinnamon and soft brown sugar with softened unsalted butter, spread over toasted brioche and grill (broil) until the butter begins to bubble. Serve with fresh berries.

## substantial starters

If you are in need of a hearty start to the day or are looking for winning Sunday brunch ideas, then try some of these toasted favourites:

- Pile oven-roasted tomatoes onto toasted bread and add sliced Cheddar cheese. Grill (broil) until the cheese starts to bubble, then serve with crispy bacon. Or team the tomatoes with ricotta cheese, a spoonful of tapenade or black olive paste and serve with toasted wholemeal bread.

- Toast wholemeal bread and top with slices of leg ham and sautéed mushrooms, spoon over the buttery pan juices from the mushrooms and serve with fresh baby English spinach leaves.

- Top a slice of toasted wholemeal bread with some sautéed spinach. Cover with a slice of Emmenthal cheese and grill (broil) until the cheese is beginning to melt. Serve with a scattering of cracked pepper.

- Top a square of focaccia with some thin slices of salami, provolone cheese, marinated artichoke hearts and thin slices of tomato, then grill (broil) until the cheese has melted. Drizzle with a little extra virgin olive oil — the classic focaccia.

- Put slices of leg ham and Gruyère cheese in between two thin slices of sourdough bread. Butter the outsides of the bread and pan-fry over low heat until the sandwiches are golden brown and the cheese is golden and melting. Serve with fruit chutney.

- For the much-loved BLT, toast two slices of plain white or sourdough bread, slather the bread with mayonnaise and then fill with crispy bacon, thin slices of tomato and shredded iceberg lettuce. Serve with a bloody or virgin Mary for a great recovery meal.

- While we're in recovery mode, here's my all-time favourite pick-me-up. Take a thick slice of sourdough bread and cut a hole in the centre. Fry the bread in a little olive oil then break an egg into the hole. When the egg starts to cook and the underside of the bread is golden brown, flip the whole thing over and cook until golden brown on the other side. Serve with a little sweet chilli sauce for a fry-up with a kick.

# classic grains

## sweet couscous

Put 175 g (6 oz/1 cup) couscous into a saucepan with
3 teaspoons honey and 500 ml (17 fl oz/2 cups) boiling
water. Cover and cook over low heat for 5 minutes, or until
all the liquid has been absorbed. Fluff the couscous with a
fork, then cover again and remove from the heat. Allow to sit
for 10 minutes, then add 1/2 teaspoon ground cinnamon,
1 teaspoon finely grated orange zest, 3 tablespoons currants
and 3 tablespoons toasted flaked almonds. Toss to combine
and serve with plain yoghurt. Serves 4

## bircher muesli

Put 200 g (7 oz/2 cups) rolled oats and 250 ml (9 fl oz/
1 cup) apple juice into a bowl and soak for at least 1 hour
or overnight. Grate 2 green apples and add them to the
soaked oats with 125 g (41/2 oz/1/2 cup) plain yoghurt and
1/2 teaspoon ground cinnamon. Mix well and serve with fresh
berries or stewed rhubarb (page 27). Serves 4

## sticky black rice

Soak 200 g (7 oz/1 cup) black rice in plenty of cold water for 1 hour. Drain, then rinse. Drain again and put into a saucepan with 500 ml (17 fl oz/2 cups) water. Bring to the boil, stirring occasionally, then reduce the heat to low, cover with a lid and allow to simmer for 35 minutes. Remove the lid and stir through 4 tablespoons soft brown sugar or grated palm sugar, a pinch of salt and 125 ml (4 fl oz/$^{1}/_{2}$ cup) coconut milk. Simmer over low heat for a further 10 minutes, then remove and allow to cool. Serve spooned over sliced red papaya or banana and drizzle with coconut milk. Serves 4

## honey-toasted fruit muesli

Preheat the oven to 150°C (300°F/Gas 2). Put 500 g (1 lb 2 oz/5 cups) rolled oats into a large bowl. Add 125 g (4$^{1}/_{2}$ oz/1 cup) unsalted sunflower seeds, 125 g (4$^{1}/_{2}$ oz/ 1 cup) slivered almonds, 100 g (3$^{1}/_{2}$ oz/1 cup) triticale, 60 g (2$^{1}/_{4}$ oz/1 cup) shredded coconut and 2 tablespoons sesame seeds. Stir to combine. Heat 250 g (9 oz/$^{3}/_{4}$ cup) honey and 4 tablespoons vegetable oil in a saucepan over low heat. Pour the warm honey mixture over the dry ingredients and stir until they are well coated. Spread the mixture on a baking tray and bake for 30 minutes, stirring occasionally. Remove from the oven and allow to cool. Add 50 g (1$^{3}/_{4}$ oz/$^{1}/_{4}$ cup) finely sliced dried apricots, 25 g (1 oz/$^{1}/_{4}$ cup) finely sliced dried apples and 50 g (1$^{3}/_{4}$ oz/ $^{1}/_{4}$ cup) finely sliced dried peaches. Toss to combine. Store the muesli in an airtight container. Makes 12 serves

# healthy essentials

If you like to start your day on a light note, then there is no better beginning than fresh fruit. Add the nutritional bonus of grains and you'll be bouncing through your day.

For fruit, stick with the seasonal variations that Mother Nature provides. If you choose fruits in season, you're getting them at their best. Summer brings the wonders of tropical fruit, berries and stone fruit, while in winter it's time to think of the warming possibilities of stewed rhubarb or apple and lightly spiced marinated fruit salads.

Grains are both nutritional and filling and can be as simple as a sprinkle of bran flakes or as hearty as a saucepan of porridge or sticky rice. All grains keep well in an airtight container, so it's possible to have a selection that will suit every season. For example, quick and easy muesli or couscous in summer and the warming flavours of oats and rice in the colder months.

## fresh starts

Here are a few ideas that will not only ensure that every day starts in a fresh and healthy way, but will hopefully tempt you away from your coffee and toast habit:

- Make breakfast trifles by layering muesli, seasonal fruit and plain yoghurt in large glasses.
- Toss a selection of fresh berries through sweet couscous (page 24) and serve with plain yoghurt.
- Serve creamy porridge with a sprinkle of soft brown sugar and chopped banana, stewed rhubarb (at right) or poached peaches (page 346).
- Serve thin slices of mango and banana with a squeeze of lime juice, a spoonful of sticky black rice (page 25) and a drizzle of coconut milk.

## summer fruit

There is no better way to celebrate the rising sun than with a plate of summer fruit. The fruit can either be fresh or cooked; here are a few summer fruit favourites:

- Slice a selection of stone fruits and put them into a bowl with some orange juice, a little lime juice and the pulp of several passionfruit. Gently toss to combine and serve with sweet couscous (page 24), a dollop of plain yoghurt or simply by itself.

- Thinly slice 6 ripe plums and put into a saucepan with 3 tablespoons water, 2 tablespoons sugar and a split vanilla bean. Cook until the plums are beginning to break up. Spoon over toasted brioche or yoghurt and muesli.
- Cut peaches in half and sprinkle with a little sugar. Grill (broil) for a few minutes until the sugar is beginning to caramelize. Serve with yoghurt and toasted flaked almonds.
- Combine 3 tablespoons unsalted pistachio kernels, 3 tablespoons toasted desiccated coconut and 2 tablespoons grated palm sugar in a blender or food processor. Process until the mixture is the consistency of coarse breadcrumbs. Sprinkle over a plate of sliced pineapple, mango, papaya and banana. Serve with fresh lime wedges.

## winter fruit

If you love starting your day with fruit, then the cooling months are not necessarily a sign for change. Winter fruits work just as well though they will require a little more preparation. However, if you stew fruit in batches it can be kept in a bowl in the refrigerator and raided every morning.

- Winter strawberries need a little help to bring the taste of summer to your cereal bowl. Mash 250 g (9 oz/1 2/3 cups) strawberries and add 2 tablespoons sugar, 1 tablespoon lemon juice and 3 tablespoons water. Bring to the boil in a stainless-steel saucepan, then reduce the heat and simmer for 10 minutes. Spoon over toasted brioche, yoghurt, toasted muesli or pancakes.
- To make stewed rhubarb, trim 500 g (1 lb 2 oz/1 bunch) rhubarb and roughly cut the stalks into 5 cm (2 in) pieces. Put the rhubarb into a large stainless-steel saucepan with 3 tablespoons sugar and 3 tablespoons water. Cover and simmer over medium heat for 10 minutes. Remove from the heat and allow to cool. Serve with Greek-style yoghurt, bircher muesli, toasted brioche or creamed rice.
- Stewed apples can be eaten by the bowlful when served with yoghurt and a touch of cinnamon or spooned into a bowl and topped with hot porridge and a sprinkle of soft brown sugar. Green apples have a nice tartness when stewed and both green and red apples need little or no sugar when stewing for breakfast. Peel and quarter the apples, removing the core, then put in a saucepan with a few tablespoons of water, apple juice or orange juice. Cover and simmer over low heat until the apples have almost dissolved. Test for sweetness and add sugar to taste. For a richer version, add a tablespoon of butter.

# The golden-baked goodness of

# muffin basics

1 Preheat the oven to 180°C (350°F/Gas 4). Combine 2 eggs, 2 tablespoons honey, 1 tablespoon caster (superfine) sugar and 3 tablespoons vegetable oil in a large bowl. Whisk together until the ingredients are just combined. Cut 1 green apple in half and grate one half. Add the grated apple to the bowl along with 185 ml (6 fl oz/$^3$/4 cup) milk and 150 g (5$^1$/2 oz/1 cup) blueberries and stir together.

2 Sift 250 g (9 oz/2 cups) plain (all-purpose) flour, 1 teaspoon ground cinnamon and 2 teaspoons baking powder into a bowl. Lightly fold the dry ingredients into the muffin mixture. Spoon the batter into a 6-hole muffin tin or patty case.

3 Finely slice the remaining half of the apple and put the slices on top of the muffins. Sprinkle each muffin with a little caster (superfine) sugar, then bake for 30 minutes, or until the tops are golden. Makes 6 large muffins

## hints & tips

- The key to good muffins is never over-stir the batter. Fold the ingredients together only until they are just combined. This prevents the mixture from becoming overworked and tough.

- Blueberries are classic muffin ingredients but they can be replaced with an equal quantity of raspberries or strawberries depending on what's in season. If fresh berries are unavailable, use frozen berries.

- Muffins are best eaten on the day they are baked and in an ideal world served warm straight from the oven. If reheating, it is preferable to heat them in the oven rather than a microwave (which tends to toughen them) and serve with unsalted butter.

fruit and spiced batter is a great start to the day.

# classic breads

## banana

Preheat the oven to 180°C (350°F/Gas 4). Put 90 g (3¹/₄ oz) softened butter, 115 g (4 oz/¹/₂ cup) caster (superfine) sugar, 2 eggs, 1 teaspoon natural vanilla extract, 250 g (9 oz/ 2 cups) plain (all-purpose) flour, 2 teaspoons baking powder, 2 large ripe bananas and the grated zest of 1 orange into a food processor. Process to a smooth batter. Spoon into a greased and lined 8 x 16 cm (3¹/₄ x 6¹/₄ in) loaf tin. Bake for 1 hour, or until a skewer inserted into the centre comes out clean. Serve in warm slices or toasted with butter and a drizzle of honey or maple syrup. Makes 1 loaf

## corn

Preheat the oven to 180°C (350°F/Gas 4). Put 125 ml (4 fl oz/ ¹/₂ cup) milk into a saucepan with 90 g (3¹/₄ oz) butter. Heat over low heat until the butter has melted, then remove from the heat. Sift 250 g (9 oz/2 cups) plain (all-purpose) flour, 2 teaspoons baking powder and 2 teaspoons bicarbonate of soda into a bowl. Add 250 g (9 oz/1²/₃ cups) fine polenta and 1 teaspoon sea salt and make a well in the centre. In a separate bowl, whisk together 2 eggs, 125 ml (4 fl oz/¹/₂ cup) buttermilk, a roughly chopped handful of coriander (cilantro) leaves, and 2 seeded and finely chopped red chillies. Fold the buttermilk mixture through the dry ingredients, then fold through the warm milk mixture. Pour the batter into a greased 24 cm (9¹/₂ in) springform tin and mark the top into wedges. Bake for 25 minutes, or until the cornbread is golden brown and a skewer inserted into the centre comes out clean. Serve warm with crispy bacon and roasted tomatoes. Makes 1 loaf

## coconut

Preheat the oven to 180°C (350°F/Gas 4). Put 2 eggs and 300 ml (10$^1$/$_2$ fl oz) milk into a bowl and lightly whisk. Melt 70 g (2$^1$/$_2$ oz) unsalted butter and set aside. Sift 300 g (10$^1$/$_2$ oz/2$^1$/$_2$ cups) plain (all-purpose) flour, 2 teaspoons baking powder and 2 teaspoons ground cinnamon into a mixing bowl. Add 225 g (8 oz/1 cup) caster (superfine) sugar and 150 g (5$^1$/$_2$ oz/2$^1$/$_2$ cups) shredded coconut. Make a well in the centre and gradually stir in the milk mixture until combined. Add the melted butter and stir until the mixture is just smooth. Pour into a greased and lined 21 x 10 cm (8$^1$/$_4$ x 4 in) loaf tin and bake for 1 hour, or until a skewer inserted into the centre comes out clean. Allow to cool before removing from the loaf tin. Serve in buttery toasted slices with or without sliced banana. Makes 1 loaf

## walnut and soda

Preheat the oven to 200°C (400°F/Gas 6). Put 450 g (1 lb/ 3$^2$/$_3$ cups) plain (all-purpose) flour, 1 heaped teaspoon bicarbonate of soda, 1 heaped teaspoon cream of tartar, 1 tablespoon sugar and 1 teaspoon sea salt into a large bowl. Make a well in the centre and gradually add 500 ml (17 fl oz/2 cups) buttermilk, combining to form a soft dough. Add 4 tablespoons finely chopped walnuts and slowly fold through the dough. Melt 2 tablespoons butter and brush the insides of a 21 x 10 cm (8$^1$/$_4$ x 4 in) loaf tin with the melted butter. Put the dough into the greased tin and pour over any remaining butter. Bake for 30 minutes, then reduce the oven temperature to 150°C (300°F/Gas 2) and bake for a further 30 minutes, or until a skewer inserted into the centre comes out clean. Turn out the bread onto a wire rack to cool. Serve warm or toasted with butter, apricot jam, honey or fresh ricotta cheese. Makes 1 loaf

# pancake basics

1 Sift 125 g (4$^1$/$_2$ oz/1 cup) self-raising flour into a bowl, add 2 tablespoons caster (superfine) sugar and make a well in the centre. In a separate bowl, whisk together 2 eggs and 185 ml (6 fl oz/$^3$/$_4$ cup) milk. Add the egg mixture to the dry ingredients and whisk until you have a smooth batter. Allow to sit for 10 minutes.

2 Heat a nonstick or crepe pan over medium heat and grease with a little butter. Add the batter to the pan in large spoonfuls, making sure the pancakes do not touch each other.

3 Cook for 1 minute, or until bubbles form on the surface. Flip the pancakes over with a spatula and cook for a further 1 minute. Repeat the process with any remaining mixture. Eat immediately, served with maple syrup. Serves 4

## hints & tips

- Pancakes can be served with so many things, from the classic maple syrup or lemon juice, butter and sugar to golden syrup, fresh berries, sliced banana or crisp bacon.

- Make flavoured butter to serve with your pancakes. Add crushed honeycomb, dried berries or cinnamon to softened butter in a food processor and blend. Put a line of the butter onto a length of plastic wrap, roll up and store in the refrigerator or freezer.

- For a variation on the classic pancake, put thinly sliced bananas or fresh blueberries on top of the pancake while it's cooking. Flip and allow the fruit to cook into the surface. Serve with maple syrup.

- For savoury pancakes, omit the sugar and add a pinch of salt to the batter. Add finely chopped chives, dill or basil for flavour, or a little finely grated Parmesan cheese or finely grated zucchini (courgette). Serve with bacon or smoked salmon.

- To make crepes, sift 60 g (2$^1$/$_4$ oz/$^1$/$_2$ cup) plain (all-purpose) flour into a bowl and add a pinch of salt and 1 teaspoon sugar. In a separate bowl, whisk together 2 eggs and 250 ml (9 fl oz/1 cup) milk. Whisk the egg mixture into the dry ingredients to form a smooth batter. Cover and set aside for 30 minutes.

# lavish essentials

When it comes to breakfast there's always room for extravagance on special occasions. There's no better start to a birthday than a morning filled with Good Things — but there are many other reasons for indulging in a luxurious Sunday morning. A hard week at work will do! Whatever the reason, start thinking Champagne, smoked salmon, caviar, raspberries and other luscious fruit and rich dark chocolate. Buy in some delicate pastries, fill the fruit bowl, offer blended drinks of tropical fruit and warm the pan for scrambled eggs or freshly flipped pancakes.

## a little fizz at breakfast

- Pour chilled Italian Prosecco or sparkling wine into a parfait glass filled with raspberries and serve with a long spoon. Or serve the Prosecco with freshly squeezed orange juice or white peach juice.

- White peach juice is available in cartons and is worth tracking down. It brings a taste of summer to any morning and when mixed with Champagne or sparkling wine it makes an easy and glamorous cocktail.

- While thinking of drinks, remember that in this age of off-the-shelf juices there really is nothing nicer than freshly squeezed orange juice. Such a simple thing, but direct from juicer to glass, real orange juice is one of the best ways to begin the day.

- Serve Champagne chilled and by itself.

## salmon and caviar

- Buy a side of smoked salmon and indulge — serve with pancakes flavoured with some finely chopped dill or layer over wholemeal toast and serve with sliced avocado and a wedge of lemon.

- Curl slices of smoked salmon on a plate and serve with scrambled eggs and a scatter of finely chopped chives.

- Toast brioche and top it with slices of smoked salmon and a poached egg. Season with freshly ground black pepper and serve with baby rocket (arugula) or English spinach.

- Top of the list of lavish ingredients is real caviar. Wildly expensive and nowadays quite difficult to obtain, caviar is the roe, or eggs, of the female sturgeon. This fish is mostly harvested in the Caspian Sea — depending on the species harvested, the caviar will be one of three main varieties: beluga, osciotre and sevruga. Beluga is the most expensive and delicately flavoured. Caviar is best served by itself on small shell or bone spoons with chilled Champagne or set on blinis or small squares of toast. For a very lavish breakfast it can also be spooned over creamy scrambled eggs.

- More affordable forms of fish roe are red caviar or salmon roe. With their salty flavour, they make a colourful and luxurious addition to egg dishes. Serve poached eggs with sautéed spinach and a spoonful of salmon roe or simply serve it over scrambled eggs. For a cute touch, spoon scrambled eggs back into the egg shells and spoon a little roe on top. Perch in egg cups and serve with a teaspoon.

- Flying fish roe is delicately flavoured and its tiny eggs can be bought tinged with red or gold or as a green wasabi-flavoured roe. Serve savoury pancakes topped with smoked salmon, light sour cream and a spoonful of the coloured roe.

- If you're in search of something different, try kippers. They are definitely not everyday breakfast fare. These smoked herrings are traditionally served lightly grilled (broiled) with butter, lemon juice and toast. You can also make them into a paste that can be served on toast. Remove the skin and bones from the kipper and mash the flesh with a fork. Blend with unsalted butter and add lemon juice and freshly ground black pepper to taste.

## sweet beginnings

If your idea of indulgence heads more into the sweet end of the breakfast spectrum, then head towards your nearest chocolate speciality shop or delicatessen to buy a good-quality block of chocolate. When it comes to breakfast chocolate it is best to buy one that is dark and slightly bitter with a high cocoa content.

- Grate the chocolate into coffee glasses and pour over warm milk. Serve with croissants, small brioche or baked sticks of sugary puff pastry that can be dipped into the rich hot chocolate.

- Shave the bitter chocolate with a sharp knife or vegetable peeler and pile onto a serving plate with a small bowl of cinnamon sugar. Serve with warm pancakes and allow your guests to help themselves.

# + drinks

## egg flip

Put 250 ml (9 fl oz/1 cup) milk, 1 tablespoon plain yoghurt, 1 fresh organic egg and 1 tablespoon honey in a blender. Blend until the honey has dissolved, then pour into a chilled glass. Drink immediately. Serves 1

## banana cardamom lassi

Remove the small seeds from 1 cardamom pod and put them in a blender along with 1 roughly chopped ripe banana, 250 g (9 oz/1 cup) plain yoghurt and 8 ice cubes. Blend until smooth. Serve in chilled glasses. Serves 2

Some days, all I want for breakfast is a creamy but

## pear and honey smoothie

Put 2 Bartlett pears or other green-skinned pears, 125 g (4$^1$/$_2$ oz/$^1$/$_2$ cup) plain yoghurt, 125 ml (4 fl oz/$^1$/$_2$ cup) water, 1 tablespoon honey and 8 ice cubes in a blender. Blend until smooth. Pour into tall glasses. Serves 2

## hot chocolate

Put 125 g (4$^1$/$_2$ oz) dark chocolate in a double boiler and cook over low heat, stirring occasionally, until the chocolate has melted. Spoon into two coffee glasses. Gently swirl the chocolate around inside the glass. Heat 400 ml (14 fl oz) milk over low heat and then slowly pour it into the two glasses. Serve with a spoon to stir. Serves 2

nutritious meal in a glass. Here are some classics.

# + drinks

## rhubarb smoothie

Combine 250 ml (9 fl oz/1 cup) cooled stewed rhubarb,
375 g (13 oz/1$^1$/$_2$ cups) plain yoghurt, $^1$/$_2$ teaspoon ground
cinnamon and 16 ice cubes in a blender. Blend until smooth.
Pour the mixture into chilled glasses and drink immediately.
Serves 4

## banana and honey smoothie

Put 1 roughly chopped ripe banana, 175 g (6 oz/ $^3$/$_4$ cup)
plain yoghurt, 1 tablespoon honey, a generous pinch of
ground nutmeg and 8 ice cubes in a blender. Blend until
smooth and serve immediately. Serves 2

For a simple kickstart to the day, blend fruit, plain

## berry smoothie

Put 70 g (2$^1$/$_2$ oz/$^1$/$_2$ cup) strawberries and 60 g (2$^1$/$_4$ oz/ $^1$/$_2$ cup) each of blackberries and raspberries in a blender. Add 60 ml (2 fl oz/$^1$/$_4$ cup) sugar syrup, 3 tablespoons plain yoghurt and 6 ice cubes and blend until smooth. Pour into chilled glasses. Serves 2

## fig and honey smoothie

Put 2 chopped ripe black figs, 175 g (6 oz/$^3$/$_4$ cup) plain yoghurt, 1 tablespoon honey and 8 ice cubes in a blender. Blend until smooth. Pour into glasses and stir through 3 tablespoons finely chopped walnuts. Serves 2

yoghurt and ice — smoothie perfection.

# + drinks

## mango and strawberry chiller

Put the peeled flesh of 1 large mango, 250 ml (9 fl oz/1 cup) apricot nectar, 6 strawberries and 6 ice cubes in a blender. Blend until smooth and pour into tall glasses. Serves 2

## honeydew and pineapple whip

Put 250 ml (9 fl oz/1 cup) pineapple juice, 140 g (5 oz/1 cup) chopped honeydew melon, 1 tablespoon lime juice and 6 ice cubes in a blender. Blend until smooth and pour into tall glasses. Serves 2

## rockmelon ginger whip

Put 280 g (10 oz/2 cups) chopped ripe rockmelon (or other orange-fleshed melon), 125 ml (4 fl oz/1/2 cup) orange juice, 1 tablespoon chopped fresh ginger and 8 ice cubes in a blender. Blend until smooth and pour into tall glasses. Serves 2

## bloody mary

Put 150 g (51/2 oz/3/4 cup) finely chopped tomato and 1/4 teaspoon salt in a bowl and allow to sit for 30 minutes. Transfer the tomato to a blender, add 4 tablespoons tomato juice and blend until smooth. Put the blended tomato into a cocktail shaker with 3 tablespoons vodka, 1 teaspoon lime juice, 1 teaspoon horseradish cream, 1/4 teaspoon Worcestershire sauce and 1/4 teaspoon Tabasco sauce and shake vigorously. Pour into a glass filled with ice and garnish with a celery stalk, a slice of lime and some freshly ground black pepper. Serves 1

# breakfast recipes
...to help you ease into the day
## waffles and muffins
sugary cinnamon toast
## savoury fritters
aromatic and spiced fruit
grab the newspaper
## and back to bed

nectarine salad

citrus compote

## nectarine salad

8 nectarines, stones removed, cut into eighths
150 g (5¹/2 oz/1¹/4 cups) raspberries
1 tablespoon grated fresh ginger
3 tablespoons soft brown sugar
juice of 1 lime
crème fraîche or plain yoghurt, to serve

Put all the ingredients into a large bowl and gently toss together. Allow the salad to marinate for 1 hour. Serve with crème fraîche or plain yoghurt. Serves 6

## citrus compote

3 limes
3 oranges
2 pink grapefruits
1 vanilla bean, finely chopped
1 teaspoon sugar
250 g (9 oz/1 cup) honey-flavoured yoghurt, to serve

Zest 1 lime and 1 orange and put the zest in a bowl. Peel the remaining limes and oranges and the grapefruits with a sharp knife. Cut all the flesh into segments, or thinly slice, reserving any juice, then put in the bowl. Add the vanilla bean, sugar and reserved citrus juice and mix to combine. Serve with honey-flavoured yoghurt. Serves 4

## banana and berry muffins

250 g (9 oz/2 cups) plain (all-purpose) flour
2 teaspoons baking powder
¹/2 teaspoon ground cinnamon
2 ripe bananas, mashed
150 g (5¹/2 oz/1 cup) fresh or frozen blueberries
3 tablespoons honey
3 tablespoons vegetable oil
1 large egg
185 ml (6 fl oz/³/4 cup) milk
cinnamon sugar and strawberries, to garnish

Preheat the oven to 180°C (350°F/Gas 4). Sift the flour, baking powder, cinnamon and a pinch of salt into a large bowl. Add the banana and blueberries and, using a fork, lightly toss the fruit through the flour. Whisk together the honey, vegetable oil, egg and milk in a small bowl. Add the liquid ingredients to the dry ingredients and lightly combine.

Spoon the batter into a greased 8-hole muffin tin or patty case and top with a sprinkle of cinnamon sugar and a halved strawberry if using. Bake for 20 minutes. Serve immediately. Makes 8

Fruit can be made quite a glamorous affair simply by adding a luxurious ingredient such as vanilla or with a generous drizzling of rich honey.

banana and berry muffins

# cinnamon french toast

4 thick slices white bread, crusts removed
1 egg
1 tablespoon sugar
1 teaspoon ground cinnamon
125 ml (4 fl oz/1/2 cup) milk
butter, for frying
extra sugar, for sprinkling
175 g (6 oz/3/4 cup) plain yoghurt, to serve
fresh seasonal fruit, to serve
100 ml (31/2 fl oz) maple syrup, to serve
2 tablespoons finely chopped toasted pecans, to serve

Cut each slice of bread in half to make rectangles. Beat the egg, sugar and cinnamon in a bowl, then add the milk and combine well. Melt 1 tablespoon butter in a frying pan over medium heat. Dip the bread into the milk mixture, covering both sides. Sprinkle one side of each piece of bread with sugar and gently fry, sugar-side down, for 3 minutes, or until the undersides are golden. Sprinkle the tops with a little sugar and flip over. Cook until golden. Serve with yoghurt, fresh fruit, maple syrup and a sprinkle of pecans. Serves 4

# panettone fingers with rhubarb

6 rhubarb stalks, trimmed
1/2 teaspoon grated fresh ginger
1 teaspoon finely chopped orange zest
4 tablespoons orange juice
3 tablespoons soft brown sugar
1 tablespoon unsalted butter
1/2 vanilla bean, split and scraped
12 fingers panettone, cut into lengths 2 x 12 cm (3/4 x 41/2 in)
icing (confectioners') sugar, to serve

Preheat the oven to 180°C (350°F/Gas 4). Cut each rhubarb stalk into two 12 cm (41/2 in) lengths. Put the ginger, orange zest, orange juice, soft brown sugar, butter and vanilla bean on a stainless-steel baking tray and place in the oven for 1–2 minutes, or until the butter has melted. Remove from the oven and stir to combine. Add the rhubarb and toss together so that the rhubarb is well coated in the sugary mix. Bake for 10 minutes. Turn the rhubarb over and bake for 10 minutes. Allow to cool.

Toast the panettone fingers until golden and then put a strip of rhubarb along each of them. Drizzle with a little of the syrup, sprinkle with icing sugar and serve. Makes 12

# pineapple muffins

225 g (8 oz/13/4 cups) plain (all-purpose) flour
2 teaspoons baking powder
150 g (51/2 oz/scant 3/4 cup) sugar
1/2 teaspoon ground cinnamon
115 g (4 oz/11/4 cups) desiccated coconut
50 g (13/4 oz) unsalted butter, melted
185 ml (6 fl oz/3/4 cup) milk
2 eggs
200 g (7 oz/heaped 1 cup) finely diced fresh pineapple

Preheat the oven to 180°C (350°F/Gas 4). Sift the flour, baking powder and a pinch of salt into a bowl. Add the sugar, cinnamon and coconut and stir to combine. Make a well in the centre and add the melted butter, milk and eggs. Mix until just combined, then fold the pineapple through.

Grease or line with paper patty cases a 6-hole muffin tin or patty case, then spoon the mixture into the holes. Bake for 25–30 minutes, or until golden brown. Makes 6

# peach waffles

115 g (4 oz/1/2 cup) sugar
1/2 vanilla bean, split and scraped
juice of 1 lemon
4 large freestone peaches, peeled and cut into eighths
250 g (9 oz/2 cups) self-raising flour
2 teaspoons cinnamon
175 g (6 oz/3/4 cup) caster (superfine) sugar
75 g (21/2 oz) butter, melted
3 eggs, separated
570 ml (20 fl oz/21/2 cups) milk

Put 400 ml (14 fl oz) water, the sugar, vanilla bean and lemon juice in a saucepan and bring to the boil, stirring to dissolve the sugar. Add the peach segments and return to the boil. Reduce the heat and simmer gently for 2 minutes. Transfer the peaches to a bowl and reduce the liquid in the saucepan over medium heat for 10–15 minutes. Pour over the peaches.

To make the waffles, sift the flour and cinnamon into a bowl. Add the sugar, mix and make a well in the centre. In a jug, mix together the melted butter, egg yolks and milk and pour quickly into the flour mixture, whisking to form a smooth batter. In a bowl, whisk the egg whites until soft peaks form. Fold through the batter. Preheat and grease a waffle iron. Spoon a small amount of the mixture onto the iron, close and cook the waffle until golden. Repeat with the remaining mixture.

Evenly divide the peach segments among the waffles and drizzle over their syrup. Serves 4

rosewater fruit salad

## spiced yoghurt with fresh fruit

2 cinnamon sticks
2 star anise
2 cloves
2 vanilla beans, split lengthways
2 cardamom pods, split lengthways
250 ml (9 fl oz/1 cup) cream
1 tablespoon sugar
300 g (10$^1$/$_2$ oz/1$^1$/$_4$ cups) Greek-style yoghurt
fresh fruit and pomegranate seeds, to serve

Put the cinnamon, star anise, cloves, vanilla beans, cardamom pods and cream into a small saucepan over low heat. Simmer for 30 minutes. Remove from the heat, strain the cream, then stir in the sugar. Allow to cool. Fold the spiced cream through the yoghurt and serve drizzled over a fresh fruit or rosewater fruit salad. Scatter with pomegranate seeds before serving. Serves 6

## rosewater fruit salad

70 g (2$^1$/$_2$ oz/scant $^1$/$_2$ cup) dried figs
70 g (2$^1$/$_2$ oz/scant $^1$/$_2$ cup) dried apricots
70 g (2$^1$/$_2$ oz/$^1$/$_3$ cup) pitted prunes
3 tablespoons sugar
3 tablespoons orange juice
1 cinnamon stick
2 star anise
$^1$/$_2$ teaspoon rosewater
250 g (9 oz/1 cup) plain yoghurt, to serve
90 g (3$^1$/$_4$ oz/1 cup) flaked toasted almonds, to serve

Cut the dried fruit into bite-sized pieces and put in a small heatproof bowl. Put the sugar, 250 ml (9 fl oz/1 cup) water, the orange juice, cinnamon and star anise in a saucepan and bring to the boil over medium heat, stirring to dissolve the sugar. Boil gently for 5–6 minutes until a light syrup forms. Remove from the heat and stir the rosewater through. Pour

the liquid over the prepared dried fruit and allow to soak for several hours, or preferably overnight. Serve accompanied with yoghurt and sprinkled with the flaked almonds. Serves 6

## gruyère baked eggs

1–2 tablespoons butter, softened
4 slices prosciutto, finely chopped
4 tablespoons finely chopped flat-leaf (Italian) parsley
8 eggs
2 tablespoons grated Gruyère cheese
buttered toast, to serve

Preheat the oven to 180°C (350°F/Gas 4). Generously butter four 8 cm (3$^1$/$_4$ in) ramekins and put them into a roasting tin half-filled with water.

Divide the prosciutto and parsley among the ramekins. Put the eggs into a bowl, season and lightly whisk together. Fill the ramekins with the egg mixture, sprinkle with the cheese and put the roasting tin into the oven. Bake for 25–30 minutes, by which time the egg should be just set. Serve with buttered toast. Serves 4

Escape to exotic locations with the brilliant colours of pomegranate seeds and the heady scents of cinnamon, cardamom and rosewater.

gruyère baked eggs

## zucchini and marjoram frittatas

1 tablespoon butter
1 red onion, finely sliced
1 teaspoon finely chopped marjoram
200 g (7 oz/1$^1$/$_2$ cups) grated zucchini (courgette)
6 eggs
50 g (1$^3$/$_4$ oz/$^1$/$_2$ cup) grated Parmesan cheese

Preheat the oven to 180°C (350°F/Gas 4). Gently heat the butter in a frying pan and sauté the onion and marjoram over medium heat for 7–10 minutes, or until the onion is soft and caramelized. Spoon the mixture into two lightly greased, deep, 12-hole patty cases and top with the zucchini.Whisk the eggs with 1 tablespoon water and season with salt and ground white pepper. Fill each of the patty cases with the egg mixture and sprinkle with the Parmesan cheese. Bake for 10 minutes, or until set. Makes 24

## spinach and ricotta omelette

4 tablespoons butter
1 onion, finely sliced
$^1$/$_2$ teaspoon ground cumin
pinch of ground nutmeg
500 g (1 lb 2 oz/1 bunch) English spinach, washed and trimmed
6 eggs, separated
4 tablespoons roughly chopped flat-leaf (Italian) parsley
2 tablespoons finely chopped dill
200 g (7 oz/heaped $^3$/$_4$ cup) ricotta cheese
3 tablespoons grated Parmesan cheese
wholemeal toast, to serve

Heat a large heavy-based ovenproof frying pan over medium heat and add 1 tablespoon butter, the onion, cumin and nutmeg. Cook until the onion is soft, then add the spinach. Cover and steam for 2 minutes, then remove from the heat and cool. Beat the egg whites in a bowl until they form stiff peaks. Squeeze any excess liquid from the spinach and roughly chop. Combine the spinach and onion mixture with the egg yolks, parsley, dill and ricotta cheese. Season with sea salt and freshly ground black pepper, then lightly fold in the egg whites.

Return the pan to high heat and melt the remaining butter. Pour in the egg mixture then reduce the heat to medium. Cook for 1–2 minutes. Sprinkle with Parmesan cheese, then put the frying pan under a medium hot grill (broiler) and cook until the omelette is golden. Serve with wholemeal toast. Serves 4–6

## vanilla-poached apricots

200 g (7 oz/heaped 1 cup) dried apricots
1 vanilla bean, split
$^1$/$_2$ teaspoon rosewater
1 tablespoon honey
4 tablespoons toasted slivered almonds, to serve
250 g (9 oz/1 cup) plain yoghurt, to serve

Put the apricots in a saucepan with the split vanilla bean and 600 ml (21 fl oz) water. Bring to the boil, then cover and simmer over low heat for 1 hour.

Remove the vanilla bean and stir in the rosewater and the honey. Serve with the toasted almonds and yoghurt — a swirl of warm custard is also a nice idea. Serves 6

## salmon and chive fritters

250 g (9 oz) salmon fillet, boned and skin removed
3 teaspoons finely chopped lemon zest
2 eggs, lightly beaten
125 g (4$^1$/$_2$ oz/1 cup) plain (all-purpose) flour
1 teaspoon baking powder
2 tablespoons plain yoghurt
4 tablespoons finely sliced garlic chives
125 g (4$^1$/$_2$ oz/1 cup) finely sliced spring onions (scallions)
vegetable oil, for cooking
lemon wedges, to serve

Finely slice the salmon fillet. Put in a small bowl, cover and refrigerate until ready to use.

Whisk the zest, eggs, flour, baking powder and yoghurt in a bowl until smooth. Just before cooking, fold the salmon, chives and spring onion through the batter until evenly mixed. Season well with salt and freshly ground black pepper.

Heat a frying pan over medium heat and add 1 tablespoon oil. Put heaped teaspoons of the mixture into the pan and press down to form flat fritters. As they become golden on the bottom, turn over and cook until golden on both sides. Drain on paper towels. Repeat with the remaining batter, adding a little more oil to the pan as necessary. Serve the fritters warm, accompanied with lemon wedges. Makes 36

# kitchen bench

Once you have mastered a few of the classic recipes and techniques of lunch you'll never look back. Bread just out of the oven, shortcrust tart waiting for great flavours, home-made sauces and real mayonnaise — these things turn a meal into a celebration.

# kitchen bench inspiration

pummel pasta dough

## whisk and pour

slice, dice, pound and chop

## sandwiches piled high

golden, sizzling cheese

everyone mucks in

and helps themselves

There is nothing more welcoming

# focaccia basics

1 Put 450 g (1 lb/3$^2$/$_3$ cups) plain (all-purpose) flour into a large bowl with a good pinch of sea salt. Put 2 teaspoons dried yeast or 15 g ($^1$/$_2$ oz) fresh yeast in a small bowl with 250 ml (9 fl oz/1 cup) warm water and 1 teaspoon sugar. Set aside for 10 minutes. When the mixture has started to froth, add it to the flour along with 3 tablespoons olive oil. Work the ingredients together to form a rough dough before turning out onto a floured board.

2 Knead the dough until it is smooth and elastic. Put into an oiled bowl and cover with a tea towel. Leave the bowl in a warm place for 1 hour until the dough has doubled in size.

3 Preheat the oven to 200°C (400°F/Gas 6). Put the dough onto an oiled 34 x 24 cm (13$^1$/$_2$ x 9$^1$/$_2$ in) baking tray and press it out until it covers the tray. Use your fingers to make dimples in the dough and then drizzle with 2 tablespoons extra virgin olive oil and sprinkle with 1 tablespoon sea salt. Allow to rise for a further 20 minutes. Bake for 20 minutes, or until the focaccia is cooked through and golden brown on top. Makes 1 loaf

## hints & tips

- Warmth is essential to activate the yeast so if the day or more precisely your kitchen is cool, the dough may take a little longer to rise. You can wrap a towel around the bowl to keep the warmth in, place it near a window to catch the sunlight or turn on the oven and place the bowl close to its warmth.

- On the other hand, dough that is left too long will lose its oomph. If possible, plan your day to accommodate the rising times of the dough since it is not a good idea to leave the dough for longer than is required. If you do need to slow the process down, you can place the dough in the refrigerator, but this really isn't ideal.

- To test if the focaccia is ready, tap the surface with your finger. It will sound hollow when it is cooked.

- Flavour the focaccia with a scatter of black olives, caramelized onions, rosemary, thyme or finely chopped sun-dried tomatoes or preserved lemon rind. These flavourful additions can be scattered over the focaccia dough just before it is placed into the oven for baking.

than the smell of fresh bread.

# classic focaccia flavours

## hummus

Put 175 g (6 oz/1 cup) cooked chickpeas, 2 tablespoons lemon juice, 3 tablespoons tahini, 1 teaspoon ground cumin, 1 garlic clove and a pinch of cayenne pepper into a blender or food processor. Blend to a purée, adding a little water if necessary to make it smooth. Season with sea salt and freshly ground black pepper, then fold through 2 tablespoons extra virgin olive oil. Makes 500 ml (17 fl oz/2 cups)

## tapenade

Put 80 g (2 3/4 oz/1/2 cup) pitted Kalamata olives, 1 garlic clove, 1 roughly chopped handful flat-leaf (Italian) parsley, 10 basil leaves, 2 anchovy fillets and 1 teaspoon capers into a blender or food processor and blend to a rough paste. Add 3 tablespoons olive oil in a stream until you reach the desired consistency. Season with freshly ground black pepper to taste. Makes 250 ml (9 fl oz/1 cup)

## tomato relish

Put 1.5 kg (3 lb 5 oz) coarsely chopped tomatoes, 1 finely sliced red onion, 3 finely chopped garlic cloves, 1 tablespoon finely grated fresh ginger, 1/2 teaspoon ground allspice, 2 teaspoons yellow mustard seeds, 1/4 teaspoon red chilli powder, 2 teaspoons sea salt and 200 ml (7 fl oz) white wine vinegar into a large pot and bring to the boil. Simmer, covered, for 1 hour before adding 250 g (9 oz/heaped 1 cup) sugar. Continue to simmer, uncovered, for 40 minutes, stirring occasionally. Pour into sterilized jars and allow to cool before storing. Makes 750 ml (26 fl oz/3 cups)

## flavoured butters

The simplest way to add more character to sandwiches is by softening the butter and stirring in some flavour-packed ingredients. Try finely chopped herbs, lemon zest, sun-dried tomatoes or olives, or perhaps a little curry powder, blended with the butter in a bowl or combined in a food processor until smooth. Simply add the flavoured butter to your favourite sandwich combination.

# A dollop of velvety mayonnaise

## mayonnaise basics

1 Separate the yolks from 2 eggs and put the yolks in a large bowl with 1 teaspoon white wine vinegar and 1 teaspoon Dijon mustard.

2 Whisk until the mixture is thick and creamy.

3 While whisking continuously, slowly drizzle in about 250 ml (9 fl oz/1 cup) light olive oil or vegetable oil, until the mixture thickens. When it is thick enough to dollop, season to taste with a little sea salt and freshly ground black pepper. Makes 250 ml (9 fl oz/1 cup)

### hints & tips

● Mayonnaise can be made in a blender or food processor but you'll need to add the oil in a constant, steady stream to offset the speed of the blades. If the mayonnaise splits, you can still rescue the mixture. Remove it from the blender or food processor, put 1 extra egg yolk in a large bowl and whisk the egg yolk with a few teaspoons of the original mixture. As it thickens, slowly add the split mayonnaise a few spoonfuls at a time while whisking.

● If your mayonnaise is too thick, you can thin it with a little warm water, added drop by drop and whisked into the mixture.

● As long as the eggs are fresh, mayonnaise will keep for a week in the refrigerator. Spoon into a clean jar, glass bowl or plastic container and seal with a lid or plastic wrap.

● Never make mayonnaise with an extra virgin olive oil as the flavour is too strong and will destroy the light creaminess that you are after.

● A flavoursome version of mayonnaise is the classic rouille sauce, which is often served with seafood dishes such as bouillabaisse. To make, simply tear 1 thick slice of sourdough bread into pieces and put in a bowl. Put a pinch of saffron threads and 3 tablespoons water in a saucepan and bring to the boil. Simmer for 1 minute. Pour the hot saffron water over the bread. Allow to sit for 1 minute before putting in a food processor or blender. Add the flesh of 1 roasted capsicum (pepper), 1/4 teaspoon paprika and 2 garlic cloves and blend to form a smooth paste. Add 125 ml (4 fl oz/1/2 cup) olive oil in a stream until a thick mayonnaise forms. Season with salt to taste.

raises the sandwich or salad to a culinary treat.

# sandwich essentials

Years ago I worked in a cafe where each day we made a fresh bowl of mayonnaise and baked slabs of focaccia, which were timed so that they were coming out of the oven just as the first lunch orders were hitting the wall.

I can still recall those sandwiches: a big square of warm salt-flecked bread, slathered with freshly made mayonnaise and filled with a few well-chosen ingredients — truly raising the sandwich to great culinary heights. Now, I'm not for a minute advocating that you bake your own bread every day, I merely wish to comment on the fact that the humble sandwich can be a wonderful thing if enough care is taken with its essential elements.

With the wealth of breads that now line most supermarket and delicatessen shelves there really is no excuse not to enjoy a superb sandwich. In fact, a perfect sandwich can be as simple as a fresh baguette enriched with a ripe brie or can be as complex as a multi-layered American-style sandwich with meat, salad and all the trimmings of tangy mustards, pickles, chutneys and relishes. It's no surprise then that sandwiches are so popular as a lunchtime meal. They're quick and easy to prepare, easy to transport and can combine all your favourite flavours in a mouthful. What is surprising is that people often settle for less when the sandwich really is about more, more, more.

## filling fantastic

My firm belief is that sandwiches are limited only by the imagination. With your own focaccia and mayonnaise, you're off to the best of possible beginnings. Here are a few of my favourite combinations:

- smoked salmon, sliced cucumber and lemon mayonnaise
- sliced roasted beef, Cheddar cheese and tomato relish
- tinned tuna, thinly sliced gherkins, iceberg lettuce and caper mayonnaise
- oven-roasted tomatoes, fried eggplant (aubergine) and olive tapenade
- sliced roasted beef, watercress and garlic mayonnaise
- sliced ham, tomato, cucumber and mustard
- fried eggplant (aubergine), rocket (arugula) and hummus
- sliced ham, Gruyère cheese and mustard pickles
- sliced roasted beef, tomato, rocket (arugula) and pesto
- boiled egg, cress mix and mayonnaise
- poached chicken, finely sliced gherkins and dill mayonnaise

- sliced roasted lamb, rocket (arugula) and mango chutney
- chopped roasted chicken and fresh dill, a little lemon zest and just enough mayonnaise to bind the mixture together

## a sandwich classic

Roast a head of garlic until it is soft and the cloves are creamy. Blend the roasted garlic to a purée and whisk it into a mayonnaise made with a base of balsamic vinegar instead of white wine vinegar. This garlic mayonnaise adds a rich twist to the classic steak sandwich, and you could further crown the steak with some caramelized onions.

## mayonnaise marvels

Mayonnaise is one of those wonderful flavour boosters that is equally at home on a slice of fresh bread as it is dolloped on a leafy green salad. And, while the classic mayonnaise is perfect for smoothing the edges of strong ingredients, it can also have its own array of flavours. If you don't have time to make your own, you can buy a good-quality egg-based mayonnaise and add flavours for oomph. Here are a few suggestions to get you started:

- Add finely chopped fresh herbs, oven-dried tomatoes, roasted capsicum (pepper), olives or capers to the basic mayonnaise. Or replace the vinegar in the recipe with lemon juice and add some grated lemon zest for tang.
- Blend mayonnaise with a tablespoon of black olive purée and serve it dolloped onto a salad of rare roasted beef, blanched green beans and cherry tomatoes.
- Add some finely sliced fresh basil leaves to mayonnaise and stir to combine. Serve with a salad of sliced roasted lamb, roasted tomatoes and baby English spinach leaves.
- Grind 1/2 teaspoon fennel seeds in a mortar and pestle and blend with mayonnaise, a dash of lemon juice and finely chopped dill. Serve with a salad of watercress and smoked salmon.
- Toss together cooked crab meat with quartered cherry tomatoes, coriander (cilantro) leaves, finely chopped chilli, grated lime zest and a little mayonnaise. Serve warm with crusty bread and a baby leaf salad.
- Mix mayonnaise with finely chopped capers, finely grated lemon zest and freshly ground black pepper. Spread over sliced rye bread and serve with smoked salmon and finely sliced cucumber.
- Mix together mayonnaise with drained tinned tuna, finely chopped parsley and finely diced roasted red capsicum (pepper). Spoon the mixture into pitta bread with baby rocket (arugula) leaves.

Kneading a ball of dough lets you release pent-up

frustrations and the dough loves it!

# pizza dough basics

1   Put 2 teaspoons dried yeast or 15 g ($^1/_2$ oz) fresh yeast into a small bowl with 1 teaspoon sugar and 4 tablespoons warm water. Lightly stir to combine. Set aside for 10–15 minutes, or until the mixture starts to froth. Sift 250 g (9 oz/ 2 cups) plain (all-purpose) flour into a bowl and make a well in the centre. Add 1 egg, $2^1/_2$ tablespoons milk, 1 teaspoon sea salt and the yeast mixture. Gradually work the ingredients together to form a stiff dough.

2   Turn the dough out onto a floured surface and knead until smooth and elastic. Oil a large bowl with a little olive oil and put the dough in it. Rub a little oil over the dough before covering it with a damp cloth. Put the bowl in a warm place for 2 hours until the dough has doubled in size.

3   Preheat the oven to 200°C (400°F/Gas 6). Divide the dough in half and roll it out on a floured surface. Put the dough onto two oiled baking trays and add your toppings. Bake for 15 minutes. This makes 1 quantity pizza dough or 2 medium pizza bases, approximately 23 cm (9 in) in diameter depending on the preferred thickness.

## hints & tips

- You can double this recipe if you need to make several pizzas. For more than that, it is easier to make the dough in batches rather than trying to handle a large amount of dough.

- You can make the pizza dough in a food processor. Put the flour and salt into the bowl of the processor and pulse once or twice to sift. Then add the egg, milk and finally the frothy yeast mixture. Process only until the dough forms a ball. Remove and knead briefly.

- You can bring extra flavour to your dough by adding a sprinkle of dried herbs to the dough. Try a little rosemary, thyme or oregano.

- If you are serious about making pizzas often, then you may like to invest in a pizza stone. These porous baking stones replicate the cooking conditions of the traditional ovens and will result in a wonderful crisp crust. Special pizza trays are also available from speciality kitchenware shops.

# classic pizzas

## romano

Preheat the oven to 200°C (400°F/Gas 6). Finely slice 500 g (1 lb 2 oz) bocconcini cheese or fresh mozzarella cheese and spread half of the cheese over 2 medium pizza bases. Roughly chop 6 anchovy fillets and scatter half of them over the bases. Bake for 15 minutes. Remove from the oven and top with the remaining cheese and anchovies. Drizzle with extra virgin olive oil, season with a little sea salt and return to the oven. Bake until the cheese has just melted. Scatter over basil leaves before serving. Serves 4

## patate

Preheat the oven to 200°C (400°F/Gas 6). Peel and finely slice 4 medium-sized potatoes and arrange the slices on 2 medium pizza bases. Drizzle liberally with extra virgin olive oil and scatter with 1 tablespoon finely chopped rosemary. Sprinkle over sea salt and bake for 20 minutes. Remove from the oven and drizzle with a little olive oil. This simple pizza is wonderful partnered with hearty winter soups or served as a pre-dinner snack. Serves 4

## capriciosa

Preheat the oven to 200°C (400°F/Gas 6). Drain and finely chop a 400 g (14 oz) tin Roma (plum) tomatoes. Put the tomato in a saucepan with 2 tablespoons extra virgin olive oil and simmer over medium heat for 5 minutes. Allow to cool. Spread the tomato over 2 medium pizza bases. Season with sea salt, drizzle with a little extra virgin olive oil and bake for 15 minutes. Remove from the oven and top with 250 g (9 oz) sliced bocconcini cheese, 100 g (3¹/2 oz) sliced ham, 50 g (1³/4 oz/¹/2 cup) sliced button mushrooms, 110 g (3³/4 oz/ ¹/2 cup) sliced marinated artichoke hearts and 80 g (2³/4 oz/ ¹/2 cup) pitted Kalamata olives. Sprinkle with 2 tablespoons grated Parmesan cheese and return to the oven for a few minutes until the cheese has melted. Serves 4

## margherita

Preheat the oven to 200°C (400°F/Gas 6). Drain and finely chop a 400 g (14 oz) tin Roma (plum) tomatoes. Put the tomato in a saucepan with 2 tablespoons extra virgin olive oil and simmer over medium heat for 5 minutes, or until the tomatoes are no longer watery. Allow to cool. Spread the tomato evenly over 2 medium pizza bases. Season with a little sea salt, drizzle with a little extra virgin olive oil and bake for 15 minutes. Remove from the oven and top with 250 g (9 oz) sliced bocconcini cheese and 2 tablespoons grated Parmesan cheese. Return to the oven for a few minutes until the cheese has melted. Scatter with fresh oregano leaves. Serves 4

Feel like you are lost in Italy with

# pasta dough basics

1 Put 400 g (14 oz/3$^1$/$_4$ cups) plain (all-purpose) flour into a food processor with $^1$/$_2$ teaspoon salt. Add 4 eggs and process until the mixture begins to come together in a rough dough.

2 Put the dough on a lightly floured board and dust with 50 g (1$^3$/$_4$ oz/heaped $^1$/$_3$ cup) semolina flour. Knead until the dough is smooth. Divide the dough into four equal portions and wrap in plastic wrap. Refrigerate for 30 minutes.

3 Put the dough through a pasta machine according to the manufacturer's instructions. When it has reached the desired thickness and cut, set it on a clean tray liberally sprinkled with more semolina flour or plain (all-purpose) flour. Gently toss the pasta through your fingers to separate it, then lay it on a floured tray while you cut the remaining dough. Makes enough pasta for 4 main servings

## hints & tips

● Always make pasta dough in a cool place so that the dough does not dry out.

● When cooking pasta, fresh or dried, make sure you use a large pot of boiling water — pasta needs a lot of water around it. Add at least 1 tablespoon sea salt to the water, then allow the water to return to the boil before adding your pasta. This will season the pasta. If your sauce is quite light, add more salt to the cooking water.

● When cooking pasta it is important to cook it only until it is al dente. The aim is to have a pasta that is cooked through but still gives a sense of firmness when you bite into it. Pastas need different cooking times depending on their shape, size and whether they are fresh or dried, so for bought pasta, it is essential to check the manufacturer's cooking instructions. Fresh pasta needs only a few minutes in boiling water before it is al dente.

● When buying or cooking pasta one should usually allow around 100 g (3$^1$/$_2$ oz) per serve. If the pasta is a starter to a heavy meal then reduce this quantity to approximately 70–80 g (2$^1$/$_2$–2$^3$/$_4$ oz).

egg-yellow pasta spilling over your kitchen bench.

# classic pasta sauces

## pesto

Put 125 g (4$^1/_2$ oz/1 bunch) basil leaves, 1 handful flat-leaf (Italian) parsley, 100 g (3$^1/_2$ oz/1 cup) grated Parmesan cheese, 1 garlic clove and 85 g (3 oz/$^1/_2$ cup) toasted pine nuts into a food processor, or use a mortar and pestle. Blend together and add 170 ml (5$^1/_2$ fl oz/$^2/_3$ cup) olive oil in a steady stream until you have a spoonable consistency. Lightly toss the pesto through freshly cooked pasta and serve. Serves 4

## roasted tomato

Preheat the oven to 200°C (400°F/Gas 6). Put 6 Roma (plum) tomatoes on a baking tray and roast until the skins are beginning to blacken all over. Put the whole tomatoes, including the charred skin and any juices, into a food processor or blender with 10 basil leaves, 1 garlic clove, 2 tablespoons extra virgin olive oil, 1 teaspoon balsamic vinegar and 1 teaspoon sugar. Blend to form a thick sauce, thinning the mixture with a little warm water if necessary. Toss the sauce through warm pasta and serve with grated Parmesan cheese and a few basil leaves. Serves 4

## lemon

Finely grate the zest of 3 lemons into a bowl. Add the juice of 2 of the lemons to the bowl and add the juice of the other lemon to the cooking water for the pasta. Add 1 chopped handful flat-leaf (Italian) parsley, about 10 torn basil leaves, 100 g (3$^{1}/_{2}$ oz/1 cup) coarsely grated Parmesan cheese and 3 tablespoons extra virgin olive oil to the bowl. Mix together well. Toss freshly cooked pasta through the lemon sauce and serve. Serves 4

## mushroom

Heat 2 tablespoons butter in a large frying pan over medium heat. Add 1 crushed garlic clove, 400 g (14 oz) halved button mushrooms and 2 large roughly chopped field mushrooms. Sauté for 5 minutes, then add 1 teaspoon thyme leaves and 4 tablespoons white wine. Simmer for a further 1 minute. Toss the sauce through warm pasta, then drizzle with extra virgin olive oil, add 50 g (1$^{3}/_{4}$ oz/$^{1}/_{2}$ cup) grated Parmesan cheese and toss to combine. Serves 4

# pasta essentials

For a quick-fix meal, it's hard to go past pasta. In winter or at night, I usually prefer the richer, more traditional style of sauces that are tomato or cream based — they always hit the spot. However, at lunchtime, I'm just as likely to throw together a tin of tuna, capers, basil, tomato and a handful of baby rocket (arugula), add some warm penne, a swirl of olive oil and a scattering of Parmesan cheese and — hey presto! — a wonderful bowl of satisfying goodness.

Simple sauces for pasta depend on what lies in your cupboard and refrigerator so it's best to stock up on the essentials — good-quality extra virgin olive oil, tinned Italian-style tuna, capers, olives, anchovies and tinned tomatoes. From the refrigerator, you could add some baby English spinach or rocket (arugula) leaves, ruby-red fresh tomatoes, celery, broccoli, lemon or fresh herbs.

And, of course, there's the pasta. Never swamp fresh pasta with a thick, heavy sauce. You want to appreciate its flavour and texture, so just add a splash of lemon sauce or pesto, or olives and finely chopped tomatoes, or herbs and lightly seared prawns (shrimp). Dried pastas are more robust and are better with heavier-style sauces. You can be as adventurous as you like with their sauces but always buy a good-quality dried pasta.

## getting saucy

One of the best things about pasta is that once you've mastered a few sauces, the combinations are endless. Here are some quick sauce suggestions:

- Cut eggplant (aubergine) into small chunks and lightly fry in olive oil with a minced garlic clove and 1 finely diced red capsicum (pepper). When the eggplant is soft and beginning to get a little mushy, add a 400 g (14 oz) tin chopped Roma (plum) tomatoes. Simmer for 5 minutes, then toss with warm pasta, 1 chopped handful flat-leaf (Italian) parsley leaves and grated Parmesan cheese.
- Toss warm pasta with olive oil, sea salt and black pepper, 1/2 finely chopped red onion, a generous amount of chopped flat-leaf (Italian) parsley, a few torn anchovies, olives and lemon zest. Serve with grated Parmesan cheese.
- Toss warm pasta with sliced grilled (broiled) capsicums (peppers), anchovies, capers and basil.
- Finely chop Roma (plum) tomatoes and toss them with anchovies, capers, parsley and olive oil. Toss with warm pasta and serve with grated Parmesan cheese.

- Finely slice pine mushrooms, field mushrooms and oyster mushrooms and sauté them with some butter, garlic and prosciutto. Add to warm pasta with a light scattering of oregano leaves and shaved Parmesan cheese.
- Make a great start to any warming pasta sauce by sautéing several finely sliced leeks with a little prosciutto. Then add your favourite flavours — perhaps tomato and olive, fresh parsley and tuna, or ricotta and grated Parmesan cheese.
- Put diced ripe tomatoes in a bowl and generously sprinkle them with sea salt. Set them aside for 30 minutes before adding olive oil, plenty of roughly chopped flat-leaf (Italian) parsley and grated Parmesan cheese. Toss with warm pasta and sprinkle with small olives.
- If you'd like to lighten a pesto pasta, then add some fresh ricotta and torn basil leaves to the warm pasta along with the pesto. Toss to combine, then serve immediately.

## twists on lemon

Lemon is always beautiful in pasta. For a start, you can make a flavoured oil with virgin olive oil, finely grated lemon zest, a little lemon juice, sea salt and freshly ground black pepper. Toss warm pasta in the oil and add a generous amount of grated Parmesan cheese. To up the flavour but retain the delicacy, add some finely sliced smoked salmon and capers; or for a heartier version, add tinned tuna and blanched broccoli florets or a few chopped anchovies.

## cooking pasta

When it comes to cooking the perfect pasta dish there are a few key points to remember and most of them are about the speed with which the dish should be served. Always have the sauce ready before you start cooking the pasta. If it is a cooked sauce have it ready in a saucepan over low heat. If it is a fresh-flavoured pasta have all the ingredients, including a healthy drizzle of olive oil, ready in a large bowl. Cook the pasta until it is al dente, then quickly drain it and return the hot pasta to the warm pot that you cooked it in. This will ensure that the pasta stays warm. Never leave pasta sitting around; serve it straight away or it will become a gluggy mess. Add the pasta sauce or fresh ingredients and quickly swirl it all together with a pair of tongs. Serve in individual plates or in a warm serving bowl. If you are serving a very light sauce of fresh herbs or lemon it is a good idea to add most of the Parmesan cheese to the pasta before you add the other ingredients. Return the pasta to the warm pot, add some olive oil and finely grated Parmesan and toss so that all the individual pieces of pasta are lightly coated in the cheese. Then add the herbs or lemon.

# shortcrust pastry basics

1 Put 200 g (7 oz/1$^2$/$_3$ cups) plain (all-purpose) flour into a food processor with 100 g (3$^1$/$_2$ oz) chilled unsalted butter, cut into cubes. Add a pinch of salt and process for 1 minute. Add 2 tablespoons chilled water and process until the mixture comes together. Wrap the dough in plastic wrap and chill for 30 minutes.

2 Using a rolling pin, roll out the pastry as thinly as possible, working from the centre outwards. The pastry can be rolled out on a floured surface, between two layers of plastic wrap or on baking paper. Use the pastry to line a 25 cm (10 in) tart tin. Chill for a further 30 minutes.

3 Preheat the oven to 180°C (350°F/Gas 4). Prick the base of the pastry case, line it with crumpled baking paper and fill with uncooked rice or baking weights. Bake the case for 10–15 minutes, or until the pastry looks cooked and dry. Remove from the oven, remove the baking paper and rice or weights and allow the case to cool. Makes 1 tart case

## hints & tips

- The most important point to remember when making pastry is to always keep everything chilled — chilled butter and chilled water for the dough and a chilled tart case for baking.

- To make small tartlet cases, simply follow the above recipe, using the pastry to line six 9 cm (3$^1$/$_2$ in) tartlet tins. You can also make tiny bite-sized pastry cases by pressing the pastry into well-greased small patty cases.

- Uncooked tart cases that are not used immediately can be stored in the freezer for several weeks. Put the prepared tart case into a preheated oven direct from the freezer. This is also a great idea if you don't have baking weights or rice at hand. Freezing the pastry and placing it directly into a preheated oven will prevent the pastry from collapsing in on itself.

- The easiest way to get your finished tart out of the tin is to put the base of the flan tin on the lip of a medium-sized bowl, allowing the metal ring that forms the side of the tin to fall away. If serving the tart warm, run a sharp knife carefully between the pastry and the tart tin to check that no filling has caught on the side before trying to remove it.

# classic tarts

## quiche lorraine

Preheat the oven to 180°C (350°F/Gas 4). Melt 1 teaspoon butter in a heavy-based frying pan over medium heat. Thinly slice 6 rashers of lean bacon, add to the pan and cook until lightly brown and crisp. Remove with a slotted spoon and drain on paper towel. Put 2 eggs, 2 egg yolks and 250 ml (9 fl oz/1 cup) thick (double/heavy) cream into a bowl and whisk together. Season with sea salt and white pepper, then stir in 100 g (3½ oz/1 cup) grated Parmesan cheese. Scatter the bacon in a prebaked 25 cm (10 in) tart case and pour the cream mixture over it. Carefully put the tart into the oven and bake for 25 minutes, or until the filling is set and golden brown. Serve with a green salad. Serves 6

## crab and tomato

Preheat the oven to 180°C (350°F/Gas 4). Put 10 saffron threads in a small saucepan with 4 tablespoons cold water. Put over high heat and simmer until the liquid has reduced to approximately 1 tablespoon. Remove from the heat and add 250 ml (9 fl oz/1 cup) thick (double/heavy) cream. Stir to combine, then whisk in 4 egg yolks. Season with sea salt and freshly ground black pepper and then add 3 tablespoons finely chopped chives. Finely chop 2 ripe Roma (plum) tomatoes and scatter the tomato in a prebaked 25 cm (10 in) tart case. Shred 150 g (5½ oz) fresh crab meat and scatter it over the tomato. Pour the cream mixture over the tomato and crab. Bake the tart for 25 minutes, or until the filling has set and is lightly golden. Serve with a watercress salad. Serves 6

## sweet onion and herb

Preheat the oven to 180°C (350°F/Gas 4). Using a large frying pan (with a lid), melt 1¹/2 tablespoons butter over medium heat along with ¹/2 teaspoon finely chopped rosemary and ¹/2 teaspoon finely chopped thyme. Add 800 g (1 lb 12 oz) finely sliced brown onions and sauté until the onion is soft and transparent. Add 125 ml (4 fl oz/¹/2 cup) white wine and cover the pan. Reduce the heat and gently simmer for 40 minutes, or until the onion is richly caramelized. Spread the onion mixture in a prebaked 25 cm (10 in) tart case. Put 250 ml (9 fl oz/1 cup) thick (double/heavy) cream into a bowl with 4 egg yolks and whisk together. Season with sea salt and freshly ground black pepper and stir in 70 g (2¹/2 oz/ ¹/2 cup) grated Gruyère cheese. Pour the cream mixture over the onion and carefully put the tart into the oven. Bake for 30 minutes, or until the filling has set and is lightly golden. Serve with a bitter leaf salad. Serves 6

## provençal

Preheat the oven to 180°C (350°F/Gas 4). Peel 4 large red onions and cut each into six wedges. Put them into a heavy-based frying pan with 2 tablespoons olive oil and a few sprigs of thyme. Sauté over low heat for 20 minutes, or until the onion is beginning to soften and lightly caramelize. Add 1 tablespoon balsamic vinegar, stir to combine and cook for a further 5 minutes. Remove from the heat and spread the onion in a prebaked 25 cm (10 in) tart case. Thickly slice 3 ripe Roma (plum) tomatoes and arrange the slices over the onion. Remove the pits from 10 Kalamata olives and scatter the torn olives over the sliced tomato. Season with salt and freshly ground black pepper. Cover with aluminium foil and bake for 20 minutes. Remove the foil and bake for a further 15 minutes. Remove from the oven, drizzle with a little extra virgin olive oil and add a scatter of torn basil leaves. Serve with a green salad or a round of goat's cheese. Serves 6

# shortcrust tart essentials

A freshly baked tart is not just a clever way of bringing all your favourite ingredients together in one crumbly pastry-encased mouthful, it looks great as well. Think caramelized onions, bacon and eggs, rich and gooey cheeses, grilled capsicums (peppers), slivers of pink smoked salmon and rich and creamy herbed custards. Served alongside a crisp green salad, you have a lunchtime treat that will suit just about every occasion from a smart affair or celebration through to a springtime picnic. While it may look as if you've gone to a lot of trouble, tarts really don't demand lots of cooking time, so don't let the thought of making your own pastry deter you from an easy lunch. You can use ready-made frozen pastry, but do try to choose one that is made with butter as it will take you closer to the taste of a home-made pastry.

## a simple tart

You can fill a prebaked tart case with almost any of your favourite flavours, but keeping it simple always works well. Here are a few ideas:

- Sauté 4 finely sliced leeks in 2 tablespoons butter. Cover and cook over low heat for 20 minutes, or until the leek is soft and almost caramelized. Spread the leek over a prebaked tart case, season and cover with a mixture of 250 ml (9 fl oz/1 cup) cream, 2 eggs and 2 egg yolks whisked together. Bake in a preheated 180°C (350°F/Gas 4) oven for 30 minutes. You could also add flaked smoked trout with the sautéed leeks, then cover with the cream mixture and sprinkle with a little fresh dill before baking. Serve with a salad of mixed greens and finely sliced cucumber.

- Whisk together 300 g (10 1/2 oz) goat's cheese, 3 eggs, 5 egg yolks, 500 ml (17 fl oz/2 cups) cream and a little freshly ground black pepper. Pour into a prebaked tart case and bake in a preheated 180°C (350°F/Gas 4) oven for 30 minutes, or until the filling is golden brown and set. Serve with oven-roasted tomatoes and rocket (arugula).

- Sauté 2 finely sliced brown onions and 200 g (7 oz) sliced button mushrooms in 2 tablespoons butter until they are soft. Add 1 roughly chopped handful flat-leaf (Italian) parsley and spread over a prebaked tart case. Cover with a mixture of 60 g (2 1/4 oz/1/2 cup) grated Cheddar cheese and 50 g (1 3/4 oz/1/2 cup) grated Parmesan cheese. Bake in a preheated 180°C (350°F/Gas 4) oven for 10 minutes, or until the cheese is golden brown and melted.

- Sauté 1 kg (2 lb 4 oz/2 bunches) chopped baby English spinach and spread over a prebaked tart case. Scatter over some finely chopped black olives and finely sliced prosciutto and finish with crumbled goat's cheese over the top. Bake in a preheated 180°C (350°F/Gas 4) oven for 10 minutes, or until the cheese is soft and slightly brown.

- Soak 10 g (1/4 oz) dried porcini mushrooms, then drain. Sauté the mushrooms with 500 g (1 lb 2 oz) assorted fresh mushrooms until they have softened and reduced in size by half. Stir the mushrooms through 250 g (9 oz/heaped 1 cup) mascarpone cheese, then fold in 4 egg yolks and 4 tablespoons grated Parmesan cheese and season with sea salt and freshly ground black pepper. Pour into a prebaked tart case and bake in a preheated 180°C (350°F/Gas 4) oven for 30 minutes.

## round about

For a lighter, less rich alternative to shortcrust pastry tarts, you can make small tarts using rounds of puff pastry. Top the rounds with some of your favourite delicatessen ingredients — prosciutto, olives, goat's cheese, artichoke hearts, bocconcini cheese, sun-dried tomato, salami, blue cheese — then bake in a preheated 180°C (350°F/Gas 4) oven until puffed and golden brown.

## creamy brie

A layered brie cheese tart is somewhat of a cross between a tart and a pizza. Simply arrange slices of brie cheese in a concentric circle over the base of an uncooked shortcrust tart case. Place a layer of thin slices of tomato and basil leaves over the cheese. Sprinkle with thyme leaves and cracked black pepper and bake in a preheated 180°C (350°F/Gas 4) oven for 30 minutes. Serve with a green salad. Alternatively, you can make this layered tart with thin slices of pear rather than tomato; serve it with ham and a fruit chutney.

# cheese essentials

There can be nothing more simply sublime than sitting down to a plate of cheese and bread. It may be one of the most basic of meals, yet the options and combinations are infinitely variable. Soft cheese, hard cheese, blue cheese, baguette, rye, oatcake, nuts, fruit, pickles — I could go on.

Cheese doesn't only come in a variety of styles, it's also food for any time of the day — think breakfast and finely grated Parmesan cheese folded through your scrambled eggs or the soft milkiness of fresh ricotta cheese drizzled with honey and served with fingers of toast and fresh or poached fruit. At lunchtime, enjoy a salad of farmhouse cheese nestled into crisp greens or the bite of rocket (arugula) with Parmesan cheese and pear or richly matured Cheddar cheese melted over toast.

It's simply a matter of picking your favourite cheese and finding a few nice things to eat with it. Have fun with the research. Visit a delicatessen that has a good cheese section or better still a speciality store with a cheese room. There are now so many quality cheesemakers that there is always a wonderfully diverse range to choose from. Since cheeses can be somewhat seasonal and dependent upon ripeness, always ask which cheeses are at their best. Talk to the cheese specialist and try a selection to suit your own style. With cheese, you can be sure that as soon as you think you've found a favourite there will be another one around the culinary corner waiting to surprise you.

## quick fixes

One of the wonderful things about cheese is that it's an instant food fix. Already packed with flavour, texture and substance, it only needs a few extras — be they salad, bread, biscuits or nuts — to transform it into a deliciously satisfying meal or snack.

- Blend together feta cheese, olives and a little cream to create a flavour-packed spread for bruschetta. Top with a scatter of torn basil leaves or thyme and finely sliced fig, pear or tomato.

- Marinate chunks of goat's cheese overnight in olive oil flavoured with peppercorns, bay leaves, thyme and lemon zest. Serve on a bed of rocket (arugula) leaves with oven-baked croûtons to soak up the flavoursome oil.

- Stuff ripe figs with a little goat's cheese, wrap in prosciutto and bake in a hot oven for a few minutes. Serve on a bed of salad greens, drizzled with extra virgin olive oil and balsamic vinegar.

- Make a quick and easy salad of finely sliced leg ham, shaved Parmesan cheese, sliced pear and rocket (arugula) leaves. Serve with fingers of lightly oiled toasted sourdough bread.

- Mix fresh ricotta cheese with herbs and a little olive paste. Serve with a salad of ripe tomatoes and baby English spinach leaves.

- Make a salad of roasted pumpkin and baby beets, toasted hazelnuts and crumbled goat's cheese.

- Spread some caramelized onions over toasted rye bread and top with slices of leg ham and Gruyère cheese for a ham and cheese melt with a difference.

- Drizzle a little olive oil over large field mushrooms and grill (broil) for a few minutes. Spread with soft goat's curd and grill (broil) until lightly golden. Serve on toasted rye bread with a scatter of finely chopped walnuts.

## a light touch

For a light approach to lunch, team cheese with puffed pastry and a few fuss-free toppings. Preheat the oven to 180°C (350°F/Gas 4) and line a greased baking tray with ready-made puff pastry. Arrange slices of tomato, without overlapping, over the top of the pastry, then add some very finely sliced red onion rings. Scatter with fresh thyme, cover with a layer of grated Parmesan cheese and bake until golden brown. Cut into squares and serve topped with a salad of baby leaves. Another option is crumbling blue cheese or goat's cheese over the puff pastry. Sprinkle with thyme leaves and bake until the pastry is golden. Serve with a salad of tomato, basil and baby rocket (arugula) leaves.

## baked ricotta

Freshly baked ricotta cheese, warm from the oven, is always welcome in a wintry lunch. Put 200 g (7 oz/heaped 3/4 cup) ricotta cheese on a lined baking tray or in a small lined cake tin. Top with fresh herbs, a little chopped chilli, finely chopped black olives and a little grated Parmesan cheese. Cover with another 200 g (7 oz/heaped 3/4 cup) ricotta cheese and drizzle with a little olive oil. Bake in a preheated 180°C (350°F/Gas 4) oven for 30 minutes. Serve with warm bread and a tomato salad.

When ripe plump fruit meets creamy ripe cheese the result is divine.

# classic cheese

## brie with apple and walnuts

Thinly slice 2 red apples and put in a bowl. Drizzle with the juice of $1/2$ lemon and toss so that the lemon juice coats the apple. Finely slice 2 witlof (chicory/Belgian endive) lengthways and add to the apple along with 10 finely chopped walnut halves. Drizzle with extra virgin olive oil and season with freshly ground black pepper and sea salt. Divide the salad among four plates and top each with a generous slice of ripe brie cheese. Serve with toasted rye bread and quince paste (optional). Serves 4

## baguette with grilled goat's cheese

Slice a baguette on the diagonal into four long thin slices. Lightly toast the slices, then top with sliced goat's cheese. Grill (broil) until the cheese is golden brown. Serve on a dressed salad of baby leaves and season with freshly ground black pepper. To pep up the salad, you could add a scatter of small olives, pomegranate seeds or marinated artichoke hearts. Serves 4

Who can resist the classic combinations of crisp

## rocket, pear and parmesan salad

Put 200 g (7 oz/2 small bunches) rocket (arugula) leaves
in a bowl with 2 thinly sliced beurre bosc pears and 150 g
(5 1/2 oz/1 1/2 cups) shaved Parmesan cheese. Drizzle with
extra virgin olive oil and balsamic vinegar and lightly toss
together. Serves 4 as a side salad

## ploughman's lunch

While the ploughman's lunch found in many an English pub
can leave a lot to be desired, the easy combination of a
richly matured buttery Cheddar cheese, fresh crusty bread
and good-quality pickles remains a favourite. Add some
oatmeal biscuits, thinly sliced leg ham and fresh figs, grapes
or apples and you have a simple lunch or perfect picnic.

## fruit, full-flavoured cheeses and bitter leaves?

# + drinks

## iced lychee and mint

Drain 5 lychees from a tin and reserve 125 ml (4 fl oz/$^1$/$_2$ cup) of the syrup. Put the lychees, reserved syrup, 15 large mint leaves, 1 tablespoon lime juice and 10 ice cubes in a blender and blend until smooth. Pour into chilled glasses. Serves 2

## mango lassi

Combine 250 g (9 oz/$^3$/$_4$ cup) roughly chopped mango flesh, 125 g (4$^1$/$_2$ fl oz/$^1$/$_2$ cup) plain yoghurt, 1 teaspoon honey, 1 teaspoon lime juice and 8 ice cubes in a blender. Blend until smooth, then pour into chilled glasses. Serves 2

Indulge in some fruity fun with these quick tropical

## mint and ice cream smoothie

Combine 2 large scoops of vanilla ice cream, 3 tablespoons crème de menthe (or other mint-flavoured liqueur), 6 mint leaves and 4 ice cubes in a blender. Blend until smooth, then pour into small chilled glasses. Serves 2

## strawberry lassi

Combine 150 g (5$^1$/$_2$ oz/1 cup) hulled strawberries, 250 g (9 oz/1 cup) Greek-style yoghurt, 1 teaspoon honey and 8 ice cubes in a blender. Blend until smooth and pour into chilled glasses. Serves 2

delights or try an ice cream smoothie with a kick.

# + drinks

## almond sherbet

Combine 200 ml (7 fl oz) water, 225 g (8 oz/1 cup) sugar, 4 tablespoons ground almond and 4 split cardamom pods in a small saucepan. Boil until the mixture thickens. Cool, add 1 teaspoon rosewater and 2 drops almond extract. Pour a few tablespoons into chilled glasses and top up with cold sparkling mineral water. Serves 8

## watermelon and chilli cooler

Blend 250 ml (9 fl oz/1 cup) watermelon juice, 1 tablespoon chilli syrup and 1 tablespoon lime juice. Pour into a glass filled with ice and garnish with sprigs of fresh mint. (To make chilli syrup, put 2 large red chillies, 115 g (4 oz/1/2 cup) sugar and 125 ml (4 fl oz/1/2 cup) water in a small saucepan and bring to the boil. Reduce the heat and gently simmer for 5 minutes. Remove the chillies, cool the syrup and pour into a jar or bottle. Store extra syrup in the refrigerator.) Serves 1

## pimm's classic

Put 150 ml (5 fl oz) dry ginger ale, 3 tablespoons Pimm's and
1 teaspoon lime juice into a tall, chilled glass and top with
ice. Stir to combine, then garnish with thin slices of orange
and strips of cucumber. Serves 1

## rose petal sherbet

Remove the petals from 4 organic red roses and put the
petals in a large saucepan with 225 g (8 oz/1 cup) sugar and
300 ml (10$^1$/$_2$ fl oz) water. Bring to the boil, then reduce the
heat and simmer for 8 minutes, or until the mixture becomes
a light syrup. Remove any scum as it forms. Cool and stir in
1 tablespoon rosewater. To serve, pour a few tablespoons of
the syrup into chilled glasses and top with cold sparkling
mineral water. Serves 8

# kitchen bench recipes
a dollop of pesto

your favourite pizza

or pasta

thick crusty bread

bold flavours

olives, anchovies, capers

hearty and healthy in one

## lavash with pastrami

2 red capsicums (peppers)
1 telegraph cucumber
4 pieces lavash bread
8 slices pastrami
4 dill pickles, finely sliced
50 g (1³/4 oz) baby English spinach leaves

Put the two whole capsicums under a hot grill (broiler) and grill (broil) until the skin is beginning to blacken and blister all over. Put the capsicums into a bowl and cover with plastic wrap. When the capsicums have cooled, remove the skin and seeds and finely slice the flesh. Set aside. Slice the cucumber into long thin strips using a vegetable peeler.

Put one piece of lavash onto a clean dry surface. Put two pieces of pastrami along one side and top with some strips of cucumber, sliced capsicum, dill pickles and spinach leaves. Roll up and set aside. Repeat with the remaining three pieces of bread. Cut the lavash rolls in half and put onto a serving platter. Serves 4

## duck and mango rolls

1 teaspoon Sichuan peppercorns
1 teaspoon black peppercorns
¹/2 teaspoon sea salt
¹/2 Chinese roasted duck
8 round rice paper wrappers
4 tablespoons plum sauce
2 ripe mangoes, peeled and sliced
50 g (1³/4 oz) snowpea (mangetout) shoots

Put both types of peppercorn and the sea salt into a spice grinder and grind to form a coarse seasoning. Set aside. Remove the skin from the duck and slice it into thin strips with a pair of clean kitchen scissors. Remove the flesh and shred it. Soak the rice paper wrappers in hot water, one at a time, until they become soft, then remove them and pat dry.

Put some of the plum sauce along the centre of a softened wrapper and top with some duck flesh, duck skin, sliced mango, snowpea shoots and a sprinkle of the seasoning. Roll up, folding in the sides to make a neat parcel. When ready to serve, cut the parcels in half and put on a serving platter. Serves 4

## artichoke, sage and prosciutto pizza

2 vine-ripened tomatoes
4 tablespoons olive oil
1 quantity pizza dough (page 69)
8 slices prosciutto, cut in half
175 g (6 oz) jar of marinated artichoke hearts, drained and sliced
100 g (3¹/2 oz) goat's cheese
a few oregano leaves

Preheat the oven to 200°C (400°F/Gas 6). Cut the tomatoes into eighths and put them onto a baking tray. Season with a little sea salt and drizzle with 2 tablespoons olive oil. Roast the tomatoes for 15 minutes. Remove from the oven.

Roll out 4 small circles of the pizza dough, each one about 12 cm (4¹/2 in) in diameter. Put onto a baking tray and top with the prosciutto, roasted tomatoes, artichoke hearts and goat's cheese. Drizzle with a little olive oil and season with sea salt. Bake for 15 minutes, then garnish with a few oregano leaves. Makes 4

## pan bagna

1 baguette
1 tablespoon virgin olive oil
1 garlic clove, peeled and halved
2 red capsicums (peppers), roasted, skin and seeds removed
1 tablespoon salted capers, rinsed and drained
175 g (6 oz) tin tuna, drained
15 black olives, pitted
¹/2 small red onion, finely sliced
15 basil leaves
1 handful flat-leaf (Italian) parsley, roughly chopped
10 anchovies
100 g (3¹/2 oz) marinated artichoke hearts, drained

Using a sharp knife, slice the baguette in half lengthways and remove the bread filling from both the top and bottom portions. Brush the interior of the loaf with olive oil and rub with the cut garlic.

Cut the roasted capsicums into thin strips and combine with the remaining ingredients in a bowl. Season with salt and freshly ground black pepper and spoon inside the bottom half of the loaf, heaping it up. Reassemble the loaf, making sure that the sides meet neatly. Wrap in plastic wrap, put a weight on top (a bread board or heavy saucepan is suitable) and refrigerate overnight. Slice into 5 cm (2 in) widths and serve. Makes 10 slices

braised mushrooms with buttered angel hair pasta

pissaladière

## braised mushrooms with buttered angel hair pasta

700 g (1 lb 9 oz) mixed mushrooms (button, Swiss brown, shiitake, oyster and enoki)
3 tablespoons olive oil
3 garlic cloves, crushed
1 tablespoon thyme leaves
250 ml (9 fl oz/1 cup) white wine
250 g (9 oz) fresh angel hair pasta or dried linguine
2 tablespoons butter
2 tablespoons finely chopped flat-leaf (Italian) parsley
4 tablespoons finely grated Parmesan cheese, to serve

Bring a large pot of salted water to the boil. Cut the mushrooms into halves or quarters. Heat the oil in a large saucepan over medium heat and add the garlic, mushrooms and thyme. Toss the mushrooms in the pan and cook until the garlic begins to soften. Add the white wine and season with sea salt. Cover with a lid and simmer for 7 minutes. Add the pasta to the water and cook until al dente.

Drain the pasta, then retun it to the hot saucepan. Stir the butter and parsley through the pasta, then pile onto four warmed plates. Make a well in the centre of the pasta and fill with the mushrooms. Drizzle with the mushroom cooking liquid and season with freshly ground black pepper. Serve sprinkled with the Parmesan. Serves 4 as a starter

## pissaladière

4 tablespoons olive oil
4–5 large onions, peeled and finely sliced
1 teaspoon finely chopped rosemary
1 teaspoon finely chopped thyme
1 teaspoon caster (superfine) sugar
1 quantity pizza dough (page 69)
12 anchovy fillets
16 black olives, pitted
12 basil leaves, to garnish

Preheat the oven to 220°C (425°F/Gas 7). Heat a large frying pan over medium heat and add the olive oil, onion, rosemary and thyme. Cover and cook over low heat for 20 minutes, or until the onion is very soft. Add the sugar and cook for a further 1 minute before setting aside.

Turn out the risen dough onto a floured surface and punch it down. Divide into four equal sections, then roll out each piece to form a thin oval, about 12 cm (4½ in) in diameter. Turn over the edges a little to form a slightly thicker crust. Put on a large oiled baking tray and cover the surface of the dough with the onion. Tear the anchovies and olives into small pieces and scatter over the top of the onion. Bake for 15 minutes. Remove from the oven and garnish with freshly torn basil leaves. Serves 4

## spring chowder

1.5 kg (3 lb 5 oz) cleaned clams (vongole)
1 tablespoon light olive oil
1 garlic clove, crushed
2 rashers streaky bacon, chopped
2 white onions, diced
1 red chilli, seeded and finely chopped
1 carrot, grated
1 bay leaf
2 large desiree potatoes, peeled and diced
2 celery stalks, thinly sliced
1 large handful flat-leaf (Italian) parsley, roughly chopped

Throw away any clams that don't close when you tap them. Bring 500 ml (17 fl oz/2 cups) water to the boil in a large saucepan, add the clams, then cover and cook for 2–3 minutes until they open. Discard any that stay closed. Take most of the clams out of their shells, keeping some whole for the garnish. Strain and reserve the clam liquid.

Put the olive oil, garlic and bacon in the saucepan and cook over medium heat until the bacon has browned. Add the onion, chilli, carrot and bay leaf. When the onion is soft and transparent, add the potato, clam liquid and 250 ml (9 fl oz/1 cup) water. Cover and simmer for 35 minutes. Add the celery, clams and parsley and season with sea salt and ground white pepper. Ladle the chowder into four soup bowls and garnish with the reserved whole clams. Serves 4

spring chowder

# red lentil soup

3 tablespoons olive oil
1 onion, finely diced
1 tablespoon grated fresh ginger
1 tablespoon ground cumin
2 carrots, peeled and grated
250 g (9 oz/1 cup) red lentils
1 litre (35 fl oz/4 cups) vegetable stock or water
2 red onions, finely sliced
90 g (3¼ oz/1 bunch) coriander (cilantro), with roots attached

Put 1 tablespoon olive oil into a large saucepan and add the diced onion, ginger and cumin. Cook over medium heat until the onion is soft and transparent. Add the carrot, lentils and stock. Bring the soup to the boil, then reduce to a gentle simmer. Cook for 30 minutes, or until the lentils have completely disintegrated.

Meanwhile, heat the remaining olive oil in a frying pan over medium heat and add the red onion. Thoroughly wash the coriander. Finely chop the roots and stems, setting aside the top leafy section for the garnish. Add the chopped coriander roots and stems to the red onion and continue to cook, stirring occasionally, until the onion has caramelized.

To serve, ladle the soup into four soup bowls, garnish with a generous sprinkling of coriander leaves, then top with a spoonful of the caramelized onion. Serves 4 as a starter

# prawn sandwich

20 medium raw prawns (shrimp), peeled and deveined
3 tablespoons lime juice
3 tablespoons light olive oil
2 tablespoons oil
mayonnaise (page 64)
8 slices white sourdough bread
coriander (cilantro) leaves

Put the prawns, lime juice and olive oil into a bowl and leave to marinate in the refrigerator for 30 minutes.

Heat some of the oil in a heavy-based frying pan over high heat. Put a few prawns into the pan and sear them for about 2 minutes, until they begin to curl. Flip them over and cook them for a further 1 minute, or until they are cooked through. Cook the rest of the prawns, a few at a time, in the same way.

Spread some mayonnaise onto each piece of bread. Divide the prawns among four slices, scatter over coriander leaves and season with white pepper. Top with the remaining bread. Serves 4

# cheese and olive sandwiches

100 g (3½ oz/⅔ cup) grated mozzarella cheese
3 tablespoons grated Parmesan cheese
4 tablespoons pitted and finely sliced green olives
2 tablespoons roughly chopped flat-leaf (Italian) parsley
8 slices white bread, crusts removed
2 tablespoons olive oil

Preheat the oven to 180°C (350°F/Gas 4). Put the mozzarella, Parmesan, olives and parsley in a bowl and gently mix to combine. Brush four slices of bread with half the olive oil and put them, oiled-side down, on a greased baking tray. Divide the cheese mixture evenly among the four slices of bread and top with the remaining four slices. Brush the tops of the sandwiches with the remaining oil and bake for 10 minutes, turning if necessary. Remove and slice each piece into three fingers. Makes 12

# chicken and coconut soup

1 teaspoon sesame oil
1 red chilli, seeded and finely sliced
2 chicken breast fillets, sliced thinly across the grain
4 spring onions (scallions), trimmed and sliced on the diagonal
1 red capsicum (pepper), finely sliced
1.5 litres (52 fl oz/6 cups) chicken stock
400 ml (14 fl oz) coconut milk
3 tablespoons lime juice
1 tablespoon fish sauce
1 handful coriander (cilantro), chopped
100 g (3½ oz) snowpea (mangetout) shoots, cut into short
  lengths
lime wedges, to serve

Put the sesame oil, chilli and chicken into a wok or large saucepan over medium heat and stir-fry until the chicken is beginning to brown. Add the spring onion, capsicum, chicken stock, coconut milk, lime juice and fish sauce. Bring to the boil, then reduce the heat and simmer for 10 minutes.

Add the coriander and snowpea shoots. Season to taste with salt and freshly ground black pepper and serve immediately with lime wedges to squeeze over. Serves 4

field mushrooms on puff pastry

zucchini and caper spaghettini

# field mushrooms on puff pastry

4 field mushrooms
2 tablespoons olive oil
1 garlic clove, crushed
1 sheet butter puff pastry
150 g (5$^1$/2 oz/1 bunch) rocket (arugula), stalks removed
70 g (2$^1$/2 oz/$^3$/4 cup) shaved Parmesan cheese
1 tablespoon balsamic vinegar

Preheat the oven to 180°C (350°F/Gas 4). Remove the stem from each of the mushrooms and put the caps into a large bowl with the olive oil, garlic and some sea salt and freshly ground black pepper. Toss to coat the mushrooms in the garlicky oil.

Cut the pastry into four squares and lay them on a baking tray. Roll over the edges of each square to form a raised edge, then put a mushroom into the centre of each square. Bake for 20 minutes, or until the pastry is puffed and golden.

Tear the rocket leaves into bite-sized pieces, put them into a bowl, toss them with the Parmesan and vinegar and season to taste. Pile the rocket salad on top of the mushroom tartlets and serve while they are still warm. Serves 4

# zucchini and caper spaghettini

3 tablespoons extra virgin olive oil
2 garlic cloves, crushed
6 zucchini (courgettes), grated
400 g (14 oz) spaghettini
1 handful flat-leaf (Italian) parsley, roughly chopped
2 tablespoons small capers
110 g (3$^3$/4 oz/heaped 1 cup) grated Parmesan cheese

Bring a large saucepan of salted water to the boil for the pasta. Heat a deep frying pan over medium heat and add the olive oil and garlic. Move the garlic around the pan with a spatula until it is lightly golden, then add the grated zucchini. Slowly braise the grated zucchini, stirring it as it cooks, for about 15 minutes, or until it begins to dry out and catch on the bottom of the pan.

Cook the pasta until it is al dente, about 10 minutes, then drain and return it to the saucepan. Add the parsley, capers, most of the Parmesan cheese and the zucchini. Toss the ingredients together and divide the pasta among four pasta bowls. Sprinkle with the remaining Parmesan. Serves 4

# sardines on toast

3 ripe tomatoes, finely diced
$^1$/2 red onion, finely sliced into rings
2 tablespoons white wine vinegar
2 tablespoons virgin olive oil
1 tablespoon oregano leaves
1 teaspoon butter
8 or 16 sardine fillets, depending on their size (you want 300 g/10$^1$/2 oz in total)
4 thick slices wholemeal bread, toasted

Put the tomato, onion, vinegar, olive oil and oregano leaves in a small bowl. Stir to combine and season with sea salt and freshly ground black pepper.

Put a nonstick frying pan over high heat and add the butter. Fry the sardine fillets for 1–2 minutes on both sides until they are opaque and slightly browned. Pile the sardines onto the toast. Top with the tomato salad and any remaining dressing. Serves 4

Parmesan and pastry, caper-flecked pasta and just-fried sardines on toast.

sardines on toast

# gazpacho

4 Lebanese (short) cucumbers
8 ripe tomatoes, roughly chopped
1 tablespoon sea salt
1 teaspoon ground roasted cumin seeds
1 small beetroot, peeled and chopped
1 red capsicum (pepper), diced
3 spring onions (scallions), finely sliced
1/2 red onion, finely diced
2 tablespoons chopped coriander (cilantro) leaves
extra virgin olive oil, to serve
melba toasts, to serve

Roughly chop two of the cucumbers and finely dice the remaining two. Put the tomato and chopped cucumber into a large bowl with the sea salt and the ground cumin seeds, stir well and then allow to marinate for 2 hours. Put the tomato and cucumber mixture into a blender or food processor with the beetroot and blend to a purée. Pour the purée into a muslin-lined strainer over a bowl, twist the muslin into a ball and squeeze out all the liquid into a bowl.

Discard the pulp and chill the juice. When the juice is cold, add the diced vegetables and coriander, stir well and then chill the gazpacho for a further 1 hour. Season to taste, ladle into individual bowls and serve with a drizzle of extra virgin olive oil and melba toasts. Serves 4

# pea and lettuce soup

2 tablespoons olive oil
1 leek, finely sliced
1 garlic clove, crushed
1 litre (35 fl oz/4 cups) vegetable or chicken stock
1 butter lettuce, stem removed, finely sliced
150 g (5 1/2 oz/1 cup) fresh peas
1 teaspoon sugar
20 mint leaves
finely grated Parmesan cheese, to serve

Put the oil, leek and garlic into a large saucepan and sauté until the leek is soft. Add the stock, lettuce and peas and bring to the boil. Reduce the heat and simmer for 15 minutes, or until the peas are soft, then remove the pan from the heat and add the sugar and mint leaves.

Pour the soup mixture into a blender or food processor and blend until it is smooth. Season well. Serve the soup with some grated Parmesan to sprinkle over. Serves 4

# risoni with sweet and sour capsicum

1 red onion, finely sliced
2 red capsicums (peppers), cut into thick slices
2 tablespoons balsamic vinegar
2 tablespoons soft brown sugar
250 g (9 oz) risoni
2 large ripe tomatoes, roughly chopped
10 large basil leaves, roughly torn
150 g (5 1/2 oz/1 bunch) baby rocket (arugula), stalks removed
4 tablespoons extra virgin olive oil

Preheat the oven to 180°C (350°F/Gas 4). Put the onion, capsicum, vinegar and sugar in a baking dish and toss them together. Season the vegetables with a little sea salt, cover with aluminium foil and bake for 30 minutes.

Remove the baking dish from the oven and allow the vegetables to cool. Cook the risoni in a large pan of rapidly boiling water for 10 minutes, or until al dente, then drain it well.

Put the risoni in a large bowl with the capsicum mixture, tomatoes, basil and rocket and toss to combine. Season to taste and drizzle with olive oil. Serves 6

# pappardelle with basil, feta and roast capsicum

4 red capsicums (peppers)
3 tablespoons extra virgin olive oil
1 teaspoon balsamic vinegar
125 g (4 1/2 oz/1 bunch) basil
400 g (14 oz) pappardelle
150 g (5 1/2 oz) feta cheese

Preheat the oven to 200°C (400°F/Gas 6). Rub the capsicums with a little oil, slice them in half lengthways and put them, skin-side up, on a baking tray. Bake for 20 minutes, or until the skin blackens and blisters. Put the capsicums in a plastic bag or bowl covered with plastic wrap, allow them to cool, then remove the skin and seeds. Put the capsicum flesh into a blender with the vinegar and 10 basil leaves, season and blend. Add the strained liquid from the baking tray and a little olive oil to make a sauce consistency. Put the sauce in a large saucepan over low heat to keep it warm.

Cook the pappardelle until it is al dente, then drain the pasta and add it to the warm capsicum sauce. Crumble half the feta over the pasta and gently toss the ingredients together. Serve garnished with basil leaves and the rest of the feta crumbled on top. Serves 4

# salads

I have to admit that I often find myself standing before an open refrigerator or cupboard thinking that I'd quite like a little bit of everything. It's a condition my father used to describe as 'eyes too big for her belly', and it was always getting me into trouble. It was only later that I discovered the perfect antidote — the salad.

# salad inspiration
freshly picked herbs

crisp leaves

tangy dressings

the salty bite of capers and anchovies

# a handful of nutty grains
dive into big bowls of crunch

and colour

# vinaigrette basics

1 Put 1 tablespoon lemon juice and 3 tablespoons extra virgin olive oil into a bowl and season with a pinch of sea salt and a grind of black pepper.

2 Bruise 1 garlic clove once with the wide blade of a large knife or a mallet.

3 Add the garlic to the dressing, lightly stir and allow it to sit for 30 minutes to infuse. Remove the garlic, stir the dressing again, then use. Pour over salads that feature chicken or seafood. Makes 4 tablespoons

## hints & tips

● The most important part of making great salad dressings is to use the best extra virgin olive oil and vinegar that you can afford. Good-quality olive oils can vary in flavour from smooth to green to quite peppery, so choose one that you like. Vinegars also vary and the best are sweet and smooth and not at all like the industrial-style vinegars which are sold in large bottles and which are to be avoided. Those vinegars are only good for pickling or for splashing over chips by the seaside!

● If you love the taste of garlic, you can finely mince the garlic clove and add it to the dressing instead of infusing it (see step 3), but be careful — the other ingredients in the salad must be strong enough not to be overpowered by the taste and aroma of raw garlic.

● The simplest vinaigrette of all contains nothing more than balsamic vinegar and extra virgin olive oil. Put 1 part vinegar to 4 parts oil into a small bowl and season with a pinch of sea salt and a grind of black pepper. Stir together well. Serve drizzled over salads that feature tomatoes, beans, roasted beef, seared lamb, roasted capsicums (peppers), figs and pears.

● Another simple vinaigrette includes herbs. Combine 1 tablespoon white wine vinegar and 4 tablespoons extra virgin olive oil and season with a pinch of sea salt and a grind of black pepper. Stir together well, then add 1 teaspoon finely chopped fresh herbs, such as tarragon, oregano, basil, chervil or thyme. Pour over simple green salads.

# salad essentials

For me salads are all about flavour and crunch. I can think of nothing better than sitting down to a bowl of some of my favourite ingredients tossed together with a lush array of leaves and the smooth bite of a good dressing.

Now to make a salad you have to first get a bit conceptual about the whole process. Actually, the following scenario is a good thing to keep in mind when planning any meal, but it is especially important with a salad. I call it the three 't's...taste, texture and tang. Does the salad have at least two really good flavours, preferably one rich and one fresh? Does it have at least two textures, a bit of crunch and a bit of smooth, and does it have an element of zing, whether it's from a good dressing or an interesting extra flavour? If there's a tick against most of these points you are well on the way to a great meal. Think of any of the great salad classics — caesar, Niçoise, waldorf and so on — and they all conform to this test. The flavour comes from the variety of ingredients and from the dressing, which should bring the tang of acid and the depth of its seasonings to the salad. The smooth can come from cheese, mayonnaise or soft leaves and the crunch comes from the crispness of fresh salad greens and the fruit, vegetables or nuts that can be thrown into the mix.

## going green

Since crispness is essential in most salads, the care of your greens is an important factor. Always buy salad greens and herbs that are in top condition. This may mean that you decide on the main elements of the salad as you shop, depending on which leaves are looking their best. Avoid lettuce with spotted or mushy leaves and herbs that have begun to wilt. If possible, rinse the greens in cold water when you get home. Drain well and place them into plastic crisper boxes or plastic bags in the refrigerator. If your herbs have wilted, then this will often resurrect a sad bunch. Pre-picked leaves like baby rocket (arugula), English spinach, mizuna or mixed salad selections should be bought as close as possible to the day of use. And be careful when transporting them home. A squashed and bruised bag of baby greens is a waste of money and of little use in a salad.

Watercress, with its leafy bite, is a great addition to many a salad but it does have a short shelf-life. Here's the easiest way to prepare it. Untie the bunch and rinse the watercress in a large bowl of cold water. Line an airtight salad container with a clean tea towel or paper towels. Break off the sprigs of watercress and place them into the container, seal and put in the refrigerator. Your watercress is now ready to use with little fuss and should keep for a couple of days.

In summer, one of my all-time favourites is the iceberg lettuce. This good old lettuce is sometimes overlooked yet there's barely a green that's simpler to prepare. Just chill it, cut it into wedges and pile it onto a plate; season with sea salt and cracked black pepper, then drizzle with a simple dressing before serving alongside seared seafood or cold roasted chicken — divinely crisp and refreshing.

## herbs by the handful

Apart from the crisp watery crunch of fresh greens, the other great thing about salads is their varied flavours and the easiest way to add a bit of zing is with fresh herbs.

- Parsley is welcome in almost any salad. It's not too strong to overpower other flavours but still has enough freshness to lift the spirits of just about anything. In case you hadn't noticed, I use it by the handful.

- Rocket (arugula) has become a salad standard and can usually be bought as bunches of large leaves or as loose small leaves. Some varieties, in particular the small-leafed wild rocket, can be quite hot and peppery and so should be mixed in with other leaves. Because of the peppery nature of rocket, always serve it alongside other strong flavours, such as cold meats or cheeses. If you are serving rocket as the main ingredient in a salad, temper its heat with fresh sliced pear or another light-flavoured green.

- Coriander (cilantro) is a strong-flavoured herb that can hold its own against the vibrant ingredients found in most Asian salads and is usually the perfect herb for any dish that contains fresh chilli. It's also ideal for refreshing the flavours in a rich Asian-style meal or for tossing through heavily spiced Middle Eastern salads.

## a light touch

You can afford to be generous with the above herbs but other herbs need a light hand. Tarragon, with its soft aniseed flavour, is wonderful scattered over a green salad or used to flavour vinegars and sauces. Dill is marvellous with fish and potatoes, while finely chopped chives can be sprinkled over just about anything that's leafy, eggy or fishy.

Mint is a clever crossover herb that mingles well with the sweet and the savoury crowds. It comes into its own in Middle Eastern-style salads or scattered over potatoes, peas or seared lamb. Lacy chervil is a herb that adds a simple tarragon-like flavour to an elegant summer salad.

Clockwise from top: pearl barley, white rice, moghrabiyeh, brown rice and red rice

# storecupboard essentials

## small but full of flavour

Herbs are not the only fast-track to flavour, there are several other storecupboard essentials that pack a flavourful punch.

- Capers come in a variety of forms, mostly in brine, but if you love their piquant flavour choose the small capers that are preserved in salt. Their flavour is less acidic and their saltiness becomes part of the salad's seasoning. They can be scattered over a simple tomato or leaf salad, tossed through warm potatoes or used to season a puy lentil salad.

- Preserved lemons are available from most delicatessens, speciality food stores and occasionally supermarkets. Just remove the flesh and any of the salty brine, then very finely dice the rind and add to your salad for a slightly spiced citrus bite. It's a great flavour to combine with couscous, chickpeas, roasted red capsicums (peppers) and flat-leaf (Italian) parsley.

- Nuts in all their varied forms can provide a great flavour crunch in salads. Pecans and walnuts with their rich, almost caramel-like flavour combine beautifully with cheese, while almonds, lightly toasted, add a subtle flavour and are best when combined with simple salads. Peanuts, finely chopped, are perfect scattered over delicate Asian-style salads, and roasted pine nuts are perfect teamed with spinach or seared lamb and beef.

- Nuts can become rancid with age so it's always a good idea to buy them from a shop with a high turnover. This may mean buying them from a health food store or large greengrocer and once opened don't bother trying to store them for a long time. It's best to buy small packets and munch on any leftovers over the next few days.

- Seeds are another way to bring interesting texture and taste to a salad. Lightly toast sesame seeds and add them to roasted pumpkin, English spinach and roasted eggplant (aubergine) salads. Or roast pumpkin seeds and sunflower seeds and scatter them over simple salads to add a delicious crunch.

- Lightly toasting or roasting nuts and seeds brings out their flavour. You can do this in a frying pan over medium heat or by scattering the nuts and seeds onto a baking tray and placing in a 180°C (350°F/Gas 4) oven. However, because of their high oil content, they easily burn so watch your frying pan or baking tray, and remove it from the heat as soon as the nuts are turning golden brown.

## the good grain

Grains have long formed the basis of most traditional cuisines. We couldn't exist without wheat, barley, corn, oats or rice, and far from being mere staples, grains impart character and substance to meals.

Think of the nuttiness of brown rice, which gives a salad a hearty rustic flavour that will stand up to strong flavours. In particular, this rice suits heavy soy-based dressings, and works well with strong flavours like fresh ginger and rich flavours like roasted pumpkin. Its earthy flavour is also a good match for the peppery bite of rocket (arugula).

White rice, on the other hand, provides a perfect bland background for lots of interesting flavours, and works as well with the ginger-chilli-lime combinations of Southeast Asia as it does with the parsley, basil and caper accents of European dishes.

### couscous

Simply cooked, couscous is a filling and buttery grain that is perfectly designed for a side dish or salad. It's quick and easy to prepare and is also versatile.

- For a zesty twist on couscous, add a few tablespoons of orange juice to the absorption liquid and, when the couscous is cooked, add finely grated orange zest, finely chopped flat-leaf (Italian) parsley and finely sliced celery. Stir to combine. Toss through mizuna leaves and then serve with pan-fried whiting or perch.

- Moghrabiyeh are the large balls of couscous that are a Lebanese speciality and available from Middle Eastern stores. To prepare them, simply add to salted boiling water and cook for 5–7 minutes. Drain and then toss with a little oil and a light sprinkle of cinnamon and freshly ground cumin. When cool, toss through a salad of mint, parsley and coriander (cilantro) leaves and serve scattered over thickly sliced tomato.

## on the wild side

Wild rice brings a wonderful nutty flavour to salads as well as an interesting texture and colour. Wild rice is not actually 'rice' but the seed of a North American grass. The grains should be washed in cold water before cooking. Once brought to the boil, wild rice takes about 25 minutes to cook. Drain and serve warm as a side dish or allow to cool before tossing through salad ingredients.

- Toss wild rice with finely chopped roasted red capsicums (peppers), finely chopped red onion and parsley. Season and dress with extra virgin olive oil and a dash of pomegranate molasses. Serve alongside spicy grilled (broiled) sausages.

Gravlax is normally served with cured salmon is a great addition

## gravlax basics

1 Put 200 g (7 oz/1$^1$/$_2$ cups) coarse sea salt, 150 g (5$^1$/$_2$ oz/heaped $^2$/$_3$ cup) sugar, 2 teaspoons coarsely crushed black peppercorns and 60 g (2$^1$/$_4$ oz/ 1 bunch) finely chopped dill in a bowl. Stir to combine. Line a shallow dish or tray with plastic wrap and put a little of the salt mixture over the base.

2 Put one 900 g (2 lb) unskinned salmon fillet, skin-side down, over the salt and then cover the fillet with the remaining salt. Put another piece of plastic wrap over the fillet and then tightly wrap the plastic around the fish. Put a slightly smaller tray or cutting board on the fish and weigh it down with a heavy bowl or several tins. Refrigerate for 2 days, turning the fish occasionally.

3 Unwrap the fish and brush away any excess salt and herbs. Put the fillet onto a clean board and thinly slice with a very sharp knife. You should cut the fillet as you would smoked salmon, starting at the tail end, with the knife on the diagonal, cutting down towards the skin. Makes 800 g (1 lb 12 oz)

### hints & tips

● Once made, gravlax will keep in the refrigerator for at least a week. If you have time, marinating it for an extra day will allow a little extra flavour to seep in.

● If the wallet permits, make a double batch by putting 2 salmon fillets together, skin-side out, with the salty mixture laid between the fillets as well as on the outsides. It might seem a tad indulgent to have extra cured salmon in the refrigerator, but it keeps well and is an easy option for sandwiches and salads during the following week.

● Gravlax is traditionally served with rye bread and horseradish cream. It can also be served with a dill-flavoured mayonnaise or sour cream flavoured with finely chopped chives.

rye bread, but the salty sweet flavour of home-
to any salad, adding a sea-tinged velvety richness.

There is something magical about peeling back the lid of a tin to reveal the little silvery sardine soldiers.

# quick fish essentials

There are some things in my pantry that I seem to stock-pile. This is because each time I go to the supermarket I grab a few tins just in case. Then, when I'm putting away the groceries I discover that I already have eight tins of Italian-style tuna. However, other than the difficulty of trying to fit them all in, I believe that your pantry can never have too many tins of organic chickpeas, beans, Italian tomatoes — or fish!

Tins of flaky tuna, rosy salmon and succulent sardines, as well as cured salmon and delicate pink smoked trout — with a selection of precooked and cured fish at hand, you can rest easy that you'll never be at a loss for lunch or a quick and light snack. Nowadays most large supermarkets and delicatessens are stocked with a good selection of these products and it's really just a matter of adding some great bread, a green salad, fresh herbs and a squeeze or two of lemon. With this in mind it's wise to mostly avoid any of the tinned fish that have extra flavours and add your own herbs rather than be subjected to a sad version that has spent several herb lifetimes in a tin.

While tinned fish is a great storecupboard staple, don't forget the many kinds of cured fish that can be kept in the refrigerator. Smoked salmon and gravlax are both cured forms of raw salmon, with the different curing techniques flavouring the fish. Smoked salmon has a slight smoky flavour, while gravlax is slightly sweet. Both are wonderful served with simple salads of avocado and greens or piled onto sandwiches or savoury pancakes with a dollop of crème fraîche or dill mayonnaise.

## fish to go

Tinned fish is one of those foods that people either love or hate, but for me there is nothing more convenient or nutritious than a tin of sardines or tuna. Try these five-minute lunches:

- Press sardines into toasted wholemeal bread and top with some lemon juice and pepper. Serve with a side salad of rocket (arugula) and baby English spinach leaves.
- Lightly break up sardines and scatter through a salad of boiled egg, baby English spinach leaves, diced ripe tomato and roasted red capsicum (pepper).
- Toss drained tinned tuna through a salad of small boiled potatoes, black olives, finely sliced celery, salad greens and torn basil. Dress with olive oil and lemon juice.

- Drain and rinse a tin of cannellini beans, then add them to a bowl with drained tinned tuna, roughly chopped ripe tomatoes, torn radicchio leaves and some rocket (arugula) leaves. Serve with fresh olive bread.
- Stir drained tinned tuna and lots of roughly chopped flat-leaf (Italian) parsley through some freshly made mayonnaise (page 64). Serve with a green salad and crusty bread.
- Make a salad of baby English spinach leaves and chervil and top with roasted beetroot, sliced feta cheese, roughly chopped walnuts and drained tinned tuna. Drizzle with a balsamic vinegar dressing. You could also add a little drizzle of walnut oil if you've got some handy.

## smoke it

Whether you like to eat it hot, warm or cold, smoked fish is a simple yet ever-elegant addition to sandwiches and all sorts of salads:

- Arrange several slices of smoked salmon on a plate and top with a salad of julienned Lebanese (short) cucumbers, finely chopped mint and dill and a little lemon juice. Dollop with some light sour cream and sprinkle with poppy seeds. Serve with finely sliced rye or pumpernickel bread.
- Serve slices of smoked salmon with salad greens, lemon mayonnaise and sliced avocado.
- Smoked river trout is a great way to pep up a simple pasta. Use a lemon pasta sauce (page 75) as a starting point and then add rocket (arugula) leaves and flakes of the smoky fish. Toss the sauce through drained pasta and serve immediately.

If you're lucky, your supermarket will also stock varieties of hot-smoked fish: salmon, trout, mackerel or herring. Hot-smoked is a different style of curing again, where the fish is actually heated and smoked at the same time. This method results in a piece of fish that is cured with a lovely smoky flavour and has the texture of cooked fish. The wonderfully succulent flesh can be broken into flakes and scattered through salads, or simply served with steamed potatoes. Serve it with a dollop of lemon mayonnaise or a scatter of salted capers, or drizzle it with a lemon vinaigrette flavoured with fresh dill.

- For a great summer dish, try thinly sliced hot-smoked salmon with an avocado salsa, lime mayonnaise and a green salad.
- Serve a thick slice of hot-smoked ocean trout on top of a noodle salad.

From top: chickpeas, red lentils and puy lentils

# legume essentials

Legumes are indispensable in the kitchen. They are one of our most important staples and can be found in some of the great dishes of the world, from cassoulets to tempeh. Yet, legumes have acquired a reputation for being fiddly and difficult to cook with or, at the other extreme, for being grungy. If you've so far avoided cooking with beans, peas and lentils, then now is the time to be a bit adventurous.

## perfect pantry standbys

Dried and tinned beans come in quite a range and it's worth a trip to a market or health food store to discover their various colours and shapes. Most dried beans will require soaking overnight before cooking. Though this does mean a little pre planning, all you need to do is throw a handful of dried beans into a bowl of water and leave it on the kitchen counter overnight. Next day, put them into a pot, cover generously with cold water and bring to the boil. Never salt the water as this will toughen the skins. Simmer the beans for 1–2 hours until they are soft and cooked through. It's simple and the pay-off is the excellent flavours and textures that cooked beans bring — the fluffy textures and rich flavours of kidney beans, the light and creamy cannellini, the slight chalkiness and sweet nutty flavour of borlotti, mild pale butterbeans (lima beans), colourful black turtle beans and sweet adzuki.

It's a good idea to keep an assortment of tinned beans in the pantry for meal emergencies. Before using any tinned variety, always drain and rinse the beans under cold water to remove any of the starchy cooking liquid. Chickpeas are a particularly good stand by as they suit the canning process. Where possible, buy organic chickpeas or ones that have been cooked in pure water, as they have the best flavour. If time permits, however, cook your own as the texture and sweet nuttiness of freshly cooked chickpeas is incomparable.

Unlike beans, lentils don't need pre-soaking before cooking and so they're ever-ready to be thrown into a meal. There are three main types of lentils. Red lentils have a wonderful colour but they tend to cook into a mush, so they are best suited to soups and stews. Brown lentils maintain their shape and are ideal for serving with red meats and rich flavours. Puy lentils are small greeny-grey French lentils and have a wonderful flavour but are more expensive.

Always store lentils and dried beans in airtight containers, preferably in glass jars so you can see them and be reminded of their presence. The worst thing you can do is find yourself with several half-used packets of lentils of a questionable vintage stuffed into the back of a cupboard.

## easy combinations

There's something appealing about salads with sprightly leaves and soothing beans or lentils. And with all the nutritional goodness that legumes bring to any meal, they should be enjoyed as often as possible.

- Blend cooked chickpeas in a food processor with a little olive oil, lemon juice and ground cumin. Serve as a dip, or add roughly chopped flat-leaf (Italian) parsley and finely diced preserved lemon rind to the chickpeas and serve with seared lamb.

- Serve cooked chickpeas in a salad of baby English spinach leaves, tomato and feta cheese.

- Toss cooked chickpeas through couscous flavoured with finely chopped flat-leaf (Italian) parsley, coriander (cilantro) and currants.

- Toss cooked puy lentils in a balsamic vinegar dressing then add some sliced basil. Spoon lentils and basil over a salad of rocket (arugula) and baby bocconcini cheese.

- For a hearty salad, arrange blanched French beans and julienned carrots over a bed of baby English spinach leaves. Toss cooked brown lentils in a balsamic vinegar dressing with a little finely grated fresh ginger, then spoon the lentils over the salad. Serve with seared lamb.

- Try a winter salad of oven-roasted tomatoes, grilled (broiled) prosciutto, baby English spinach leaves and brown lentils, dressed with a little Dijon mustard and extra virgin olive oil.

- For a bitter-leaf salad, combine cooked cannellini beans, roughly chopped marinated artichoke hearts, flat-leaf (Italian) parsley leaves and a scatter of small salted capers. Drizzle with a lemon dressing. Serve with roasted chicken.

- Toss cooked chickpeas in extra virgin olive oil with a pinch of paprika and season with sea salt and freshly ground black pepper. Spoon over a salad of roughly chopped tomatoes, cucumber, coriander (cilantro) leaves and some finely chopped preserved lemon rind or pickled lime. Drizzle with a little fresh lemon juice and scatter over toasted flaked almonds. Serve with grilled (broiled) fish.

# classic salads

## greek

Cut 4 ripe tomatoes into chunks and arrange on a serving platter. Add 2 thickly cut Lebanese (short) cucumbers and 1/2 red onion, finely sliced into paper-thin half rings. Scatter over 175 g (6 oz/1 cup) Kalamata olives and sprinkle with 1/4 teaspoon dried oregano. Cut 200 g (7 oz) creamy feta cheese into thick slices and put them on top of the salad. Make a dressing with 1 teaspoon red wine vinegar and 2–3 tablespoons extra virgin olive oil and seasoned with salt and freshly ground black pepper. Drizzle over and serve. Serves 4 as a side dish

## tabbouleh

Soak 70 g (2 1/2 oz/heaped 1/3 cup) burghul in cold water for 10 minutes, then drain and squeeze to remove any excess water. Put the burghul into a large bowl and add 3 finely chopped ripe tomatoes. Season with 1 teaspoon sea salt and some freshly ground black pepper. Finely chop 150 g (5 1/2 oz/1 bunch) flat-leaf (Italian) parsley, gathering the leafy ends together and discarding the stems. Add to the salad with 2 finely chopped spring onions (scallions) and 1 finely chopped small handful mint. Combine 4 tablespoons olive oil and 3 tablespoons lemon juice and pour over the salad. Toss together and serve. Serves 4 as a side dish

## caesar

Whisk together 1 teaspoon Dijon mustard, 2 tablespoons lemon juice and 1 egg. Slowly add 125 ml (4 fl oz/$1/2$ cup) olive oil, whisking constantly. Stir through 3 tablespoons grated Parmesan cheese and season with sea salt and freshly ground black pepper. Boil 2 eggs for 6 minutes. Remove the crusts from 3 slices sourdough bread and chop. Put 4 tablespoons olive oil in a frying pan and fry 2 finely sliced rashers of bacon over medium heat. As the bacon cooks, remove and drain on paper towels. Add the bread to the oil and fry until golden brown. Roughly chop the hearts of 2 cos (romaine) lettuces and put onto a serving platter. Shell and quarter the eggs. Add the eggs, bacon, fried bread and 4 finely chopped anchovies to the platter. Drizzle with the dressing. Serves 4 as a side dish

## niçoise

Boil 8 small potatoes until cooked through, then drain and cut in half. Blanch 150 g (5$1/2$ oz) French beans in boiling water until emerald green, then drain and rinse. Boil 4 eggs for 6 minutes. Divide the leaves from 2 small butter lettuces among four bowls. Shell the eggs and cut in half. Divide the potatoes, beans and eggs among the bowls. Drain a 175 g (6 oz) tin Italian-style tuna and add to the bowls along with 2 ripe tomatoes, cut into chunks, and $1/2$ finely sliced red onion. Add 4–5 olives to each bowl with a light scatter of flat-leaf (Italian) parsley leaves and salted capers. Combine 2 tablespoons lemon juice, 4 tablespoons extra virgin olive oil and $1/4$ teaspoon minced garlic. Drizzle the dressing over the salads and then top each salad with 2 anchovies. Serves 4

# salad recipes
## meals with a crispy crunch
# leafy herbs
# citrus burst
# savoury fritters
## freshly diced mouthfuls of colour
# tossed or piled high

couscous with herbs and chickpeas

fennel and grapefruit salad

## couscous with herbs and chickpeas

175 g (6 oz/1 cup) couscous
1 teaspoon butter
400 g (14 oz) tin chickpeas, drained and rinsed
2 ripe Roma (plum) tomatoes, seeded and diced
1/2 red onion, finely diced
1 handful mint
1 handful coriander (cilantro) leaves
1 handful flat-leaf (Italian) parsley
1 tablespoon lemon juice
3 tablespoons olive oil
2 tablespoons diced preserved lemon rind

Put the couscous in a large bowl with the butter and cover with 250 ml (9 fl oz/1 cup) boiling water. Leave the couscous for 20–30 minutes, from time to time separating the grains with a fork. Before adding the remaining salad ingredients, rub the cooked grains between your fingers to break up any lumps.

Toss the couscous and all the salad ingredients together and season with sea salt and ground black pepper. Serves 4

## fennel and grapefruit salad

500 ml (17 fl oz/2 cups) apple juice
3 black peppercorns
1 sprig of thyme
1 tablespoon balsamic vinegar
1 teaspoon celery salt
2 fennel bulbs, very finely sliced
2 pink grapefruits, peeled and segmented
2 celery stalks, finely sliced

Put the apple juice, peppercorns and thyme into a small saucepan and place over medium heat. Lightly boil until the liquid has reduced to a syrupy consistency, resulting in about 3 tablespoons apple syrup. Set aside and allow to cool. Add the balsamic and celery salt to the syrup and stir to combine.

Pile the fennel, grapefruit and celery into a bowl or on a serving platter. Garnish with a few sprigs of the fennel tops and dress with the apple dressing. Serve with cold roasted pork loin or chicken. Serves 4 as a side dish

## chicken and papaya salad

125 ml (4 fl oz/1/2 cup) tamarind water
1 teaspoon soy sauce
2 teaspoons finely grated fresh ginger
1 tablespoon grated palm sugar
1/2 teaspoon cumin seeds, roasted and ground
1 large red chilli, seeded and finely sliced
2 roasted chicken breasts, roughly shredded
85 g (3 oz/1/2 cup) peanuts, roughly chopped
1 orange papaya, peeled, seeded and sliced
1 Lebanese (short) cucumber, diced
2 tablespoons Asian fried onions
2 spring onions (scallions), shredded
1 large handful mint
15 betel leaves

Mix the tamarind water, soy sauce, ginger, palm sugar, roasted cumin and chilli together in a large bowl and stir until the sugar has dissolved. Add the chicken to the dressing and toss it all together. Combine the remaining salad ingredients except the betel leaves in another bowl and season.

Arrange the betel leaves on a serving platter or four plates and top with the papaya salad and chicken. Top with any remaining dressing. Serves 4

Scattered leafy herbs surprise and refresh the palate — use fennel, mint and parsley to bring salads to life.

chicken and papaya salad

## chicken and preserved lemon salad

2 chicken breast fillets
1/2 teaspoon ground cinnamon
10 saffron threads
2 Lebanese (short) cucumbers
1 tablespoon finely chopped preserved lemon rind
1 large handful flat-leaf (Italian) parsley
12 mint leaves
2 tablespoons extra virgin olive oil
60 g (2$^1$/$_4$ oz/$^1$/$_2$ cup) flaked almonds, toasted

Preheat the oven to 200°C (400°F/Gas 6). Put the chicken breasts into a small pan or casserole dish. Add the cinnamon, saffron and 250 ml (9 fl oz/1 cup) water. Seal with a lid or aluminium foil and bake for 30 minutes. Remove from the oven and check that the chicken is cooked through with the point of a sharp knife. Return to the oven if it is still a little pink. Allow the cooked chicken to cool.

Meanwhile, chop the cucumbers into small pieces and put into a bowl along with the preserved lemon rind, parsley and mint. Shred the chicken into small pieces and add to the salad along with some of the cooled cooking liquid. Season to taste with a little sea salt and freshly ground black pepper. Drizzle with olive oil, add the toasted almonds and toss together. Serve with couscous or a green salad. Serves 4

## chicken and pink grapefruit salad

1 spring onion (scallion), finely sliced
2 tablespoons white wine vinegar
4 tablespoons extra virgin olive oil
4 tablespoons crème fraîche
175 g (6 oz/1 cup) shredded roasted chicken meat
2 pink grapefruits
3 handfuls mixed salad leaves, such as mizuna, lambs lettuce and baby English spinach leaves
8 walnuts, finely chopped

Put the spring onion, vinegar, olive oil and crème fraîche in a bowl and stir to combine. If too thick, add a little warm water. Add the shredded chicken and toss until the chicken pieces are coated all over. Using a sharp knife, peel the grapefruit and remove the segments by slicing between each of the membranes. Arrange a bed of mixed salad leaves on a serving plate and top with the chicken. Scatter the grapefruit segments and walnuts over the top of the salad and season with a little sea salt and freshly ground black pepper. Serves 4 as a starter

## fennel and orange salad

2 tablespoons balsamic vinegar
4 tablespoons olive oil
1 teaspoon Dijon mustard
2 fennel bulbs, finely sliced
2 oranges, segmented
1 large handful flat-leaf (Italian) parsley
3 tablespoons walnuts, roughly chopped
20 Niçoise olives

Put the vinegar, oil and mustard in a small bowl and stir to combine. Toss the fennel, orange, parsley, walnuts and olives together in a large serving bowl and drizzle with the dressing. Serves 4 as a side dish

## green bean and pistachio salad

300 g (10$^1$/$_2$ oz) green beans, trimmed
400 g (14 oz) tin butterbeans (lima beans), drained and rinsed
85 g (3 oz/1 bunch) mint
70 g (2$^1$/$_2$ oz/$^1$/$_2$ cup) pistachio kernels, toasted
grated zest and juice of 2 mandarins
3 tablespoons extra virgin olive oil

Blanch the green beans in boiling salted water for a few minutes, or until they turn a bright emerald green. Drain and rinse the beans under cold running water.

Put the green beans into a salad bowl along with the rinsed butterbeans. Add the mint leaves, pistachio kernels and the grated mandarin zest and toss together. Blend together the mandarin juice and the olive oil in a small bowl, then season with salt and freshly ground black pepper. Dress the salad and serve. Serves 4–6 as a side dish

Salads can be comforting like this three bean
packed with all the goodness that freshly sliced

three bean salad with prosciutto

salad laced with warm prosciutto and pine nuts or
apple, cheese and bitter leaves can bring to a bowl.

apple and pecorino salad

# three bean salad with prosciutto

6 slices prosciutto
175 g (6 oz) French beans
175 g (6 oz) yellow string beans
175 g (6 oz) tin butterbeans (lima beans)
2 tablespoons extra virgin olive oil
2 tablespoons white wine vinegar
1 large handful flat-leaf (Italian) parsley, roughly chopped
2 tablespoons toasted pine nuts

Put a large saucepan of water on to boil. Meanwhile, grill (broil) or pan-fry the prosciutto until it is crisp and then drain on paper towels. Blanch the French beans and yellow string beans in the boiling water for a few minutes, or until the green beans begin to turn an emerald green. Drain the beans and briefly refresh them under cold running water.

Return the blanched beans to the saucepan with the butterbeans and add the olive oil, vinegar and parsley. Break the prosciutto into small pieces and add to the beans along with the pine nuts. Toss the ingredients together and season with sea salt and freshly ground black pepper. Pile onto a serving platter. Serves 4

# pear and walnut salad

100 g (3$^1$/$_2$ oz/1 cup) walnut halves
$^1$/$_2$ garlic clove
1 teaspoon sea salt
grated zest and juice of 1 orange
125 ml (4 fl oz/$^1$/$_2$ cup) light olive oil
300 g (10$^1$/$_2$ oz/2 bunches) rocket (arugula), stalks removed
2 beurre bosc pears
140 g (5 oz) goat's curd

Put the walnuts, garlic, sea salt, grated orange zest and olive oil in a blender or food processor and blend to form a sauce. Toss the rocket leaves in the orange juice and divide the leaves among four plates.

Core the pears, slice them thinly and arrange the slices over the rocket. Top with the goat's curd, gently pour the walnut dressing over the salad and season. Serves 4 as a starter

# apple and pecorino salad

2 teaspoons honey
1 teaspoon Dijon mustard
3 tablespoons extra virgin olive oil
2 tablespoons lemon juice
2 pink lady apples, cored and finely sliced
2 red witlof (chicory/Belgian endive), leaves rinsed
100 g (3$^1$/$_2$ oz/1 small bunch) rocket (arugula), stalks removed
85 g (3 oz/1 cup) shaved Pecorino cheese

Combine the honey, mustard and oil in a small bowl.

Put the lemon juice into another bowl and add the apple slices. Toss in the juice so that they are well coated. Drain any excess juice into the honey dressing. Put the witlof and rocket into a serving bowl. Scatter with the shaved Pecorino and apple and then drizzle with the honey dressing. Serves 4

pear and walnut salad

# chicken and pine nut salad

1 egg yolk
1 teaspoon balsamic vinegar
125 ml (4 fl oz/$1/2$ cup) light olive oil
2 anchovy fillets, finely chopped
2 chicken breasts, poached and shredded
3 tablespoons salted capers, rinsed and drained
3 tablespoons toasted pine nuts
3 tablespoons currants
1 handful flat-leaf (Italian) parsley, roughly chopped
grated zest of 1 lemon

Put the egg yolk and vinegar in a small bowl and whisk to combine. Slowly add the oil, whisking continuously to form a thick and creamy mayonnaise. Fold the chopped anchovy fillets through the mayonnaise and season with sea salt and freshly ground black pepper. Set aside.

Put the remaining ingredients in a large bowl and toss together. Fold in the anchovy mayonnaise. Serve the salad in little bowls and season with cracked black pepper to taste. Serves 4

# coconut and green bean salad

400 g (14 oz) green beans
2 green chillies, finely chopped
1 teaspoon grated fresh ginger
4 tablespoons plain yoghurt
juice of 1 lime
1 teaspoon sea salt
$1/4$ coconut, flesh shaved
2 tablespoons vegetable oil
1 tablespoon brown mustard seeds
30 curry leaves

Bring a saucepan of water to the boil and cook the green beans for 2–3 minutes, or until they are emerald green. Drain and refresh the beans under cold running water.

Put the chilli, ginger, yoghurt, lime juice and sea salt in a bowl, add the coconut and toss together well.

Heat the oil in a small frying pan over medium heat, then add the mustard seeds and curry leaves. When the seeds begin to pop, take the pan off the heat. Add the toasted seeds and leaves to the coconut mixture along with the green beans and toss together. Serves 4 as a side dish

# potato salad

4 large Pontiac potatoes
6 spring onions (scallions), finely sliced
70 g ($2^{1}/2$ oz/$1/2$ bunch) flat-leaf (Italian) parsley, roughly chopped
60 g ($2^{1}/4$ oz/1 bunch) dill, finely chopped
125 ml (4 fl oz/$1/2$ cup) olive oil
grated zest and juice of 1 lemon

Cut the potatoes into chunks, put them in a large saucepan of salted cold water and bring to the boil over high heat. When the water has reached boiling point, cover the pan with a lid and remove it from the heat. Leave the potato to sit for 30 minutes. (This is a nice way to cook the potato because it doesn't break up or become waterlogged.)

Meanwhile, mix the spring onion, parsley, dill, olive oil, lemon zest and juice together. When the potato is ready, test it with the point of a sharp knife — it should be tender and cooked through. Drain the potato and add it to the herbed dressing while it is still hot. Toss to combine and season with salt and freshly ground black pepper. Serves 4

# crab and watercress salad

100 ml ($3^{1}/2$ fl oz) tamarind water
2 tablespoons shaved palm sugar or soft brown sugar
2 tablespoons fish sauce
2 tablespoons lime juice
250 g (9 oz) fresh cooked crab meat
2 tablespoons light olive oil
2 tablespoons finely chopped coriander (cilantro) leaves
500 g (1 lb 2 oz/1 bunch) watercress, leaves picked
1 yellow capsicum (pepper), finely julienned
3 large red chillies, seeded and finely sliced
2 spring onions (scallions), finely sliced

To make the dressing, put the tamarind water, palm sugar, fish sauce and lime juice into a small bowl and stir until the sugar has dissolved. Set aside.

Put the crab meat into another bowl and break up the meat into fine threads. Add the olive oil and coriander and stir until well combined. Season with sea salt and freshly ground black pepper. Mix the watercress, capsicum, chilli and spring onion in a large bowl. Drizzle with the dressing and toss until all the ingredients are well coated. Divide among four plates and top with a large spoonful of the crab meat. Serves 4 as a starter

Cheese, greens and a little bit of crunch.

rocket with baked saffron ricotta

wilted spinach salad

## rocket with baked saffron ricotta

500 g (1 lb 2 oz/2 cups) ricotta cheese
pinch of saffron threads
2 tablespoons olive oil
1 teaspoon balsamic vinegar
3 teaspoons walnut oil
2 fennel bulbs, thinly sliced
300 g (10$^1$/2 oz/2 bunches) rocket (arugula), stalks removed

Preheat the oven to 180°C (350°F/Gas 4). Put the ricotta cheese in an ovenproof dish lined with baking paper. Sprinkle with saffron, drizzle with olive oil and season with sea salt and freshly ground black pepper. Bake for 30 minutes. Remove from the oven and allow to cool.

Combine the vinegar and walnut oil in a bowl and add the fennel and rocket leaves. Toss together and serve with the baked ricotta. Serves 4

## wilted spinach salad

1 kg (2 lb 4 oz/2 bunches) English spinach, rinsed and
    stalks removed
12 Kalamata olives, pitted and roughly chopped
1 garlic clove, finely chopped
2 tablespoons finely chopped mint
1 small red onion, halved and finely sliced
2 tablespoons red wine vinegar
200 g (7 oz/1$^1$/3 cups) crumbled feta cheese
125 ml (4 fl oz/$^1$/2 cup) olive oil
30 g (1 oz/1 cup) croutons

Make sure the spinach is well drained before roughly chopping the larger leaves and placing into a large metal bowl. Add the olives, garlic, mint, onion and vinegar, then sprinkle with the feta cheese.

Heat the olive oil in a frying pan over high heat until it is almost smoking, then pour it over the salad. Be careful to stand well back as some of the oil may splatter. Toss the ingredients quickly and pile them into a serving bowl. Scatter over the croutons and serve immediately. Serves 4 as a side dish

## white bean salad

2 tablespoons olive oil
2 garlic cloves, crushed
1 red onion, cut into wedges
25 g (1 oz/1 bunch) thyme, broken into sprigs
3 tablespoons white wine
400 g (14 oz) tin cannellini beans, drained and rinsed
150 g (5$^1$/2 oz) cherry tomatoes, halved
1 tablespoon balsamic vinegar
1 large handful flat-leaf (Italian) parsley, roughly chopped

Heat the oil in a frying pan over medium heat. Add the garlic and cook until lightly golden, then add the onion and thyme. Continue cooking until the onion is soft and transparent, then pour in the white wine. Simmer until the wine has almost reduced completely and then add the beans. Gently stir to combine and then remove the bean mixture from the heat.

Tip the beans into a bowl and add the tomato, vinegar and parsley. Stir to combine and season to taste. You may also wish to add a little virgin olive oil to give the salad a rich gloss. Serves 4 as a side dish

This white bean salad is an autumn favourite, with its welcoming flavours of beans, garlic and thyme.

white bean salad

# summertime

When the weather turns warm, it's only natural to want to sit back and allow a certain degree of laziness to take over the kitchen. And with the great produce that abounds at this time of the year, that is exactly what you will be doing.

# summertime inspiration
greet the sunshine with
## ruby red tomatoes
greens of every shape
## spices for zing
fresh herbs by the handful
and super cool chilled cucumbers

# summertime essentials

Summer is all about sitting back and enjoying blue skies and warm breezes. So the summer menu needs to focus on making life easy while still containing lots of zing. The easiest way to bring summer food to life is by using the ingredients of the season — think mangoes, watermelons, hot chillies, seafood, tomatoes, cucumbers, capsicums (peppers), sweetcorn and fresh herbs. With ingredients so rich in taste and colour, you need only to add the flavour punch of a great dressing, marinade or salsa and you will have dishes that are easy to make and taste great.

## asian inspiration

For me, lime and ginger are the predominant flavour accents of the season. They highlight most of my favourite accompaniments, whether it's a salsa, sauce or dressing, with the lime contributing a fragrant tang and the fresh ginger adding a warm bite. For this reason I tend to look towards Asia for inspiration in the warmer months. Chilli zapped seafood, crunchy salads with fragrant dressings, bowls of tangy noodles and barbecued juicy meats. If you have the option, then this really is the time to take the heat out of the kitchen by getting the barbecue going. Add a simple marinade to the meat or bring a spoonful of flavour with a spicy salsa and you reallly can't go wrong.

A simple bowl of noodles or steamed rice brings a little substance to meals and balances the vivid flavours that abound. There are so many noodles available these days that it's a culinary journey in itself to discover which are your favourites. Buckwheat, rice or wheat-based noodles feature in most Asian cuisines and are all very easy to prepare. Readily available dried, most noodles require less cooking time than dried wheat pasta so check the cooking instructions on the packet before tossing the noodles into boiling water. As a broad rule, soba noodles will need about 3–4 minutes in boiling water, green tea noodles and udon noodles should be boiled for 4–5 minutes and somen noodles will take about 3 minutes to cook. Rice-based noodles often only need soaking in boiling water. Put the rice vermicelli or rice-stick noodles in a bowl and cover with boiling water. Soak for 5 minutes for rice vermicelli or 10 minutes for rice-stick noodles.

## exotic touches

So many ingredients speak of summer and exotic places, it can be hard to know where to start. Here are some of my favourites to help you choose:

- Kaffir lime (makrut) leaves make a wonderful marinade base for seafood or chicken. The easiest way to slice them finely is to use a pair of kitchen scissors — simply snip the leaves into a bowl. Add some finely chopped chilli, lime juice and olive oil and toss prawns (shrimp), fish fillets or chicken pieces in the marinade and leave for up to 1 hour.

- Dashi or bonito stock makes a wonderful dressing for noodles and salads, as well as being a great base for soups. This Japanese stock is easy to make (page 285) but you can also buy instant dashi from speciality Asian stores and some large supermarkets. The packets are usually divided into individual serves, making them very handy to have in the pantry.

- Pomegranate molasses is one of those slightly obscure but highly desirable ingredients that are worth grabbing when you see a bottle. Or visit a Middle Eastern food store where it can be found, and while you're there stock up on little bottles of rosewater and orange flower water and bags of sumac. Then head back to the kitchen and start experimenting! Pomegranate molasses has a bittersweet tang and is ideal for adding to tomato-based salsas and sauces as well as beetroot dip. Rosewater and orange flower water are divine in summer fruit salads, meringues and simple cakes or icing. You'll have guests intrigued about the secret ingredient. And you won't regret having sumac on hand. With its slightly peppery lemon flavour, this great spice is wondrous when rubbed into the skin of chicken before roasting, or with lamb fillets for grilling (broiling).

- Tamarind is a fruit native to Asia and is prized for its sour pulp. The pulp is most commonly available compressed into cakes or refined as tamarind concentrate in jars. Tamarind concentrate is widely available, and should be used according to the package instructions, while the pulp can be found in Asian supermarkets. To make tamarind water from the compressed cakes, put 100 g (3 1/2 oz) tamarind into a bowl and cover with 500 ml (17 fl oz/2 cups) boiling water. Allow to steep for 1 hour, stirring occasionally to break up the fibres, then strain.

- Kecap manis is a great storecupboard essential. This rich semi-sweet soy sauce, a staple of Indonesian cooking, is flavoured with palm sugar and is less salty than Japanese soy sauce. Simply drizzle over steamed greens or add to a dressing or easy stir-fry to bring a simple taste of the East to your meal.

# classic dressings

## peanut

Combine 1 tablespoon shaved palm sugar, 100 ml (3$^1$/$_2$ fl oz) tamarind water, 2 tablespoons kecap manis and 1 tablespoon balsamic vinegar in a small bowl. Stir until the palm sugar has dissolved. Add 1 seeded and finely chopped red chilli, 1 finely chopped garlic clove and 70 g (2$^1$/$_2$ oz/$^1$/$_2$ cup) ground roasted peanuts. This dressing is delicious spooned over a salad of julienned vegetables or fresh tofu or thinly sliced beef with cucumber and mint. Makes 185 ml (6 fl oz/ $^3$/$_4$ cup)

## sweet ginger

Put 125 ml (4 fl oz/$^1$/$_2$ cup) dashi stock into a saucepan with 3 tablespoons rice wine vinegar, 4 tablespoons light soy sauce and 3 teaspoons sugar. Bring to the boil, then remove from the heat and pour the hot liquid into a serving bowl. When the dressing has cooled, add 1 tablespoon finely grated fresh ginger. This dressing is ideal for pouring over julienned vegetable salads or mixed salads that feature crab, prawns (shrimp) or other light seafood, as well as poached chicken. Makes 250 ml (9 fl oz/1 cup)

Zappy dressings bring simple salads to life with the

## lemon and cumin

Combine 2 tablespoons lemon juice, 125 ml (4 fl oz/1/2 cup) olive oil, 2 very finely chopped garlic cloves, 1 teaspoon ground cumin and a large pinch of paprika in a bowl and stir to blend. This dressing is used on many Middle Eastern-style salads. Pour it over a salad of tomatoes and cucumbers or over freshly cooked lentils. Makes 100 ml (3 1/2 fl oz)

## lime and lemongrass

Put 4 tablespoons lime juice, 4 tablespoons fish sauce and 2 tablespoons sugar into a bowl. Stir until the sugar has dissolved. Add 2 tablespoons finely chopped lemongrass, 1 very finely chopped garlic clove and 2 seeded and finely chopped small red chillies. Stir to combine. This dressing is wonderful with seafood salads and simple salads of sliced cucumber, sprouts and fresh herbs. It can also be drizzled over chilled wedges of iceberg lettuce or poured over a rice-noodle salad. Makes 150 ml (5 fl oz)

exotic flavours and aromas of the East.

# tomato essentials

There's nothing more disappointing than a cold and tasteless tomato. So remember these two basic rules — never store tomatoes in the refrigerator, and only use them when they are ripe and a rich ruby red. At this point, all they really need is a generous sprinkle of sea salt and a drizzle of extra virgin olive oil to transform them into a great salad or side dish. In fact, the best tomato salad I've ever had was in a rough campsite in Italy — the tomatoes tasted so amazing that they needed no other assistance.

While such tomatoes are not always easy to come by, there's an inspiring range readily available in supermarkets and greengrocers. Think cherry tomatoes, multi-coloured tear-drop tomatoes, baby and full-sized Roma (plum) tomatoes, truss tomatoes, vine-ripened tomatoes and magnificent beef tomatoes, when they are in season.

When buying tomatoes always check for any tell-tale bruising or marking. If the surface of the tomato feels soft and watery then it's definitely a good idea to avoid it. If in doubt, use your nose since a bad tomato is easy to smell and, if you're lucky, instead of a rotter you'll smell that wonderful green vine smell — what tomatoes used to smell like all the time!

## freshen up

To enhance the flavours of fresh tomatoes, you can simply toss them with some torn basil leaves, small black olives, salted capers, anchovies, oregano or wild rocket (arugula) leaves, and you'll have created the perfect side to a summery meal. Try some of these quick combinations:

- Put diced tomatoes in a bowl with drained tinned white beans and tinned tuna. Lightly mash together with a little olive oil and seasoning. Serve on bruschetta as a snack or with toasted rye bread as an easy lunch.

- Finely dice tomatoes and red onion and toss with some oregano leaves. Season with sea salt and freshly ground black pepper. Drizzle with extra virgin olive oil and spoon onto toasted sourdough bread. Top with a spoonful of soft goat's curd and a sprinkle of paprika.

- Add 1 tablespoon finely chopped basil and 1 teaspoon thyme leaves to 200 g (7 oz) ricotta cheese. Mix together, then serve with a salad of halved cherry tomatoes and thinly sliced cucumber. Serve the salad with olive bread.

- Toss diced tomato with slices of preserved lemon rind and parsley. Serve with grilled (broiled) fish or roasted chicken.

- Arrange thick slices of tomato on a serving platter. Scatter with parsley leaves and sprinkle with $1/2$ teaspoon ground cumin. Dress with a balsamic vinegar dressing. Serve with grilled (broiled) lamb or tuna.

- Finely slice 1 red onion and sprinkle it with 1 tablespoon sugar and a little sea salt. Allow to sit for 30 minutes, then cover with cider vinegar. Arrange some thickly sliced tomatoes on a serving platter and top with the drained onion slices. Drizzle with extra virgin olive oil and season with freshly ground black pepper.

## the hearty tomato

If you wish to make more of a meal of tomatoes, then here are a few ideas:

- Put 500 g (1 lb 2 oz) cherry tomatoes into a large frying pan and drizzle with 3 tablespoons water and 1 tablespoon balsamic vinegar. Scatter over some rosemary sprigs and season with sea salt and a little pepper. Bring to the boil over high heat and cook until the tomato skins are just beginning to split. Remove the pan from the heat and drizzle the tomatoes with a little extra virgin olive oil. When the tomatoes have cooled, spoon them over a baby leaf salad and top with crumbled goat's cheese and small black olives.

- Roughly chop 4 tomatoes and put them into a bowl with 1 finely chopped garlic clove and the diced flesh of 2 roasted yellow capsicums (peppers). Season with sea salt, black pepper, $1/2$ teaspoon ground cumin and a pinch of hot chilli powder. Drizzle with a little extra virgin olive oil and the juice of 1 lemon. Spoon over a salad of mixed baby leaves, coriander (cilantro) leaves and mint leaves.

- Put whole Roma (plum) tomatoes on a baking tray and bake them in a 200°C (400°F/Gas 6) oven until their skin is blistered and blackened. Remove from the oven and cool slightly. Blend the whole tomatoes, including the charred skins, with a handful of basil leaves and seasoning. Put the tomato mixture in a saucepan and add enough water or vegetable stock to form a soupy consistency. Heat the soup and serve with a drizzle of extra virgin olive oil, shaved Parmesan cheese and croûtons.

153

# roasted red capsicums

1 Preheat the oven to 200°C (400°F/Gas 6). Place a small rack on or over a baking tray or roasting tin. Lightly rub several red capsicums (peppers) with olive oil and place them on the rack. Bake until the skin begins to blister and blacken. You may need to turn the capsicums several times so that the skin blisters all over.

2 Remove the capsicums from the oven and transfer them to a container. Cover with plastic wrap and allow them to cool. Covering the capsicums now will make them easier to peel later.

3 Remove the blackened skin from the capsicums by gently rubbing it away with your fingers. The skin should come away easily. Remove the stems and the seeds from inside the capsicum. Lay the cleaned flesh on a board and finely slice or chop it.

## hints & tips

- If you are not using the capsicums (peppers) straight away, put them in a bowl and cover with olive oil. The oil will help the capsicums to keep longer in the refrigerator as well as providing a great flavoured oil. You may wish to add some extra flavours to the oil, such as basil, garlic, parsley or thyme.

- Marinated roasted capsicums are a wonderful thing to have on hand in the refrigerator. They can be finely diced and tossed with basil and black olives for a simple accompaniment to grilled (broiled) lamb or beef. They can be cut into strips to liven up a green salad or a cold pasta salad.

- Roasted capsicums are used in a wide range of recipes but corn and black bean salsa is one of my favourites: Heat 2 tablespoons olive oil in a frying pan over medium heat and add 1 very finely chopped garlic clove, 1 tablespoon ground cumin and 200 g (7 oz/1 cup) fresh corn kernels. Sauté until the corn has turned a golden yellow and then remove from the heat. Finely dice the flesh of 2 roasted red capsicums and then drain and rinse a 400 g (14 oz) tin black beans. Put the corn, diced red capsicum and beans in a large bowl. Roughly chop 1 handful coriander (cilantro) leaves, and add to the bowl with 10 finely chopped mint leaves, 1 tablespoon pomegranate molasses and a few drops of Tabasco sauce. Stir to combine. Taste and add more Tabasco sauce if you like your salsa spicy.

154

# classic salsas

## tomato

Put 4 finely diced Roma (plum) tomatoes into a bowl. Add 10 finely sliced basil leaves, 2 tablespoons finely diced red onion, 1/2 teaspoon very finely chopped garlic, 3 tablespoons extra virgin olive oil, 1 tablespoon balsamic vinegar and 1/2 teaspoon sea salt. Stir to combine. Check the seasoning; you may wish to add a little more salt to taste. This salsa is a wonderful accompaniment to grilled (broiled) tuna, blue-eye cod or swordfish. It can also be served with spicy marinated chicken or seared lamb. Serves 4 as a side dish

## avocado

Put 1 finely diced avocado, 1 finely diced Lebanese (short) cucumber, 1 seeded and finely diced red chilli, 1 tablespoon finely diced red onion, 3 tablespoons lime juice and 1/2 teaspoon sea salt in a bowl. Add 1 handful coriander (cilantro) leaves and 1 tablespoon extra virgin olive oil. Lightly stir to combine. Serve with some grilled (broiled) chicken, prawns (shrimp) or white-fleshed fish. This salsa can also be served with warm tortillas or on bruschetta. Serves 4 as a side dish

## nori

Finely julienne 1 Lebanese (short) cucumber and add it to a bowl with 1/2 finely julienned daikon, 1 tablespoon finely chopped pickled ginger, 1 tablespoon rice wine vinegar, a few drops of sesame oil, 1/2 teaspoon red chilli powder and 2 teaspoons toasted sesame seeds. Take 1 nori sheet and lightly toast it in a preheated 180°C (350°F/Gas 4) oven until crisp. Using a pair of kitchen scissors, cut the toasted nori sheet into thin julienne strips approximately 3 cm (11/4 in) long. Add the strips to the other ingredients. Gently toss to combine. Serve with steamed white rice or grilled (broiled) chicken or finely sliced rare roasted beef. Serves 4 as a side dish

## mango

Dice the flesh of 1 large or 2 small mangoes. Put the mango flesh into a bowl with 1 finely sliced spring onion (scallion), 1 seeded and finely chopped red chilli, 2 tablespoons lime juice, a few drops of sesame oil and a grind of black pepper. Toss to combine. If you'd like some herbs in this salsa, add 1 handful coriander (cilantro) leaves or 4 finely sliced large basil leaves. This salsa adds a lovely summer hit to barbecued prawns (shrimp) or chicken. Serves 4 as a side dish

# Grilled prawns that have soaked ginger epitomize summer. One

## marinating basics

1 Prepare the prawns (shrimp) according to how you are going to cook them. If barbecuing, you may wish to keep their shells on. Using a small sharp pair of scissors, cut a line down the back of the prawn through the shell. Then use a sharp knife to make an incision and remove the dark vein. Otherwise simply peel and devein.

2 Put 2 tablespoons finely grated fresh ginger, 4 finely sliced kaffir lime (makrut) leaves, 2 tablespoons finely chopped lemongrass, 1 finely chopped large red chilli, 1 very finely chopped garlic clove, the juice of 4 limes and 4 tablespoons olive oil into a large bowl and stir to combine.

3 Put the prawns into a large container and pour over the marinade. Toss, ensuring that they are all well covered. Cover and allow to marinate in the refrigerator for 1 hour.

### hints & tips

- For a super simple prawn (shrimp) marinade, toss the prawns in lemon juice, olive oil and garlic. This marinade could also be used for other seafood. If you like a little bite, you could season it with $1/2$ teaspoon ground white pepper or paprika or some dried chilli flakes.

- Seafood should only be marinated for up to 1 hour. Any longer and the acid in the lime or lemon juice will 'cook' the flesh.

- Remember to always marinate seafood in a container made of glass, stainless steel or ceramic to ensure that the container does not react with the acid of the marinade.

up the flavours of lemongrass, lime, chilli and bite and you can feel the sand between your toes.

# classic marinades

## seafood

For white fish, try a light marinade of 1 teaspoon finely grated fresh ginger, 2 tablespoons coriander (cilantro) leaves, 2 tablespoons lime juice and 3 tablespoons olive oil. Put into a bowl and stir to combine, then add the fish pieces. Toss the pieces in the marinade to ensure they are well coated. Allow to marinate in the refrigerator for 30 minutes before grilling (broiling), baking or pan-frying. Serves 4

## lamb

Put 125 ml (4 fl oz/$^1$/$_2$ cup) white wine, 4 tablespoons olive oil, the juice of 1 lemon, 1 tablespoon fresh oregano leaves and 1 finely chopped garlic clove into a bowl. Add lamb cutlets, fillets or a boned leg of lamb to the marinade. Toss to thoroughly coat the pieces in the mixture, then marinate in the refrigerator for 2–3 hours. Cook the lamb until it is still a little pink in the centre and then season with sea salt and freshly ground black pepper. Allow to rest for 5 minutes before serving. Serves 4

These easy marinades add fresh herb oomph to

## chicken

Put 3 tablespoons lemon juice, 3 tablespoons olive oil, 1 tablespoon Dijon mustard, 1 teaspoon finely chopped garlic, 1 teaspoon thyme leaves and 1/2 teaspoon ground white pepper into a large bowl. Add the chicken pieces and toss to thoroughly coat the pieces in the mixture, then marinate in the refrigerator for 2–3 hours. Remove the chicken pieces from the marinade and barbecue or roast them until cooked. Season with sea salt and serve. Serves 4

## beef

Put 250 ml (9 fl oz/1 cup) red wine into a bowl with 2 finely chopped garlic cloves, 1/2 teaspoon finely chopped rosemary and 125 ml (4 fl oz/1/2 cup) olive oil. Stir to mix. Add your chosen cuts of beef and gently toss so that the pieces are thoroughly coated in the mixture. Put in the refrigerator and marinate for 2–3 hours. Remove the beef from the marinade and season well with freshly ground black pepper. Cook on the barbecue or in a pan until the beef is cooked to your liking. Remove from the heat and season with sea salt. Allow to rest for 5 minutes before serving. Serves 4

everyday meals such as grilled meat or chicken.

# summertime recipes
## celebrate the season
### with slippery noodles
## fresh seafood
### leafy coriander
### slivers of marinated beef
## light and healthy
### but packed with colour and flavour

tomato with chilli and coriander

mussels with rouille

## tomato with chilli and coriander

90 g (3¹/₄ oz/1 bunch) coriander (cilantro) leaves, roughly chopped
1 red onion, finely diced
2 large red chillies, seeded and finely chopped
1 teaspoon sea salt
3 tablespoons olive oil
1 tablespoon balsamic vinegar
4 large ripe tomatoes

Put the coriander, onion, chilli, salt, olive oil and balsamic vinegar in a bowl and toss them together.

Slice the tomatoes and arrange them on a plate. Scatter the coriander salsa on top, season and serve as a side dish or as a salad with a little seared tuna or fresh ricotta cheese. Serves 4 as a side dish

## mussels with rouille

2 kg (4 lb 8 oz) mussels
2 tablespoons olive oil
1 white onion, finely chopped
2 garlic cloves, crushed
3 large ripe tomatoes, diced
1 bay leaf
1 fennel bulb, finely sliced
pinch of saffron threads
1 teaspoon sea salt
250 ml (9 fl oz/1 cup) white wine
1 handful flat-leaf (Italian) parsley
1 quantity rouille (page 64)
crusty white bread, to serve

Clean the mussels in the sink under cold running water, scrubbing them to remove any barnacles or bits of hairy 'beard'. Throw away any that are open and that do not close when you tap them.

Put the oil, onion and garlic into a large lidded saucepan and cook them over low heat until the onion is transparent. Add the tomato, bay leaf, fennel and saffron, season with the sea salt and simmer for 10 minutes. Pour in the white wine, bring the sauce to the boil and add the mussels. Cover with the lid and cook for a few minutes, shaking the pan once or twice, then check that all the mussels have opened. Throw away any that remain closed.

Divide the mussels among four big bowls, sprinkle with the parsley and serve with the rouille and crusty white bread. Serves 4

## coconut prawns with mint and lemongrass

2 tablespoons finely chopped lemongrass
2 tablespoons lime juice
¹/₂ teaspoon grated palm or soft brown sugar
250 ml (9 fl oz/1 cup) coconut milk
1 tablespoon peanut oil
20 raw king prawns (shrimp), peeled and deveined
80 g (2³/₄ oz/1 bunch) mint
60 g (2¹/₄ oz/1 cup) shredded coconut, toasted
100 g (3¹/₂ oz/heaped 1 cup) bean sprouts
2 Lebanese (short) cucumbers, finely sliced
1 lime, quartered, to serve

Put the lemongrass, lime juice, sugar and coconut milk into a small saucepan over low heat. Simmer for 10 minutes, stirring occasionally to ensure the sugar dissolves. Remove from the heat and allow to cool in a large bowl.

Put a heavy-based frying pan over high heat and add the oil. Swirl the oil over the base of the pan, then add a few of the prawns. Cook only as many prawns as will comfortably fit into the pan. Sear the prawns for a few minutes on each side, flipping them over as they change colour. As the prawns are cooked, remove and add them to the coconut sauce in the bowl. Continue until all the prawns are cooked. Put the mint, toasted coconut, bean sprouts and cucumber into a bowl and toss together. Pile the salad mix onto four plates and top with the warm prawns. Drizzle with whatever sauce remains in the bowl and serve with fresh lime wedges. Serves 4

coconut prawns with mint and lemongrass

## teriyaki beef with wakame salad

450 g (1 lb) lean beef fillet
3 tablespoons teriyaki sauce
25 g (1 oz) dried wakame seaweed
4 tablespoons rice wine vinegar
3 Lebanese (short) cucumbers
2 tablespoons caster (superfine) sugar
1/2 teaspoon soy sauce
3 cm (1 1/2 in) piece fresh ginger, julienned
2 red radishes, finely sliced
1 large handful watercress sprigs
1 tablespoon black sesame seeds

Preheat the oven to 200°C (400°F/Gas 6). Marinate the beef fillet in the teriyaki sauce for 30 minutes. Heat a heavy-based pan over high heat and sear the fillet on all sides. Put onto a baking tray and bake for 10 minutes. Remove and set aside.

Soak the wakame in cold water for 10 minutes, or until soft. Drain, put it in a bowl and cover with 1 tablespoon vinegar. Thinly slice the cucumbers diagonally and put into a separate bowl. Sprinkle with 1/2 teaspoon salt and set aside for several minutes. Dissolve the sugar in the soy sauce and remaining vinegar and add the ginger. Rinse the salt off the cucumber and gently squeeze dry. Combine the wakame, cucumber, radish and dressing in a bowl and toss to combine.

Thinly slice the beef and divide among four small plates. Top with the salad and garnish with watercress and black sesame seeds. Serves 4 as a starter

## ocean trout in citrus marinade

4 x 150 g (5 1/2 oz) skinless ocean trout fillets, boned
2 tablespoons olive oil
1 handful flat-leaf (Italian) parsley
grated zest and juice of 1 lemon
grated zest and juice of 1 orange
500 g (1 lb 2 oz) vine-ripened tomatoes, finely diced
2 spring onions (scallions), finely chopped
1 tablespoon salted capers, rinsed

Slice the trout into 4 cm (1 1/2 in) wide slices. Heat half the oil in a large, heavy-based frying pan over medium heat and sear the trout for 1 minute on both sides. Put on a serving dish and season with sea salt and freshly ground black pepper.

Scatter the parsley over the fish. Add the lemon juice, orange juice, zest, tomato, spring onion and capers to the pan and cook for 1 minute. Pour over the fish and drizzle with the remaining olive oil. Allow to sit in the refrigerator for 1 hour before serving with a spoonful of the marinade. Serves 4

## prawns with coriander and lime

2 tablespoons chopped coriander (cilantro) root
2 tablespoons grated fresh ginger
2 garlic cloves, roughly chopped
1 lemongrass stalk, white part only, roughly chopped
125 ml (4 fl oz/1/2 cup) vegetable oil
1 teaspoon ground coriander
20 large raw prawns (shrimp), peeled and deveined
1 large handful coriander (cilantro) leaves
3 tablespoons lime juice
125 ml (4 fl oz/1/2 cup) olive oil
1/2 teaspoon sugar
20 small bamboo skewers, soaked in hot water for 20 minutes

Put the coriander root, ginger, garlic, lemongrass, oil and ground coriander in a blender and blend to form a smooth paste. Put the prawns in a ceramic or glass dish and pour over the paste. Marinate in the refrigerator, covered, for 1 hour.

Combine the coriander leaves, lime juice, olive oil, sugar and a pinch of salt in a bowl and set aside. Put a prawn on each of the bamboo skewers and grill over medium heat on a barbecue for 5 minutes. Serve with a drizzle of the coriander dressing. Makes 20

## tamarind and squid salad

1 tablespoon tamarind concentrate
1 tablespoon sugar
2 tablespoons fish sauce
1 tablespoon lime juice
1 garlic clove, crushed
1 small red chilli, seeded and julienned
4 medium squid (about 400 g/14 oz), cleaned
3 tablespoons oil
1 handful basil
1 handful coriander (cilantro) leaves
90 g (3 1/4 oz/1 cup) bean sprouts
steamed white rice or rice noodles, to serve

To make the dressing, blend the tamarind with 3 tablespoons warm water, add the sugar, fish sauce, lime juice, garlic and chilli and stir until the sugar has dissolved.

Rinse the squid under cold running water and pat it dry with paper towels. Cut the tubes down one side to open, and lightly score the outside surface in a diamond pattern to make it curl up during cooking. Heat the oil in a frying pan over high heat and fry the squid for 3–4 minutes on each side. Cut each tube into bite-sized pieces and toss in the tamarind dressing with the herbs and sprouts. Serve with steamed white rice or rice noodles. Serves 4

squid and pine nut salad

snapper with a citrus dressing

## squid and pine nut salad

450 g (1 lb) small squid
4 anchovy fillets, finely chopped
2 tablespoons olive oil
grated zest and juice of 1 lemon
2 garlic cloves, crushed
150 g (5$^1$/$_2$ oz/1 bunch) rocket (arugula), stalks removed
1 large handful flat-leaf (Italian) parsley
50 g (1$^3$/$_4$ oz/$^1$/$_2$ cup) shaved Parmesan cheese
85 g (3 oz/$^1$/$_2$ cup) toasted pine nuts

Combine the squid, anchovy fillets, olive oil, lemon zest and garlic in a bowl and toss well to coat the squid thoroughly. Cover the squid and allow it to marinate in the refrigerator for at least 1 hour.

Put a heavy-based frying pan over high heat and cook the squid, searing it on both sides for 1–2 minutes, then pour on the marinade and cook for a further 30 seconds. Turn off the heat and allow the squid to sit for a few minutes before slicing it into thin rings. Put the squid in a bowl along with the remaining ingredients, dress with the lemon juice and toss together. Serves 4

## snapper with a citrus dressing

2 oranges
2 limes
1 lemon
$^1$/$_2$ teaspoon pink peppercorns, roughly chopped
4 tablespoons light olive oil
2 tablespoons oil
4 x 200 g (7 oz) snapper fillets, skin on

Preheat the oven to 200°C (400°F/Gas 6).

To make the dressing, zest the oranges, limes and lemon and put the zest into a bowl. Juice the lemon and add the juice to the bowl. Segment the oranges and limes and put them in the bowl along with any juice, then add the peppercorns and light olive oil and stir well.

Put the oil in a large ovenproof frying pan over high heat. Rinse the snapper fillets in cold water and pat them dry with paper towels. Season the fillets liberally with sea salt and put them skin-side down in the hot pan. Sear the fillets for 1–2 minutes until the skin is crisp and golden, then turn over.

Put the frying pan into the oven and bake the snapper for 8 minutes. Transfer the fillets to a serving dish, then cover with the citrus dressing and serve immediately. Serves 4

## lemongrass chicken

grated zest and juice of 1 lime
1 lemongrass stalk, trimmed and roughly chopped
2 garlic cloves, peeled
2 cm ($^3$/$_4$ in) piece fresh ginger, peeled and roughly chopped
1 large red chilli, seeded
1$^1$/$_2$ tablespoons fish sauce
4 chicken breast fillets
2 tablespoons olive oil
steamed white rice and Chinese greens, to serve

Preheat the oven to 200°C (400°F/Gas 6).

Put the lime zest, lemongrass, garlic, ginger, chilli and fish sauce into a food processor or mortar and pestle and process or grind to a smooth paste. Rub the paste all over the chicken breasts and put them on a baking tray. Drizzle with the olive oil and lime juice and season with a little sea salt. Cover with aluminium foil and bake for 25–30 minutes. Remove from the oven and use the pointed end of a sharp knife to check that the chicken is cooked through.

Serve sliced with steamed white rice, Chinese greens and a drizzle of baking juices. You can also toss the sliced chicken with a leaf salad and sprinkle with some ground roasted peanuts. Serves 4

Choose dishes that combine perfectly with blue skies and leisurely lunches.

lemongrass chicken

# seared prawns with mint and yoghurt sauce

16 large raw prawns (shrimp), peeled and deveined, tails intact
2 tablespoons olive oil
4 tablespoons lemon juice
1 large handful mint
1 green chilli, seeded
1 teaspoon ground roasted cumin
1 teaspoon sugar
1 tablespoon grated fresh ginger
100 g (3$^1$/2 oz/heaped $^1$/3 cup) plain yoghurt
10 snowpeas (mangetout), blanched
1 Lebanese (short) cucumber, diced
1 large handful coriander (cilantro) leaves
steamed white rice, to serve

Put the prawns, olive oil and 1 tablespoon of lemon juice in a bowl and toss lightly together. Set aside. Put the mint leaves, remaining lemon juice, chilli, cumin, sugar and ginger into a blender and process to make a thin sauce. Pour the sauce into a bowl, add the yoghurt and fold through. Season to taste with sea salt and freshly ground black pepper.

Heat a frying pan over high heat and sear the prawns, a few at a time, until they begin to change colour and curl. Turn them over and cook for 1 minute on the other side.

Divide the snowpeas, cucumber and coriander among four plates and top with the warm prawns. Drizzle with the yoghurt sauce and serve with steamed white rice. Serves 4

# tuna with tomato, basil and black olives

10 cherry tomatoes, halved
10 basil leaves, roughly torn
20 small black olives
2 tablespoons balsamic vinegar
4 tablespoons extra virgin olive oil
1 teaspoon olive oil
4 x 150 g (5$^1$/2 oz) tuna fillets
150 g (5$^1$/2 oz/1 bunch) rocket (arugula), stalks removed

Put the tomatoes, basil, olives, vinegar and extra virgin olive oil into a small bowl and toss together.

Put the olive oil in a pan and heat over high heat. Add the tuna and sear on one side for 1 minute. Turn the fillets over and reduce the heat to medium. Cook for a further 3 minutes. Put the tuna onto warmed plates with some rocket leaves and top with the tomato and olive mixture. Serves 4

# watercress and duck salad

125 ml (4 fl oz/$^1$/2 cup) sherry
125 ml (4 fl oz/$^1$/2 cup) orange juice
1 tablespoon soy sauce
1 teaspoon sesame oil
1 teaspoon sugar
1 teaspoon finely grated fresh ginger
1 Chinese roasted duck
115 g (4 oz) snowpeas (mangetout), trimmed
500 g (1 lb 2 oz/1 bunch) watercress
200 g (7 oz) tin water chestnuts, drained and sliced

To make the dressing, put the sherry and orange juice into a small saucepan and bring to the boil. Reduce the heat and simmer until the liquid has reduced by half. Pour into a large bowl and add the soy sauce, sesame oil, sugar and ginger.

Remove the skin from the roasted duck and cut it into thin strips, scraping off any fat. Put the skin strips on a baking tray and grill (broil) them briefly until they are crisp, then put them on paper towels to drain off any fat.

Remove the meat from the duck and tear it into strips, then add it to the bowl of dressing. Blanch the snowpeas in boiling water and refresh them under cold running water. Toss the duck meat with the watercress, water chestnuts, snowpeas and crisp skin, and serve. Serves 4

# spiced ocean trout

550 g (1 lb 4 oz) ocean trout fillet, skin and bones removed
1 teaspoon sesame oil
4 spring onions (scallions), cut into 3 cm (1$^1$/4 in) lengths
185 ml (6 fl oz/$^3$/4 cup) cider vinegar
3 tablespoons sugar
2 cm ($^3$/4 in) piece fresh ginger, peeled and julienned
2 large red chillies, seeded and finely sliced
10 cm (4 in) piece young lemongrass, finely chopped
4 star anise
1 teaspoon Sichuan peppercorns
udon noodles, to serve

Cut the fish into 1 cm ($^1$/2 in) wide slices and put them in a single layer in a large, deep, nonmetallic dish.

Put the sesame oil and spring onion in a saucepan over medium heat and cook until the spring onion has darkened in colour. Pour 500 ml (17 fl oz/2 cups) water over the spring onion and mix in the vinegar, sugar, ginger, chilli, lemongrass, star anise and peppercorns. Bring to the boil, stirring to dissolve the sugar, then pour the hot liquid over the trout. When cool, serve with udon noodles. Serves 4

swordfish with a pine nut sauce

linguine with prawns and fresh herbs

## swordfish in a pine nut sauce

1 slice white bread, crusts removed
85 g (3 oz/$^1/_2$ cup) pine nuts
$^1/_2$ garlic clove
2 tablespoons lemon juice
1 tablespoon olive oil
4 x 175 g (6 oz) swordfish steaks
salad of tomatoes, red onion and basil, to serve

Soak the bread in cold water, then squeeze it dry. Put the pine nuts, bread, garlic and lemon juice in a food processor and process to form a smooth paste, then add 3 tablespoons water to thin it to a pourable consistency.

Heat the olive oil in a large frying pan over high heat. Sear the swordfish steaks on one side for 2 minutes, or until they are golden brown, then turn them over and reduce the heat. Cook the other side for a further 2–3 minutes, or until the steaks are cooked through — they should feel firm when you press them.

Put the fish on serving plates, spoon the sauce over and serve with a salad of tomatoes, red onion and basil. Serves 4

## linguine with prawns and fresh herbs

400 g (14 oz) linguine
100 ml (3$^1/_3$ fl oz) light olive oil
3 garlic cloves, crushed and finely chopped
16 raw king prawns (shrimp), peeled and deveined, tails intact
250 g (9 oz) cherry tomatoes, halved
1 handful flat-leaf (Italian) parsley, roughly chopped
12 basil leaves, torn
30 g (1 oz/1 bunch) chives
juice of 1 lemon

Bring a large pot of salted water to the boil. Add the linguine and cook in rapidly boiling water until al dente. Meanwhile, put the olive oil in a frying pan and heat over medium heat. Add

the garlic, stir briefly, then add the prawns. Fry the prawns until they are pink on both sides and have begun to curl up. Add the cherry tomatoes and cook for a further 1 minute. Remove from the heat.

Strain the cooked linguine and return it to the pot. Add the prawn and tomato mixture, herbs and lemon juice. Toss together and season with sea salt and freshly cracked black pepper. Serves 4

## green tea noodles with lemongrass and soy

2 lemongrass stalks, white part only, finely chopped
1 tablespoon finely grated fresh ginger
3$^1/_2$ tablespoons soy sauce
3$^1/_2$ tablespoons sesame oil
1$^1/_2$ tablespoons balsamic vinegar
2 tablespoons sugar
juice of 1 lemon
300 g (10$^1/_2$ oz) dried green tea noodles
2 spring onions (scallions), finely sliced
90 g (3$^1/_4$ oz/1 bunch) coriander (cilantro), leaves picked
1 red capsicum (pepper), finely diced
1 yellow capsicum (pepper), finely diced

Put the lemongrass, ginger, soy sauce, sesame oil, balsamic vinegar, sugar and lemon juice into a small bowl and stir until the sugar has dissolved. Set aside.

Bring a large pot of water to the boil and add the noodles. Cook for 4–5 minutes, or until al dente. Drain well and transfer the noodles to a large bowl. Drizzle with the dressing, lightly tossing the noodles to ensure they are all coated. Add the sliced shallots, coriander leaves and diced capsicum. Toss again before dividing among four bowls.

Serve as a light meal, or alongside some grilled (broiled) prawns (shrimp), fish or chicken. Serves 4

Celebrate sun-kissed skin and bare feet with a bowl of slurpy, slippery, tangy noodles, speckled with colour.

green tea noodles with lemongrass and soy

# white chicken salad

4 spring onions (scallions), finely sliced, green tops reserved
1 lemongrass stalk, bruised
90 g (3¹/₄ oz/1 bunch) coriander (cilantro)
1 tablespoon sea salt
2 chicken breast fillets
400 g (14 oz/2 cups) jasmine rice
80 g (2³/₄ oz/1 bunch) mint
1 large red chilli, seeded and finely chopped
300 g (10¹/₂ oz) silken firm tofu, cut into 4 thick slices
soy sauce and lime wedges, to serve

Put the spring onion tops into a large saucepan with the lemongrass and coriander roots and stalks. Fill the pan with water, add the salt and bring to the boil. Add the chicken to the stock, cover the pan and remove it from the heat. Set aside, covered, for 40 minutes, then lift out the fillets and check they are cooked. Finely slice them across the grain.

Put the rice and 685 ml (23 fl oz/2³/₄ cups) of the strained cooking liquid into a saucepan. Bring to the boil, cover, reduce the heat to low and cook for 25 minutes, or until the stock is absorbed and the rice is tender. Finely slice half the mint leaves. Stir the spring onion, sliced mint, coriander leaves, chilli and chicken into the rice. Divide among four plates and top with a slice of tofu. Splash with soy sauce, and serve with a lime wedge and more mint leaves. Serves 4

# baked salmon and daikon salad

2 tablespoons hijiki
6 umeboshi plums, seeds removed
4 tablespoons mirin
2 teaspoons sesame oil
4 x 200 g (7 oz) salmon fillets, skin on
2 tablespoons oil
300 g (10¹/₂ oz) daikon, julienned
1 tablespoon finely sliced pickled ginger
1 tablespoon pickled ginger juice
500 g (1 lb 2 oz/1 bunch) watercress, stalks removed

Preheat the oven to 180°C (350°F/Gas 4). Soak the hijiki in warm water for about 20 minutes, then drain. Mash the plums until soft, then combine them with the mirin and sesame oil.

Rinse the salmon fillets in cold water and pat them dry. Rub the plum glaze into the flesh. Heat the oil in an ovenproof frying pan over high heat and add the fillets skin-side down. Sear the fish for a few minutes, then bake for 10 minutes.

Meanwhile, toss the hijiki, daikon, ginger and ginger juice together in a bowl with the watercress leaves. Pile the mixture onto four plates and top with the salmon fillets. Serves 4

# soba noodle salad

4 tablespoons hijiki
1 teaspoon dashi granules
125 ml (4 fl oz/¹/₂ cup) soy sauce
3 tablespoons mirin
1 teaspoon sugar
1 tablespoon pickled ginger, finely chopped
4 spring onions (scallions), finely sliced on the diagonal
300 g (10¹/₂ oz) soba noodles
500 g (1 lb 2 oz) daikon, julienned
1 Lebanese (short) cucumber, julienned
20 mint leaves, roughly torn

Soak the hijiki in warm water for 30 minutes, then drain. Combine the dashi granules, soy sauce, mirin and sugar with 375 ml (13 fl oz/1¹/₂ cups) water in a small saucepan and bring to the boil, stirring so the sugar dissolves. Remove from the heat and allow the sauce to cool. Add the pickled ginger and spring onion.

Cook the noodles in boiling water until al dente, then drain them and rinse with cold water to remove any starch. In a large bowl, toss the noodles, daikon, hijiki, cucumber, mint and sauce together and divide among four bowls. Serve the salad as is, or top it with ocean trout in citrus marinade (page 169). Serves 4

# buckwheat noodle and herb salad

3 tablespoons soy sauce
3 tablespoons sesame oil
1¹/₂ tablespoons Chinese black vinegar
3 tablespoons grated palm sugar
3 tablespoons lime juice
1 tablespoon finely chopped lemongrass
1 red chilli, seeded and finely chopped
300 g (10¹/₂ oz) buckwheat noodles
5 cm (2 in) piece fresh ginger, peeled and finely julienned
80 g (2³/₄ oz/1 bunch) mint
90 g (3¹/₄ oz/1 bunch) coriander (cilantro)
12 cm (4¹/₂ in) piece daikon, peeled and julienned

Put the soy sauce, sesame oil, vinegar, sugar, lime juice, lemongrass and chilli into a large bowl and stir until the sugar has dissolved. Bring a large pot of water to the boil and cook the noodles until al dente, then drain and rinse them under cold running water. Put them in the bowl with the dressing and toss to coat the noodles. Add the ginger, mint, coriander and daikon to the noodles, toss together, then pile into four bowls. Serves 4

# afternoon tea

There is nothing nicer than filling the kitchen with the warm smells of baking or sharing cake and tea with friends. You may even develop the impressive knack of pulling scones out of the oven just as unexpected guests arrive.

# afternoon tea inspiration
find time in the afternoon for some
## whisking and baking
ice, drizzle and sprinkle

gooey chocolate, whipped cream

tea, coffee

or something stronger

This simple butter cake is flavoured sweet covering of drizzly icing and

# butter cake basics

1 Preheat the oven to 180°C (350°F/Gas 4). Grease and line a 23 cm (9 in) springform tin.

2 Beat 250 g (9 oz) softened unsalted butter and 225 g (8 oz/1 cup) caster (superfine) sugar in a mixing bowl until pale and creamy. Add 3 eggs, 125 ml (4 fl oz/½ cup) milk and 1 teaspoon natural vanilla extract and stir to combine. Fold in 250 g (9 oz/2 cups) sifted self-raising flour and then spoon the batter into the tin.

3 Bake for 1 hour, or until a skewer inserted into the cake comes out clean. Turn out the cake onto a wire rack to cool. When the cake has cooled, cover with lemon icing (page 190) or sprinkle with icing (confectioners') sugar.

## hints & tips

● The worst thing that can happen when baking cakes is the cake sticking to the tin. So it always pays to be particularly careful when preparing the tin. If you like your cake to look perfect, then get out the scissors and a pencil. Using the base of the tin as a template, cut out a corresponding shape in baking paper. Put the paper into the base of the greased cake tin. Cut a long strip of baking paper and use it to line the sides. If you don't mind a free-form cake, then simply press a large sheet of baking paper into the tin, crumpling it slightly to enable it to sit against the edges.

● Another option is to liberally grease the cake tin with butter and then put 1 tablespoon plain (all-purpose) flour in the centre. Shake the flour around the tin so that it sticks to the butter and the surface of the tin is covered in flour. If baking a nut-based cake, you can use ground almonds or hazelnuts instead of the flour. This will give a lovely texture and flavour to the sides of your cake.

with butter, eggs and just a touch of vanilla. Add a
you have a classic afternoon tea favourite.

# classic cakes

## citrus syrup

Preheat the oven to 180°C (350°F/Gas 4). Grease and line a 23 cm (9 in) springform tin. Beat 250 g (9 oz) softened unsalted butter and 225 g (8 oz/1 cup) caster (superfine) sugar in a mixing bowl until pale and creamy. Stir in 4 lightly beaten eggs, then fold in 250 g (9 oz/2 cups) sifted self-raising flour. Spoon the batter into the tin and bake for 50 minutes, or until a skewer inserted into the centre of the cake comes out clean. Meanwhile, make the syrup. Juice and zest 4 oranges, 4 lemons and 4 limes. Combine the juice with 225 g (8 oz/1 cup) sugar in a saucepan over medium heat and stir for 20 minutes, or until the sugar dissolves and a clear syrup is formed. Add the zest and simmer for 1 minute, then remove from the heat. Leave the cooked cake in the tin and pierce it all over with a skewer. Pour most of the syrup over the cake, reserving some of the syrup and the zest. When the cake has cooled, transfer it to a serving plate and spoon over the remaining syrup and zest. Serves 10

## cupcakes

Preheat the oven to 180°C (350°F/Gas 4). Line a 12-hole patty case with paper patty cases. Beat 175 g (6 oz) softened unsalted butter with 175 g (6 oz/$^3$/$_4$ cup) caster (superfine) sugar in a mixing bowl until pale and creamy. Add 3 eggs, 125 ml (4 fl oz/$^1$/$_2$ cup) milk and 1 teaspoon natural vanilla extract. Stir to combine, then fold in 175 g (6 oz/scant 1$^1$/$_2$ cups) sifted self-raising flour. Spoon the batter into the patty cases and bake for 15–20 minutes, or until golden and firm. Transfer the cupcakes to a wire rack to cool. When the cakes have cooled, decorate with icing or make butterfly cakes with whipped cream and halved fresh strawberries. Dust with a little icing (confectioners') sugar. Makes 12

## orange poppy seed

Preheat the oven to 180°C (350°F/Gas 4). Grease and line a 23 cm (9 in) springform tin. Beat 250 g (9 oz) softened unsalted butter and 225 g (8 oz/1 cup) caster (superfine) sugar in a large mixing bowl. Add 3 lightly beaten eggs, 2 tablespoons poppy seeds, 1 tablespoon grated orange zest and 125 ml (4 fl oz/$1/2$ cup) milk. Stir to combine and then fold in 250 g (9 oz/2 cups) sifted self-raising flour. Spoon the batter into the tin and bake for 1 hour, or until a skewer inserted into the centre of the cake comes out clean. Turn out the cake onto a wire rack to cool. When the cake has cooled, transfer it to a serving plate and drizzle with orange icing (page 190) or sprinkle with icing (confectioners') sugar. Serves 10

## chocolate

Preheat the oven to 180°C (350°F/Gas 4). Grease and line a 23 cm (9 in) springform tin. Beat 250 g (9 oz) softened unsalted butter and 225 g (8 oz/1 cup) caster (superfine) sugar in a mixing bowl. Add 3 lightly beaten eggs, 125 ml (4 fl oz/$1/2$ cup) milk and 1 teaspoon natural vanilla extract. Stir to combine and then fold in 4 tablespoons dark cocoa powder, 70 g ($21/2$ oz/$2/3$ cup) ground almond and 150 g ($51/2$ oz/$11/4$ cups) self-raising flour. Spoon the batter into the prepared tin and bake for 45–50 minutes, or until a skewer inserted into the centre of the cake comes out clean. Turn out the cake onto a wire rack to cool. When the cake has cooled, transfer it to a serving plate and drizzle with chocolate icing (page 190). Serves 10

Flavoured or coloured, sprinkled calling cards letting everyone

## icing basics

1 Blend 125 g (4¹/₂ oz/1 cup) sifted icing (confectioners') sugar and
1 tablespoon softened unsalted butter in a mixing bowl. Add 1 tablespoon
water, lemon juice or orange juice.

2 Depending on the desired thickness of your icing, add a little more liquid, a
few drops at a time. Or, if making coloured icing, add the food colouring at
this stage, a drop at a time.

3 Using a spatula or knife, spread the icing over the cooled cake. To get a
smooth surface, dip the spatula in warm water and smooth it over the icing.
Makes enough for a 23 cm (9 in) cake or 12 cupcakes.

### hints & tips

● Always allow a cake to cool completely before covering it with icing. If time is
short and you need to ice a warm cake, then it is best to make a thin icing
and drizzle it over the surface of the cake.

● For a rich creamy icing, lightly stir 3 tablespoons sifted icing (confectioners')
sugar and 1 teaspoon natural vanilla extract (essence) into 250 ml (9 fl oz/
1 cup) thick (double/heavy) cream.

● For an indulgent chocolate icing, melt 200 g (7 oz) dark eating chocolate with
150 ml (5 fl oz) cream in a small saucepan over low heat. When the chocolate
and cream have combined to form a smooth sauce, remove from the heat
and allow to cool. When the icing is just warm, drizzle it over a chocolate cake.

or unadorned, swirls of sugary icing are visual
know that a good time is about to be had.

# cake decorating essentials

Cakes are by their very nature decorative things, so it's a shame not to have some fun with them. Little more than sugar and cream, they bring a sense of fun to an occasion when perched on pretty plates and surrounded by guests eagerly awaiting the first slice.

Decorating a cake can be as simple as a drizzle of icing or as dramatic as sugared petals and candied zest. And if you don't consider yourself much of a cake stylist, or you just want to bake your cake and eat it fast, then simply shake icing (confectioners') sugar or dusty cocoa over it and serve with freshly whipped cream and a bowl of luscious fruit like berries or stone fruit.

## sprinkles and sparkles

It's hard to imagine cupcakes without thinking of brightly coloured icing. It's an opportunity to throw caution to the wind and get carried away with little bottles of colourful liquid. But make sure you blend food colouring into your icing mixture sparingly as the colours are strong — and it's easier to add an extra drop than to make more icing to soften a bowl of psychedelic colour. If you don't want to use unnatural colourings, then make pretty pink hues with the juice of mashed raspberries or strawberries or create citrus tones with the finely grated zest of oranges, lemons or limes.

If colour isn't enough to satisfy your creative urges, head down to your local kitchenware specialist and check out the large range of ready-made sprinkles available. From childhood favourites such as chocolate sprinkles and 'hundreds and thousands' to silvery balls in various sizes or coloured hearts and stars, there are shapes and sentiments to suit all tastes.

If decorating for children, have fun with confectionery and top your cakes with a variety of sweets. Or paint smiley faces and your guests' names onto smooth icing with a fine paintbrush and food colouring.

## sweet touches

There are lots of options for grown-up cakes with a touch of spectacle and magic. Try to match the flavours of your decorative touch with those that lie beneath the blanket of icing. If cooking a simple butter cake or one that is flavoured with lemon or orange, then make a beautiful pile of glistening candied citrus zest. Not only is the zest a great taste sensation but piled over the top of a cake its swirling of pastel lines looks fantastic.

- To make candied citrus zest, put finely sliced zest into a saucepan of cold water over high heat. As soon as it comes to the boil, remove from the heat and drain away the water. Cover with cold water and repeat the process twice. Put 115 g (4 oz/$1/2$ cup) caster (superfine) sugar and 125 ml (4 fl oz/$1/2$ cup) water into a small saucepan and bring to the boil, stirring until the sugar has dissolved. Reduce the heat to a simmer, then add the boiled zest. Cook for a couple of minutes, then remove and roll in a little caster sugar. Allow the zest to dry overnight on a bed of caster sugar.

- For a wonderfully girly touch you can't go past sugared flowers and petals. Speciality cake and kitchenware shops often have sugared violets amongst their cake decorating stock but if you have the time it's fun to make your own. If making sugared rose petals, bake a butter cake and add a teaspoon of rosewater to the mixture. Ice the cake with soft pink icing and scatter the petals over it. Simply perfect for a special afternoon tea, baby shower or to celebrate the birthday of a girl who is totally at home in a Laura Ashley print.

- To make sugared petals, remove the small petals from organic roses or use whole violets. Whisk 2 egg whites until light and frothy and, using a small pastry brush or paintbrush, brush the egg white onto both sides of the petals. Dip the petal in caster (superfine) sugar, ensuring that it is well coated in sugar, then place on a bed of caster sugar to dry overnight.

- Berries are such beautiful things and when they are in season it seems a shame not to use them every way you can. This is especially true in high berry season when glowing red and white currants make an appearance, as well as the small and deliciously flavoured wild strawberries. Dipped in sugar and perched atop a cake they look like a cluster of frosty jewels.

- For sugar-dipped berries, make flavoured sugar by putting caster (superfine) sugar into a blender or food processor with some finely chopped vanilla bean or citrus zest. Blend to a powdery consistency, then dip the berries into the flavoured sugar. Place the berries on top of cupcakes or large cakes.

# sponge cake basics

1 Preheat the oven to 190°C (375°F/Gas 5). Line the base of a 20 cm (8 in) round or sandwich tin, then grease and lightly flour the side and base. Separate 2 eggs. Beat the egg yolks with 115 g (4 oz/1/2 cup) caster (superfine) sugar in a mixing bowl for a few minutes, then add 2 tablespoons warm water. Continue to beat for another 8 minutes until the mixture is very pale and fluffy.

2 Sieve 70 g (21/2 oz/heaped 1/2 cup) plain (all-purpose) flour and 1/2 teaspoon baking powder onto a plate. Lightly fold the flour into the egg yolk mixture, a few spoonfuls at a time.

3 In a separate bowl, whisk the egg whites until soft peaks form and then fold the egg whites through the batter. Pour the batter into the tin and bake for 20 minutes, or until the sponge firmly springs back when tapped. Turn out onto a wire rack to cool. Serve topped with whipped cream and passionfruit. Makes a 20 cm (8 in) cake

## hints & tips

● The most important feature of a sponge cake is its lightness, so treat the mixture with care and fold the ingredients with a more gentle hand than you normally would use. Also ensure that the oven is at the correct temperature.

● If you wish to make a layered sponge, then simply double the recipe and divide it between two sandwich tins.

● If passionfruit isn't available or to your liking, then there are many other topping options. Spread strawberry jam or lemon curd over the sponge and top with whipped cream; spoon whipped cream over the sponge and then pile with fresh berries; or drizzle with cooled melted chocolate and sprinkle with crushed hazelnuts.

# classic slices

## chocolate

Preheat the oven to 180°C (350°F/Gas 4). Grease and line a 23 cm (9 in) square cake tin. Melt 250 g (9 oz) butter with 325 g (11$^1$/$_2$ oz/1$^1$/$_2$ cups) sugar in a saucepan over low heat. When the butter has melted, stir to ensure that the sugar has dissolved. Remove the pan from the heat. Sift 90 g (3$^1$/$_4$ oz/$^3$/$_4$ cup) cocoa powder, 4 tablespoons plain (all-purpose) flour and $^1$/$_2$ teaspoon baking powder into a large bowl and add a pinch of salt. Make a well in the centre and stir in the melted butter and sugar, then stir in 4 eggs. Add 125 g (4$^1$/$_2$ oz/1 cup) chopped toasted hazelnuts and 200 g (7 oz/1$^1$/$_3$ cups) chopped chocolate or chocolate bits. Lightly stir to combine, then pour into the prepared tin. Bake for 25–30 minutes. Remove from the oven and cool in the pan. Cut into pieces and dust with cocoa. Makes 20 pieces

## lemon

Preheat the oven to 180°C (350°F/Gas 4). Grease and line a 16 x 26 cm (6$^1$/$_4$ x 10$^1$/$_2$ in) slice tin. Beat 125 g (4$^1$/$_2$ oz) softened unsalted butter and 60 g (2$^1$/$_4$ oz/$^1$/$_2$ cup) sifted icing (confectioners') sugar in a mixing bowl until pale and creamy. Add 1 teaspoon natural vanilla extract. Stir in 175 g (6 oz/scant 1$^1$/$_2$ cups) sifted self-raising flour and 1 teaspoon grated lemon zest. Press the mixture into the prepared tin. Bake for 15 minutes, or until golden. Sift 90 g (3$^1$/$_4$ oz/$^3$/$_4$ cup) plain (all-purpose) flour and $^1$/$_2$ teaspoon baking powder into a bowl. Add 85 g (3 oz/$^3$/$_4$ cup) ground almonds. In a separate bowl, beat together 3 eggs, 225 g (8 oz/1 cup) caster (superfine) sugar, 185 ml (6 fl oz/$^3$/$_4$ cup) lemon juice and 2 tablespoons grated lemon zest. Stir the egg mixture into the dry ingredients and pour over the base. Bake for 20 minutes, or until firm. Cool in the tin. Cut into pieces and dust with icing (confectioners') sugar. Makes 18 pieces

## caramel

Preheat the oven to 180°C (350°F/Gas 4). Grease and line a 16 x 26 cm (6¼ x 10½ in) slice tin. Put 125 g (4½ oz/ 1 cup) plain (all-purpose) flour, 90 g (3¼ oz) unsalted butter and 3 tablespoons caster (superfine) sugar into a food processor and process until it comes together. Remove and press the dough into the base of the tin. Prick the dough with a fork and bake for 15–18 minutes, or until lightly golden. Put 400 g (14 oz) condensed milk, 1½ tablespoons unsalted butter and 2 tablespoons golden syrup into a saucepan over low heat and stir for 10 minutes. Do not boil. Remove from the heat and set aside to cool for 10 minutes. Pour the caramel over the baked base and return to the oven for 10 minutes, or until the edges of the caramel begin to brown. Remove from the oven and allow to cool and set in the pan. Melt 150 g (5½ oz) dark eating chocolate and spread it over the cooled caramel. Cut into pieces. Makes 18 pieces

## coconut and white chocolate

Preheat the oven to 180°C (350°F/Gas 4). Grease and line a 16 x 26 cm (6¼ x 10½ in) slice tin. Melt 125 g (4½ oz) unsalted butter and 150 g (5½ oz) white eating chocolate in a saucepan over low heat. Add 175 g (6 oz/¾ cup) caster (superfine) sugar and stir to combine. Pour into a large bowl and add 125 g (4½ oz/1 cup) self-raising flour and 90 g (3¼ oz/1 cup) desiccated coconut. Stir to combine, then add 2 beaten eggs. Stir lightly to just combine, then fold in 150 g (5½ oz/1¼ cups) fresh raspberries. Pour the mixture into the prepared tin and bake for 40 minutes, or until firm. Cool in the tin. Cut into pieces and dust with icing (confectioners') sugar. Makes 20 pieces

# My great aunt was miraculously out of the oven just as guests

## scone basics

1  Preheat the oven to 200°C (400°F/Gas 6). Line a baking tray with baking paper. Sift 400 g (14 oz/3¼ cups) plain (all-purpose) flour into a large bowl. Add a generous pinch of salt, 3 teaspoons baking powder, 2 tablespoons caster (superfine) sugar and 85 g (3 oz) chilled and diced unsalted butter. Rub the butter into the flour using just your fingertips until it resembles fine breadcrumbs.

2  In a separate bowl, stir 1 teaspoon lemon juice into 200 ml (7 fl oz) milk and then whisk in 2 eggs. Make a well in the centre of the dry ingredients and pour in the milk mixture. Stir until the ingredients just come together, then turn out the dough onto a floured surface. Knead once or twice to just bring the dough together.

3  Press the dough out until it is 3–4 cm (1¼–1½ in) thick. Using a round cookie cutter, cut out rounds of dough and put them onto the lined baking tray. Bake for 12 minutes, or until golden. Makes 15

### hints & tips

- Scones should really be eaten warm from the oven. If expecting visitors, then prepare the dry and liquid ingredients in advance. Just as your guests are about to arrive, combine the ingredients to form a dough and then pop the scones into the oven. By the time everyone is settled and the tea is ready, the scones should be coming out of the oven.

- To make cheese scones, omit the sugar and add ½ teaspoon ground paprika and 60 g (2¼ oz/½ cup) grated Cheddar cheese. Or try herbed scones, omitting the sugar and adding some freshly ground black pepper and finely chopped chives or dill. Serve with sour cream and smoked salmon.

able to time her scones so they would be coming tumbled through her door, in eager anticipation.

# classic biscuits

## melting moments

Preheat the oven to 170°C (325°F/Gas 3). Grease and line a baking tray with baking paper. Beat 250 g (9 oz) softened unsalted butter, 1 teaspoon natural vanilla extract and 60 g (2$^{1}/_{4}$ oz/$^{1}/_{2}$ cup) icing (confectioners') sugar in a large bowl until fluffy. Sift together 175 g (6 oz/scant 1$^{1}/_{2}$ cups) plain (all-purpose) flour and 60 g (2$^{1}/_{4}$ oz/$^{1}/_{2}$ cup) cornflour (cornstarch), then add in two batches, folding through. Roll 2 teaspoons of mixture to form balls, put them 3 cm (1$^{1}/_{4}$ in) apart on the tray and flatten slightly with a fork. If the dough is sticky, lightly flour your hands. Bake for 12–15 minutes, or until the biscuits are a pale golden colour. Cool slightly on the tray before transferring to a wire rack to cool. Blend 85 g (3 oz) softened unsalted butter, 85 g (3 oz/$^{2}/_{3}$ cup) icing sugar and 1 teaspoon strained passionfruit juice in a small bowl. Sandwich 2 biscuits together with icing in between. Dust with icing sugar. Store in an airtight container. Makes 24

## anzac biscuits

Preheat the oven to 180°C (350°F/Gas 4). Grease and line a baking tray with baking paper. Sift 125 g (4$^{1}/_{2}$ oz/1 cup) plain (all-purpose) flour into a large mixing bowl and add 100 g (3$^{1}/_{2}$ oz/1 cup) rolled oats, 90 g (3$^{1}/_{4}$ oz/1 cup) desiccated coconut, 225 g (8 oz/1 cup) sugar and a pinch of salt. Put 125 g (4$^{1}/_{2}$ oz) unsalted butter and 3 tablespoons golden syrup into a saucepan. Stir over low heat until the butter has melted. Put 2 tablespoons boiling water into a cup and dissolve 1 teaspoon bicarbonate of soda. Stir the water and soda into the melted butter, which will cause it to bubble up, then pour it over the dry ingredients. Stir to combine. Drop spoonfuls of the mixture onto the prepared tray, allowing room for the biscuits to spread. Bake for 12–15 minutes, or until dark gold. Remove from the oven and transfer the biscuits to a wire rack to cool. Store in an airtight container. Makes 30

## florentines

Preheat the oven to 180°C (350°F/Gas 4). Line two baking trays with baking paper. Finely chop 2 tablespoons raisins and add them to a mixing bowl with 2 tablespoons finely chopped preserved ginger and 100 g (3$^1$/$_2$ oz/heaped 1 cup) flaked almonds. Melt 100 g (3$^1$/$_2$ oz) unsalted butter and 100 g (3$^1$/$_2$ oz/scant $^1$/$_2$ cup) caster (superfine) sugar in a saucepan over low heat. When the sugar has dissolved, turn up the heat and allow the mixture to bubble for 1 minute. Pour the hot mixture into the mixing bowl and quickly stir to combine all the ingredients. Drop teaspoons of the mixture onto the baking trays, allowing room for the biscuits to spread considerably. Bake for 10 minutes. Allow the biscuits to cool on the trays for 5 minutes before carefully lifting them onto a wire rack. Melt 100 g (3$^1$/$_2$ oz) dark eating chocolate and use a pastry brush to paint the chocolate onto the underside of the biscuits. Eat within 2–3 days. Makes 20

## chocolate chip cookies

Preheat the oven to 180°C (350°F/Gas 4). Grease and line a baking tray with baking paper. Beat 125 g (4$^1$/$_2$ oz) softened unsalted butter with 175 g (6 oz/1 cup) soft brown sugar in a mixing bowl until light and creamy. Add 1 teaspoon natural vanilla extract, 1 tablespoon milk and 1 beaten egg and work them lightly into the butter mixture. Gently fold in 175 g (6 oz/1$^1$/$_2$ cups) sifted plain (all-purpose) flour and 1 teaspoon sifted baking powder. Stir in 275 g (9$^3$/$_4$ oz/heaped 1$^1$/$_2$ cups) dark chocolate bits. Drop heaped tablespoons of the mixture onto a baking tray, leaving about 3 cm (1$^1$/$_4$ in) between each cookie. Bake for 15 minutes, or until lightly golden. Transfer the cookies to a wire rack to cool. Store in an airtight container. Makes 20

# afternoon tea essentials

Afternoon tea appears to be fast disappearing from the entertaining vocabulary. But there's no reason why you shouldn't indulge yourself every once in a while with plates of pretty cupcakes, fine sandwiches, gooey slices and sugary biscuits.

The essentials for any afternoon tea are teacups, tea strainer, milk jug, tiny napkins and small plates. However, this doesn't mean spending a lot of money. While modern and white is nice, I can't help thinking that when it comes to high tea and cake there's room to have a little bit of fun. Hunt around secondhand stores and flea markets for wonderful old teacups, jugs and teapots with personality. Mix and match old and now. Think funky fifties and gilded treasures or all-over floral meets the simplicity of the sixties. Enjoy colour, lace, embroidered edges, tiered cake stands, tassels, coloured glass and lovely old silver teaspoons and cake forks.

## tea, anyone?

And don't forget the tea. Investigate all the amazing teas that are now available and find flavours that you really love. Or match the flavour of the tea with the food. If you're serving a citrus-flavoured cake, then team it with a citrus-tinged tea. Serve a berry-flavoured tea with scones and strawberry jam.

If you're serving a classic black tea remember there's an art to making a great pot of tea. Fill the kettle with cold water and bring it to the boil. As it boils, pour a little hot water into the teapot and swirl it around so that it warms the sides of the pot. Empty the hot water from the pot and spoon in the tea leaves. Follow the old adage — one teaspoon for each person and one for the pot. Cover with boiling water and leave for 5 minutes. Serve the tea with a jug of milk and a pot of hot water and sliced lemon for those who prefer their tea black.

If you prefer to serve coffee, always use freshly ground coffee beans to ensure a great cup. Good coffee is all about the richness of its flavour so it's preferable to make a strong, though not bitter, batch and to allow guests to mellow the flavour to their own individual taste, with a jug of warmed milk. If serving chocolate-flavoured sweets or spiced flavours, then it can be a nice touch to add one or two cardamom pods to your coffee for that fragrant taste of the Middle East.

Of course, afternoon tea doesn't have to be about traditional pots of tea and coffee. If you still want to serve a warm drink but wish to avoid the obvious you can make some beautiful warm infusions.

- Roughly chop 2 stalks of fresh lemongrass and put into a large glass jug or teapot. Cover with boiling water and allow to steep for 5 minutes. You may wish to add a little ginger to this flavouring depending on your preferences and what you are serving. Sweeten with a little honey.
- Put a generous handful of fresh mint leaves into a pot with a cinnamon stick and a teaspoon of sugar. Cover with boiling water and allow to steep for 5 minutes. Pour into small glasses garnished with fresh mint.

## a cooling brew

When the weather is warm, and you'd rather serve cooling refreshments, consider preparing lassis, sherbets and home-made cordials.

- Lassis are chilled creamy drinks made by blending fresh fruit with yoghurt. Add some ice for a cooling afternoon drink and be inspired by the best of the seasonal fruits, such as mango, stone fruit, berries and passionfruit.
- For big effect serve large icy jugs of exotic flavoured sherbets. Recipes for an almond and a rose petal sherbet are listed in the kitchen bench chapter (pages 90 and 91) but if you'd like to make a simple lemon sherbet, then put the juice of 6 lemons and 4 tablespoons of caster (superfine) sugar into a saucepan and bring to the boil. Stir until the sugar has dissolved, then remove from the heat. Allow to cool then add 3 teaspoons of rosewater. Serve diluted with sparkling mineral water. This should be enough syrup to make eight glasses.
- Home-made cordials are a great way to bring flavour to everyone's glass. Make the cordials in advance and store them in the refrigerator until ready to use. Try to hunt down some old-fashioned bottles to store and serve them in and then just add some chilled glasses, brightly coloured straws and sparkling mineral water.
- To make a fresh raspberry cordial, put 250 g (9 oz/2 cups) raspberries in a saucepan with 225 g (8 oz/1 cup) caster (superfine) sugar and 800 ml (29 fl oz) water. Bring to the boil, then reduce the heat and simmer for 30 minutes. Remove from the heat and allow to cool. To serve, blend a little of the cordial with sparkling mineral water.

# + drinks

## greyhound

Put 3 tablespoons vodka, 100 ml (3¹/₂ fl oz) grapefruit juice and a dash of either Triple Sec or Cointreau into a tall glass. Stir, then top with ice. (This drink is also suitable to serve in a large jug. Increase the quantities accordingly.) Serves 1

## sorbet vodka shot

Divide 6 tablespoons of fruit sorbet among six chilled shot glasses and pour 1 tablespoon of vodka over each. Drink immediately. Serves 6

## rhubarb, strawberry and white rum chiller

Put 125 ml (4 fl oz/$\frac{1}{2}$ cup) stewed rhubarb (page 27), 6 strawberries, 3 tablespoons white rum, 1 teaspoon natural vanilla extract and 8 ice cubes into a blender and blend until smooth. Pour into chilled glasses and garnish with a small strawberry, if you like. Serves 2

## lemon cheesecake

Put 125 g (4$\frac{1}{2}$ oz/$\frac{1}{2}$ cup) plain yoghurt, 3 tablespoons cream, 2 tablespoons caster (superfine) sugar, 2 tablespoons lemon juice, $\frac{1}{2}$ teaspoon natural vanilla extract and 6 ice cubes into a blender and blend until smooth. Pour into glasses and top with grated nutmeg. Serves 2

# + drinks

## gin fizz

Put 3 tablespoons gin, 1 tablespoon lemon juice, 1 teaspoon caster (superfine) sugar and a dash of egg white into a cocktail shaker filled with ice. Shake vigorously and pour into a chilled glass. Top with soda water. Serves 1

## mint julep

Put $1^{1/2}$ teaspoons caster (superfine) sugar, 6 mint leaves and a dash of water in a glass. Using a muddler or the end of a wooden spoon, mash the ingredients together until the sugar has dissolved and the mint is bruised. Fill the glass with crushed ice and top with 80 ml ($2^{1/2}$ fl oz) whisky. Stir well and place in the freezer for 30 minutes. Serve with a garnish of mint leaves and a straw. Serves 1

Choose your ideal response to the illicit temptation

## 'citron' pressé

Put 3 tablespoons Absolut citron vodka, 3 tablespoons sugar syrup (page 229) and 2 tablespoons lemon juice in a cocktail shaker. Shake well and pour into a highball glass containing some ice. Garnish with a generous grate of lemon zest and a twist of peel. Serves 1

## long island iced tea

Put 1½ tablespoons each of vodka, gin, rum, tequila, Triple Sec and lemon juice in a cocktail shaker with 8 ice cubes and shake well. Pour into long, chilled glasses with ice, and add enough cola to colour the drink. Garnish with lemon wedges. Serves 2

# of an afternoon's tipple on a warm summer's day.

# afternoon tea recipes
find some time for
## jam drops
shortbread and fruity tarts
## sticky cakes
glossy chocolate icing
and bright sparkles
...you know you deserve it!

## shortbread

175 g (6 oz/scant 1$^1$/$_2$ cups) plain (all-purpose) flour
125 g (4$^1$/$_2$ oz/$^3$/$_4$ cup) rice flour
200 g (7 oz) unsalted butter, softened
4 tablespoons caster (superfine) sugar
2 teaspoons finely chopped lemon zest
2 tablespoons caster (superfine) sugar, extra, for sprinkling

Preheat the oven to 190°C (375°F/Gas 5). Grease and line a 30 x 20 cm (12 x 8 in) baking tray. Sift the flours together with a pinch of salt into a bowl. Cream the butter and sugar until light and fluffy, then fold through the sifted flours until just combined.

Press the mixture into the baking tray and prick all over with a fork. Use a sharp knife to mark 3 cm (1$^1$/$_4$ in) squares. Bake for 5 minutes, then reduce the oven temperature to 150°C (300°F/Gas 2) and cook for a further 15–20 minutes, or until the shortbread is a pale golden colour.

Sprinkle the lemon zest over the top of the shortbread and cook for a further 5 minutes. Remove from the oven and sprinkle with extra caster sugar while still warm. Cut into squares and cool on a wire rack. Makes 60

## chestnut cakes with lemon icing

6 eggs
150 g (5$^1$/$_2$ oz/$^2$/$_3$ cup) caster (superfine) sugar
400 g (14 oz) tin chestnut purée
175 g (6 oz/1$^3$/$_4$ cups) ground almonds
1 teaspoon baking powder
1 quantity lemon icing (page 190)

Preheat the oven to 180°C (350°F/Gas 4). Beat the eggs until light and fluffy, then add the sugar and chestnut purée and beat for a further 1 minute. Fold in the ground almonds and baking powder.

Spoon the mixture into a greased 12-hole muffin tin or into paper patty cases and bake for 20 minutes, or until the cakes are cooked through. Remove the cakes and allow them to cool before icing with lemon icing. Makes 12

## almond and pine nut cake

2 mandarins
250 g (9 oz/1$^2$/$_3$ cups) raw almonds
300 g (10$^1$/$_2$ oz/scant 1$^1$/$_3$ cups) caster (superfine) sugar
$^1$/$_2$ teaspoon ground cinnamon
8 egg whites
85 g (3 oz/$^2$/$_3$ cup) plain (all-purpose) flour, sifted
4 tablespoons pine nuts
3 tablespoons dessert wine or Grand Marnier
icing (confectioners') sugar
whipped cream

Preheat the oven to 180°C (350°F/Gas 4). Grease a 20 cm (8 in) springform tin with the butter. Peel a mandarin and, with a sharp knife, finely chop the zest. Put 3 tablespoons of zest into a food processor. Add the almonds, sugar and cinnamon and process to a fine consistency. Beat the egg whites with a pinch of salt until stiff peaks form. Lightly fold the almond mixture into the egg whites, then add the flour. Spoon the batter into the prepared tin and sprinkle with the pine nuts. Bake for 1 hour, or until a skewer inserted into the centre of the cake comes out clean. Allow to cool before serving.

Pour the dessert wine or Grand Marnier over the cake, then dust with icing sugar. Using a sharp knife, carefully remove the segments from the mandarins and serve alongside the cake. Makes a 20 cm (8 in) cake

## cinnamon jam drops

90 g (3$^1$/$_4$ oz/$^3$/$_4$ cup) self-raising flour
1 teaspoon ground cinnamon
3 tablespoons rice flour
70 g (2$^1$/$_2$ oz) unsalted butter, softened
4 tablespoons sugar
1 egg, beaten
berry jam

Preheat the oven to 180°C (350°F/Gas 4). Sift together the flour, cinnamon and rice flour. In another bowl, cream the butter and sugar until light and fluffy, then gradually add the egg, beating well. Fold into the sifted ingredients until just combined. Roll 1 teaspoon of the dough into a ball and put on a baking tray lined with baking paper. Repeat with the remaining mixture. Press a deep indent into the centre of each ball and fill with a little berry jam. Bake for 8–10 minutes, or until golden. Makes 36

sticky pineapple cake

lemon and coconut tart

## sticky pineapple cake

350 g (12 oz/1¹/2 cups) caster (superfine) sugar
175 g (6 oz/scant 2 cups) desiccated coconut, lightly toasted
250 ml (9 fl oz/1 cup) coconut milk
280 g (10 oz/1¹/2 cups) diced fresh pineapple
4 eggs
250 g (9 oz/2 cups) plain (all-purpose) flour
2 teaspoons baking powder
1 tablespoon unsalted butter, softened
125 g (4¹/2 oz/1 cup) icing (confectioners') sugar, sifted
2 tablespoons lime juice

Preheat the oven to 180°C (350°F/Gas 4). Grease and line a 24 cm (9¹/2 in) springform tin. Put the sugar, coconut, coconut milk, pineapple and eggs into a large bowl and stir together. Sift in the flour and baking powder, then fold the ingredients together. Spoon the batter into the cake tin and bake for 1 hour.

Put the butter and icing sugar into a bowl and beat until the butter has been worked into the sugar. Slowly add the lime juice so that the icing is smooth and runny enough to be drizzled over the cake.

Test the cake with a skewer to see if it is cooked. Remove the cake from the tin, cool and then gently pour over the lime icing. Serves 8

## lemon and coconut tart

125 g (4¹/2 oz) unsalted butter, softened
350 g (12 oz/1¹/2 cups) caster (superfine) sugar
4 large eggs
150 g (5¹/2 oz/scant ²/3 cup) plain yoghurt
1 teaspoon natural vanilla extract
3 tablespoons lemon juice
2 tablespoons lemon zest
90 g (3¹/4 oz/1 cup) desiccated coconut
25 cm (10 in) prebaked shortcrust tart case (page 78)
icing (confectioners') sugar
cream or ice cream, to serve

Preheat the oven to 180°C (350°F/Gas 4). Beat the butter and sugar together until they are light and creamy. Add the eggs, one at a time, beating them into the mixture. Next add

the yoghurt, vanilla, lemon juice and zest. Stir in the coconut and pour the mixture into the prebaked tart case.

Bake for 30 minutes, or until the filling is golden and puffed. Dust with icing sugar and serve warm with cream or ice cream. Serves 8

## fig and burnt butter tart

6 figs
25 cm (10 in) prebaked shortcrust tart case (page 78)
3 eggs
175 g (6 oz/³/4 cup) caster (superfine) sugar
3 tablespoons plain (all-purpose) flour
175 g (6 oz) unsalted butter

Preheat the oven to 180°C (350°F/Gas 4). Slice the figs into quarters and arrange them in the prebaked tart case with the narrow ends pointing up.

Beat the eggs and sugar in a mixing bowl until they are pale and fluffy, then fold in the flour. Heat the butter in a saucepan over high heat. When it begins to froth and turn pale golden brown, pour the hot butter into the egg mixture and beat for 1 minute. Pour the filling over the figs and bake for 25 minutes, or until the filling is cooked and golden brown. Allow the tart to cool before serving. Serves 8

fig and burnt butter tart

# lime madeleines

2 eggs
3 tablespoons caster (superfine) sugar
1/2 teaspoon finely chopped lime zest
60 g (21/4 oz/1/2 cup) plain (all-purpose) flour
50 g (13/4 oz) unsalted butter, melted
1 teaspoon lime juice
1/2 teaspoon orange flower water
caster (superfine) sugar, extra, to serve

Preheat the oven to 200°C (400°F/Gas 6). Beat the eggs, caster sugar, lime zest and a pinch of salt in a bowl until the mixture is pale and thick. Sift the flour over the egg mixture and lightly fold it in. Gently fold through the butter, lime juice and orange flower water.

Grease a madeleine tin and drop 1 teaspoon of the batter into each of the moulds. If you don't have a madeleine tin, use a shallow muffin tin or patty case. Bake for 5 minutes. Turn out onto a wire rack and sprinkle with caster sugar. Repeat twice more with the remaining mixture. Makes 36

# nectarine and almond cake

3 eggs
125 ml (4 fl oz/1/2 cup) milk
300 g (101/2 oz/scant 11/3 cups) caster (superfine) sugar
250 g (9 oz/2 cups) plain (all-purpose) flour
2 teaspoons baking powder
1 teaspoon natural vanilla extract
8 nectarines
55 g (2 oz/1/2 cup) ground almonds
2 tablespoons unsalted butter

Preheat the oven to 180°C (350°F/Gas 4) and grease and line a 23 cm (9 in) springform tin. Combine the eggs, milk, sugar, flour, baking powder and vanilla in a food processor and process to form a thick batter. Scrape the batter into a bowl. Slice the nectarines into eighths and fold the fruit pieces through the batter.

Spoon the batter into the prepared tin and top with the ground almonds and dobs of the butter. Bake for 40 minutes. Test with a skewer to ensure that the cake is cooked through, then remove the tin from the oven and allow the cake to cool before serving. Serves 8

# quince and rosewater tarts

90 g (31/4 oz) quince paste
4 tablespoons orange juice
115 g (4 oz/1/2 cup) mascarpone cheese
1/2 teaspoon rosewater
2 teaspoons icing (confectioners') sugar
1 tablespoon ground almonds, lightly toasted
12 prebaked mini tart cases (page 78)

Melt the quince paste with the orange juice in a bowl over a saucepan of simmering water. Stir well to combine, then remove the bowl from the heat and allow the paste to cool.

Blend the mascarpone cheese with the rosewater, icing sugar and ground almonds in a bowl. Spoon the mascarpone mixture into the tart cases and top with the cooled quince paste. Makes 12

# spiced treacle tarts

50 g (13/4 oz/1/2 cup) desiccated coconut
125 ml (4 fl oz/1/2 cup) golden syrup
1/4 teaspoon ground cardamom
1 tablespoon lime juice
2 teaspoons finely chopped lime zest
1 egg yolk, beaten
24 prebaked mini tart cases (page 78)
icing (confectioners') sugar, to serve

Preheat the oven to 180°C (350°F/Gas 4). Put all the ingredients except the mini tart cases and icing sugar in a bowl and mix well. Spoon 1 heaped teaspoon of the filling into each of the tart cases and bake for 10 minutes. Remove from the oven and cool on a wire rack. Dust with icing sugar before serving. Makes 24

Afternoon tea doesn't have to mean buttery and
fresh raspberries or these tiny polenta madeleines,

raspberry ripple cake

rich…though who can resist a cake rippled with
which are just perfect for tea in the garden?

sage and polenta madeleines

## raspberry ripple cake

300 g (10$^{1}/_{2}$ oz/2 cups) frozen raspberries
250 g (9 oz/2 cups) plain (all-purpose) flour
2 teaspoons baking powder
$^{1}/_{4}$ teaspoon salt
125 g (4$^{1}/_{2}$ oz) unsalted butter, softened
225 g (8 oz/1 cup) caster (superfine) sugar
3 eggs, lightly beaten
250 g (9 oz/1 cup) sour cream
1 tablespoon butter, melted
125 g (4$^{1}/_{2}$ oz/1 cup) icing (confectioners') sugar, sifted

Preheat the oven to 180°C (350°F/Gas 4). Grease and line a 23 cm (9 in) springform tin. Put the frozen raspberries into a bowl and lightly crush them. Reserve 1 tablespoon of their juice in another bowl to make the icing.

Sift the flour, baking powder and salt into a large bowl. Cream the butter and sugar until pale and fluffy, then stir in the eggs. Add the dry ingredients, alternating with the sour cream, and mixing well after each addition. Spoon approximately one-third of the batter into the prepared tin, then spoon over half the raspberries. Repeat with another third of the batter and the remaining raspberries and top with the remaining batter. Bake for 50 minutes, or until a skewer comes out clean. Allow the cake to cool in the tin before turning out and icing it.

To make the icing, add the melted butter to the reserved raspberry juice. Slowly stir in the sifted icing sugar until the icing has a smooth runny consistency. Spoon over the cake. Serves 10

## sage and polenta madeleines

150 g (5$^{1}/_{2}$ oz) unsalted butter, softened
2 teaspoons sugar
2 egg yolks
2 eggs
4 tablespoons plain (all-purpose) flour
4 tablespoons fine polenta
1$^{1}/_{4}$ teaspoons baking powder
24 small sage leaves

Preheat the oven to 180°C (350°F/Gas 4).

Put 1$^{1}/_{2}$ tablespoons of the butter in a small saucepan and cook over high heat until it begins to brown. Remove from the heat and set aside. Cream the remaining butter and the sugar in a mixing bowl until pale and fluffy. Gradually add the egg yolks and whole eggs, beating well after each addition. Gently fold in the dry ingredients, plus 1$^{1}/_{4}$ teaspoons each of salt and coarsely ground black pepper.

Grease a madeleine tin with the browned butter, put 1 sage leaf in the base of each mould and top with 1 teaspoon of batter. If you don't have a madeleine tin, use a shallow muffin tin or patty case. Bake for 7–10 minutes, or until the cakes are golden and springy to the touch. Remove from the tray and cool on a wire rack. Makes 24

## pear and cardamom tart

175 g (6 oz/scant 1$^{3}/_{4}$ cups) ground almonds
115 g (4 oz) unsalted butter
125 g (4$^{1}/_{2}$ oz/heaped $^{1}/_{2}$ cup) caster (superfine) sugar
3 eggs
$^{1}/_{2}$ teaspoon ground cardamom
3 teaspoons cocoa powder
25 cm (10 in) prebaked shortcrust tart case (page 78)
2 ripe beurre bosc pears

Preheat the oven to 180°C (350°F/Gas 4). Put the ground almonds, butter, all the sugar except for 2 tablespoons, the eggs, cardamom and cocoa into a food processor and process to form a thick paste. Carefully spoon the mixture into the prebaked tart case, spreading it evenly.

Quarter and core the pears, then slice them thickly. Arrange the slices in a fan over the top of the almond mixture. Bake for 20 minutes.

Take the tart out of the oven and sprinkle the top with the rest of the sugar. Return it to the oven for a further 10 minutes, then check that the filling is firm at the centre to ensure that the tart is cooked all the way through. Allow it to cool slightly before transferring it to a serving plate. Serves 8

pear and cardamom tart

## chocolate creams

150 g (5$^1$/2 oz/1$^1$/4 cups) plain (all-purpose) flour
2 tablespoons Dutch cocoa powder
1 teaspoon baking powder
100 g (3$^1$/2 oz) unsalted butter
175 g (6 oz) dark chocolate
115 g (4 oz/$^1$/2 cup) caster (superfine) sugar
2 eggs
100 g (3$^1$/2 oz) dark chocolate
2 tablespoons cream
cocoa powder, extra, to serve

Sift together the flour, cocoa, baking powder and $^3$/4 teaspoon salt into a bowl. Melt the butter and chocolate in a medium-sized bowl over a saucepan of simmering water, stirring until smooth. Remove from the heat and add the sugar, stirring until fully dissolved. Add the eggs, one at a time, stirring until well combined, then fold through the dry ingredients. Refrigerate the mixture for 20 minutes, or until just firm.

To make the chocolate cream, melt the chocolate and cream in a bowl over a saucepan of simmering water, stirring until smooth. Remove from the heat and allow to cool.

Preheat the oven to 180°C (350°F/Gas 4). Pipe teaspoon-sized buttons of the mixture onto baking trays lined with baking paper and bake for 5–7 minutes, or until firm. Cool slightly on the trays before transferring to a wire rack.

Sandwich the biscuits together with the chocolate cream and lightly dust with cocoa. Store in an airtight container. Makes 40

## rich chocolate cake

250 g (9 oz) butter
200 g (7 oz) dark cooking chocolate
375 ml (13 fl oz/1$^1$/2 cups) strong coffee
450 g (1 lb/2 cups) caster (superfine) sugar
175 g (6 oz/scant 1$^1$/2 cups) plain (all-purpose) flour
1 teaspoon baking powder
3 tablespoons cocoa powder
2 eggs
2 teaspoons natural vanilla extract
1 quantity chocolate icing (page 190)
whipped cream or vanilla ice cream (page 353), to serve

Preheat the oven to 180°C (350°F/Gas 4). Grease and line a 25 cm (10 in) springform tin. Put the butter, chocolate and coffee in a saucepan over low heat and cook until the chocolate has melted. Add the sugar and stir to dissolve. Remove from the heat and pour into a bowl. Whisk in the dry ingredients,then add the eggs and vanilla. Whisk to combine.

Pour the batter into the prepared tin and bake for 1 hour. Allow the cake to cool in the tin before removing it and covering with chocolate icing. Serve with whipped cream or vanilla ice cream. Serves 10

## bitter chocolate tartlets

150 g (5$^1$/2 oz) unsalted butter
200 g (7 oz) dark chocolate
3 egg yolks
2 eggs
3 tablespoons caster (superfine) sugar
2 tablespoons Tia Maria
6 prebaked mini shortcrust tart cases (page 78)
cocoa powder, to serve

Preheat the oven to 180°C (350°F/Gas 4). Melt the butter and chocolate together in a saucepan over very low heat. Beat the egg yolks, eggs and sugar until they are light and fluffy. Pour the melted chocolate and Tia Maria into the egg mixture and continue to beat for 1 minute. Pour the chocolate filling into the tart cases and bake for 5 minutes.

Remove from the oven and allow to sit for 1 hour before serving. Dust with cocoa and serve with whipped cream, fresh berries or raspberry sauce, if you like. This recipe will also fill a 25 cm (10 in) tart case if you prefer to make a whole tart. Serves 6

## ice cream trifles with turkish delight

250 g (9 oz/2 cups) raspberries or strawberries
6 cubes Turkish delight
12 plain chocolate biscuits
6 scoops vanilla ice cream
85 g (3 oz/$^1$/2 cup) blanched almonds, toasted

Purée the berries to form a sauce and set aside. Cut each piece of Turkish delight into eight small cubes. Break the biscuits into small pieces. Layer the ice cream, chocolate biscuits, Turkish delight and blanched almonds in six chilled glasses and top with the berry sauce. Serve immediately. Serves 6

# cocktails

For most of us, cocktails signify a special occasion. But that doesn't mean we should lose our mantra of simple, simple, simple. This way, rather than spending the night worrying about wayward twists of smoked salmon, you'll feel like a guest at your own party.

# cocktail inspiration
citrus curls and twirls
fabulous canapés
steamed and fried
spiced and marinated
drinks shaken or stirred?
and that perfectly placed olive

# cocktail essentials

Cocktails conjure up icy flavours and cool fun, so invite your friends around and ply them with your latest offering. Whether it's a cocktail of your own invention or a classic martini, Manhattan or mai tai, remember when throwing a party to keep the cocktail menu reduced to one or two great drinks. It also pays to be a little organized…and not to test the menu before your guests arrive!

## the perfect host

If you're serious about entertaining with cocktails, then there are a few must-haves when setting up a bar. Soda water, tonic water, dry ginger ale, sugar syrup, a small bottle of bitters and fresh lemons and limes should all be at the ready. And you'll need a selection of spirits such as gin, vodka, brandy, Cointreau, dry and sweet vermouth, tequila, Campari, whisky and white, golden and dark rum. Remember that most cocktails have to be made one at a time, so being prepared can make a big difference.

Martini shakers are not essential but they are useful. The purpose of a shaker is not only to combine but to chill the alcohol. If you don't have a shaker, improvise with a large glass or small jug: fill with plenty of ice, add your cocktail blend and stir well until the surface of the glass or jug starts to get frosty, then strain the cocktail into a glass and serve immediately.

Great cocktails rely on perfectly matching the flavours, so if you want to get the blend just right, invest in a two-sided measure or jigger. As well, cocktail spoons, with their long corkscrew handles, are ideal for stirring drinks and for layering spirits. Muddlers are wooden pestles, mainly used for crushing ice, limes and mint, or you can easily substitute with a wooden spoon.

Ice is essential to any party or small gathering and if you party often, then it's worth hunting around for a large bin or container that you can fill with ice for chilling bottles. Always buy more ice than you think you'll need. Fill ice buckets for easy access during the cocktail hours, and remember to add an ice scoop or ice tongs. If making blended cocktails, always use ice that has been out of the freezer for a few minutes to make for easier blending and smoother drinks.

Often cocktail recipes will call for sugar syrup. Make the sugar syrup in advance and store it in the refrigerator. The syrup is also handy when you think you'll be serving non-alcoholic drinks. Add 3 tablespoons of sugar syrup to a blender filled with ice and fresh fruit like mangoes, pineapple, berries or ripe stone fruit. Blend to an icy smoothness for perfect fruit frappés.

To make sugar syrup, put 225 g (8 oz/1 cup) sugar into a small saucepan with 250 ml (9 fl oz/1 cup) water. Bring to the boil, stirring until the sugar has dissolved. Cool, then store in a bottle in the refrigerator until ready to use. If you don't have time to make sugar syrup and you aren't embarking upon an evening of frozen daiquiris, then caster (superfine) sugar is a suitable substitute.

## fruity sides

Many cocktails involve some form of food preparation as part of the drink, whether it's cutting fruit for blending, making garnishes or slicing and squeezing citrus. Always reserve a small chopping board solely for preparing fruit — this ensures that other unwanted flavours don't creep in. A small sharp knife is essential for any fruit garnish, while a channel knife will help you make a perfect citrus zest curl.

One of the best things about cocktails, apart from drinking them of course, is having fun with their decoration. You can be elegant with just a twist of lemon or a slice of fresh lime but I always think that when it comes to fruit-based cocktails you really need to lash out and let your imagination run wild. Have fun with twirly umbrellas, track down some retro or wild swizzle sticks, pick up some coloured straws, have gravity-defying fruit perched on the rim of the glass, fluoro mermaids and sea horses resting their toes in alcohol and of course, always have a jar of olives at the ready for that perfect martini.

# classic cocktails

## martini

Put 1 teaspoon dry vermouth into a chilled martini glass. Fill a cocktail shaker with ice and add 3 tablespoons gin. Swirl the vermouth around the glass, then pour it out. Strain the iced gin into the glass and serve immediately with a whole olive or lemon zest garnish. Serves 1

## bellini

Purée 1/2 ripe white peach with 1 teaspoon caster (superfine) sugar. Pour a little Champagne into 2 champagne flutes and then divide the peach purée between the glasses. Lightly stir, then top with Champagne. Serves 2

Be your own James Bond with a classic martini to

## manhattan

Fill a glass with ice, then add 3 tablespoons blended whisky, 1¹/₂ tablespoons sweet vermouth and a dash of Angostura bitters. Stir until the alcohol has chilled, then strain into a chilled cocktail glass. Serve with a twist of lemon zest. Serves 1

## champagne cocktail

Moisten 1 sugar cube with 3 dashes of Angostura bitters and place it into a champagne flute. Pour in 3 teaspoons brandy and then top with Champagne. Serves 1

get the night going: the ultimate in solitary cool.

# classic cocktails

## margarita

Fill a cocktail shaker with ice and add 3 tablespoons tequila, 1¹/2 tablespoons Triple Sec and 1 tablespoon lime juice. Shake vigorously. Wet the rim of a cocktail glass with lime juice and then dip it into sea salt. Strain the cocktail into the glass and serve. Serves 1

## cosmopolitan

Fill a cocktail shaker with ice. Add 3 tablespoons vodka, 1¹/2 tablespoons Cointreau, 1¹/2 tablespoons cranberry juice and 1 teaspoon lime juice. Shake vigorously, then strain into a chilled cocktail glass. Serves 1

## classic daiquiri

Fill a cocktail shaker with ice and add 3 tablespoons rum, 1 tablespoon lime juice, 1 teaspoon Triple Sec and 1 teaspoon caster (superfine) sugar. Shake well and strain into a chilled cocktail glass. Garnish with a fine slice of lime. Serves 1

## fruit daiquiri

Put 90 g (3$^{1}$/$_{4}$ oz/$^{1}$/$_{2}$ cup) diced mango and 70 g (2$^{1}$/$_{2}$ oz/ $^{1}$/$_{2}$ cup) diced honeydew in a blender. Add 125 ml (4 fl oz/ $^{1}$/$_{2}$ cup) white rum, 1$^{1}$/$_{2}$ tablespoons lime juice, 2 teaspoons Triple Sec or Cointreau, 2 teaspoons sugar and 6 ice cubes and blend until smooth. Pour into 2 chilled glasses. Serves 2

# classic cocktails

## negroni

Fill 1 chilled glass with ice. Add 1¹/₂ tablespoons Campari, 1¹/₂ tablespoons sweet vermouth and 1¹/₂ tablespoons gin. Lightly stir to 'marble' the different coloured alcohols. Garnish with slices of orange zest. Serves 1

## ripe cherry

Put 1¹/₂ tablespoons framboise into a cocktail shaker with 3 teaspoons Malibu and 3 teaspoons white crème de cacao. Shake well, then pour into a small cocktail glass filled with crushed ice. Serve immediately. Serves 1

Serve it sweet with a ripe cherry blend or tempt

## mai tai

Fill a cocktail shaker with ice. Add 1 tablespoon lime juice, 2 tablespoons Grand Marnier, a dash of Angostura bitters, 3 tablespoons dark Jamaican rum, 4 tablespoons pineapple juice, 1 teaspoon grenadine syrup and 2 drops almond extract (essence). Shake well, then pour over ice. Garnish with pineapple and mint. Serves 1

## campari classic

Pour 125 ml (4 fl oz/$1/2$ cup) orange juice and 3 tablespoons Campari into a tall glass and top with ice. Garnish with sliced orange. Serves 1

newcomers with the tropical delights of a mai tai.

# classic nibbles

## spiced nut blend

Preheat the oven to 170°C (325°F/Gas 3). Put 1 teaspoon cumin seeds, 1 teaspoon coriander seeds, 1 teaspoon mustard seeds, $^1/_4$ teaspoon fennel seeds, $^1/_2$ cinnamon stick, $^1/_2$ teaspoon black peppercorns and 1 teaspoon ground turmeric into a spice grinder or blender and grind to a fine powder. Transfer the mixture to a large bowl and add 2 tablespoons soft brown sugar, 2 teaspoons sea salt and 350 g (12 oz) mixed nuts, such as pecans, cashews, peanuts and macadamias. Stir to combine, then add 2 tablespoons olive oil and mix well. Spread the nut blend out on a baking tray. Bake for 10–15 minutes, or until the nuts have coloured a little, stirring occasionally. Allow to cool. Store in an airtight container until ready to serve. Makes 350 g (12 oz)

## quail eggs with za'atar mix

Put 2 tablespoons lightly toasted sesame seeds, 1 tablespoon dried thyme leaves, 1 tablespoon sumac, $^1/_2$ teaspoon ground roasted cumin and 1 teaspoon sea salt in a bowl and mix together. To prepare the quail eggs, bring a large saucepan of lightly salted water to the boil. Lower 24 quail eggs in, stir them for 1 minute, then simmer for 4 minutes. Remove and submerge them in a bowl of cold water before tapping them all over on a hard surface. Peel. Serve the za'atar mix in a small bowl accompanied by the shelled quail eggs. Makes 24

## marinated olives

Put 500 g (1 lb 2 oz) mixed olives in a bowl. Add 4 long strips of orange zest, 2 crushed garlic cloves, 1 seeded red chilli and several sprigs of thyme. Pour over 3 tablespoons extra virgin olive oil and toss to combine. Cover the olives and allow to marinate in the refrigerator overnight. Makes 500 g (1 lb 2 oz)

## Parmesan cheese biscuits

Put 125 g (4$^{1}$/$_{2}$ oz) chilled, cubed butter in a food processor. Add 60 g (2$^{1}$/$_{4}$ oz/$^{1}$/$_{2}$ cup) grated Cheddar cheese, 50 g (1$^{3}$/$_{4}$ oz/$^{1}$/$_{2}$ cup) grated Parmesan cheese, 150 g (5$^{1}$/$_{2}$ oz/ 1$^{1}$/$_{4}$ cups) plain (all-purpose) flour, 1 teaspoon paprika and $^{1}$/$_{4}$ teaspoon salt. Using the pulse action, process until the ingredients just come together. Remove the dough and form it into a ball. Divide in half, then roll and shape each portion into a sausage 23 cm (9 in) long x 3 cm (1$^{1}$/$_{4}$ in) wide. Roll in baking paper and chill for 1 hour. The dough can be frozen at this point until ready to use. Preheat the oven to 180°C (350°F/Gas 4). Line a baking tray with baking paper. Unwrap the dough rolls and cut into 5 mm ($^{1}$/$_{4}$ in) slices. Spread slices on the baking tray and bake for 12–15 minutes, or until pale gold. Transfer the biscuits to a wire rack to cool. Store in an airtight container until ready to serve. Makes 60

# seafood party essentials

There's something about a wonderful display of seafood that brings a sense of indulgence to any occasion. I'm not talking about a groaning table complete with ice sculptures and tortured fish, but the sort of impact that one item can make when served in lavish quantities or finely presented.

Platters of smoked salmon, plates piled with thinly sliced rye bread or blinis and bowls of crème fraîche flecked with dill will look spectacular. As will mountains of prawns (shrimp) served with a golden dipping sauce made from lemon mayonnaise coloured with a little saffron. And, when it comes to fresh seafood, remember that you'll also need an equally generous amount of ice to serve it on.

## doing it in style

If you want to take indulgence to extremes, and there are certainly occasions in life that warrant it, then serve up the following luxury party food ideas:

- The all-time ultimate party food has to be chilled French Champagne and caviar. Serve the caviar on its own, presented on little shell or bone spoons, or perched on a dollop of sour cream atop blinis or small pancakes.

- Put thinly sliced medallions of fresh cooked lobster on rounds of toasted brioche. Drizzle with warm herbed butter.

- Scallops on the shell always look magnificent. Lightly grill (broil) them and serve with a little lemon-tinged butter or top with a spoonful of crème fraîche and a jewelled garnish of colourful fish roe.

- Smoked salmon is another favourite and can be served simply on platters for guests to help themselves or can be served as small canapés. Try salmon in delicate sandwich fingers with mayonnaise and cucumber, piled on top of herb pancakes or served with horseradish-flavoured sour cream spooned into mini Yorkshire puddings (page 292).

- Prawns (shrimp) are always a big hit at parties. Marinate them with your favourite flavours and skewer them on small bamboo sticks. Barbecue or grill (broil) them quickly and then pass around while still warm.

- Roughly chop freshly cooked prawn (shrimp) meat and blend it with a little lemon mayonnaise. Spread over fresh white bread or fill tiny buns or baby brioche for a substantial canapé that will be an instant hit.

- Serve freshly peeled prawns (shrimp) with a selection of dipping sauces including sweet chilli sauce, mayonnaise tinged with Tabasco and avocado purée.

## in the shell

Oysters are made for parties — they're exotic, impressive and serving is as easy as putting them on a nice plate. Having said that, however, I do think oysters are better served at the table rather than handed around on a platter: with a drink in one hand it can be difficult for guests to slurp an oyster in style. If passing oysters around, perch them on rock salt to stop them from slipping about. If serving them at a table, pile them on ice.

Fresh oysters already come with their own flavour of the sea, but if you don't want to serve them naturally, there are a number of sauces you can serve them with:

- Make a simple creamy garnish of light sour cream or crème fraîche blended with wasabi or horseradish to taste, and then season with a little sea salt and freshly ground black pepper.

- Serve oysters drizzled with a simple dressing of lime juice sweetened with a little Japanese mirin.

- For oysters with bite, make a Thai-style dressing by combining 1 tablespoon grated palm sugar, 1 tablespoon fish sauce and 2 tablespoons lime juice in a bowl. Stir until the sugar has dissolved, then add some finely chopped red chilli and coriander (cilantro) leaves. Spoon the dressing over the oysters just before serving.

- Cooler weather is the perfect time to serve oysters hot. Remove the oysters from their shells and put the shells in a slightly warm oven. Heat vegetable oil in a deep frying pan. Whisk 2 eggs in a bowl with a splash of Tabasco sauce and put some fine polenta on a plate. Dip each oyster into the egg and then toss in the polenta. Fry until golden brown, then return the oysters to their warm shells. Serve with a bowl of lemon mayonnaise and a small bottle of Tabasco sauce.

# blini basics

1 Put 100 g (3$^{1}$/$_{2}$ oz/heaped $^{3}$/$_{4}$ cup) plain (all-purpose) flour, 70 g (2$^{1}$/$_{2}$ oz/ $^{1}$/$_{2}$ cup) buckwheat flour and $^{3}$/$_{4}$ teaspoon dry yeast in a bowl. Stir to combine, then make a well in the centre. Heat 200 ml (7 fl oz) milk in a small saucepan until warm and then pour it into the bowl. Stir to form a smooth batter, then cover and leave overnight in the refrigerator.

2 An hour before serving, remove the batter from the refrigerator. Separate 2 eggs. Stir the egg yolks and 2 tablespoons sour cream into the batter. In a separate bowl, whisk the egg whites until they form soft peaks and then fold them through to form a thick batter. Cover and allow to sit for 30 minutes.

3 Heat a pan and, when hot, grease with a little butter. Spoon teaspoons of batter into the pan to form small pancakes. When bubbles form on the surface of the pancakes, flip and cook for a further 1 minute. Makes 40 small blinis

## hints & tips

● Blinis are traditionally served with sour cream and smoked salmon or caviar. You can flavour the sour cream with a little lemon juice, grated lemon zest or finely chopped chives or dill. If serving with smoked salmon, then these fresh herbs can also be used to garnish the top of the blinis.

● If you don't have time to make authentic blinis but like the flavour of buckwheat, you can cheat by adding a few tablespoons of buckwheat flour to a simple pancake batter.

● Like most pancakes, blinis are best served fresh from the pan. If you do need to make them in advance, make them on the day you are going to serve them. Store covered with a damp cloth until ready to use. To reheat, put onto a tray and cover with aluminium foil. Put in a preheated 180°C (350°F/Gas 4) oven until they are just warm. Serve immediately.

# classic crostini and bruschetta

## mozzarella cheese, artichoke and parsley

Preheat the oven to 150°C (300°F/Gas 2). Drain a 175 g (6 oz) jar marinated artichoke hearts and put them into a food processor with 1 tablespoon roughly chopped flat-leaf (Italian) parsley. Season with a little ground white pepper and process to a smooth paste. Cut 12 thin slices from a baguette and brush one side of each slice with olive oil. Put the slices on a baking tray and bake until golden brown, turning them once. Remove from the oven and spread the artichoke paste on top of the crostini slices. Top with thinly sliced fresh mozzarella and garnish with a parsley leaf and a light drizzle of extra virgin olive oil. Makes 12 pieces

## olive and pine nut

Preheat the oven to 150°C (300°F/Gas 2). Put 3 tablespoons red wine vinegar, 6 anchovy fillets, 2 garlic cloves, 115 g (4 oz/³/₄ cup) toasted pine nuts, 2 teaspoons salted capers, 4 hard-boiled egg yolks and 12 large pitted green olives into a food processor. Process to a smooth paste and spoon into a bowl. Finely chop 1 small handful flat-leaf (Italian) parsley and add it to the bowl. Cut 12 thin slices from a baguette and brush one side of each slice with olive oil. Put the slices on a baking tray and bake until golden brown, turning once. Spoon the topping onto the crostini slices and top with some crumbled goat's cheese or shaved Parmesan cheese. Season with freshly ground black pepper. Makes 12 pieces

## mushroom and pancetta

Thinly slice 200 g (7 oz) button mushrooms and 200 g (7 oz) oyster mushrooms. Thinly slice 6 pieces of pancetta. Heat 25 g (1 oz) butter in a frying pan over medium heat. As the butter melts, add the pancetta. Cook for 1 minute and then stir in the mushrooms. Cover the pan and reduce the heat to low. Allow the mushrooms to cook for a further 5 minutes, then remove from the heat and season to taste with a little sea salt and freshly ground black pepper. Cut 8 thick slices of a rustic country-style bread. Grill (broil) or toast the bread on both sides. Rub the top of each toasted slice with a garlic clove that has been lightly crushed. Spoon the cooked mushrooms onto the bread slices and top with some shaved Parmesan cheese. Makes 8 pieces

## tomato and basil

Cut 8 ripe tomatoes in half and scoop out most of the seeds. Discard the seeds and finely dice the flesh. Put the tomato into a bowl and season liberally with sea salt and freshly ground black pepper. Cut 8 thick slices of a rustic country-style bread. Grill (broil) or toast the bread on both sides. Rub the top of each toasted slice with a garlic clove that has been lightly crushed. Put the diced tomato onto the bread slices and top with torn basil leaves. Drizzle with olive oil and serve. Makes 8 pieces

# Nothing says 'summer party' swimming in an irresistible blend

## party punch basics

1 First make a ginger syrup. Combine 3 tablespoons grated fresh ginger, 115 g (4 oz/$^1$/$_2$ cup) sugar and 3 tablespoons water in a small saucepan. Bring to the boil over high heat, then reduce the heat and simmer for 5 minutes. Remove from the heat and strain the syrup into a glass jar or bottle. When cool, store in the refrigerator until needed.

2 Put 200 g (7 oz/heaped 1 cup) finely chopped pineapple in a large glass bowl or punch bowl. Peel and finely slice 3 white peaches and add to the bowl. Add 3 tablespoons lime juice, 4 tablespoons ginger syrup and 250 ml (9 fl oz/ 1 cup) dark rum and stir to combine. Chill until ready to serve.

3 Just before serving, stir in 1 litre (35 fl oz/4 cups) chilled ginger beer or ginger wine and 500 ml (17 fl oz/2 cups) chilled peach nectar. Add some ice cubes and garnish with finely sliced lime and torn mint leaves. Serves 8

## hints & tips

- Non-alcoholic punches are ideal for children or anyone who doesn't want to drink alcohol. Simply remove the rum from the above recipe and you have a great party drink that everyone can enjoy.

- For those who like their punch to have more of a kick, half-fill a punch bowl with ice, add 1 bottle of Sauternes, 125 ml (4 fl oz/$^1$/$_2$ cup) brandy, 125 ml (4 fl oz/$^1$/$_2$ cup) Cointreau and 125 ml (4 fl oz/$^1$/$_2$ cup) Grand Marnier. Garnish with thin slices of orange and lime and top up with sparkling mineral water. Serves 6

- For a night-time party drink, make spiced wine. Put 500 ml (17 fl oz/2 cups) Vermouth Rosso into a saucepan with the strips of zest from 2 oranges, 5 crushed cardamom pods, 6 cloves, 2 cinnamon sticks, 1 tablespoon grated fresh ginger and 225 g (8 oz/1 cup) sugar. Bring to the boil over medium heat, then reduce the heat and simmer for 5 minutes. Remove from the heat and allow to cool. Strain into a bowl and add 2 bottles of red wine and 100 ml (3$^1$/$_2$ fl oz) dark rum. Garnish with twists of orange or some toasted almonds. Serve warm or chilled depending on the season. Serves 10

better than a large icy bowl filled with drunken fruit of spicy ginger, alcohol and fizz.

# classic party cocktails

## lychee and champagne chillers

Put a 400 g (14 oz) tin lychees and their syrup into a blender with the juice of 1 lime. Blend until smooth and then strain into a jug. Cover and put in the refrigerator for 1 hour to chill. Pour the lychee syrup into eight champagne or cocktail glasses and slowly top with Champagne. Serves 8

## pina colada

Put 85 g (3 oz/1/2 cup) fresh pineapple pieces into a blender. Add 6 ice cubes, 2 tablespoons lime juice, 3 tablespoons sugar syrup, 3 tablespoons white rum and 3 tablespoons coconut cream and blend until smooth. Pour into two cocktail glasses and decorate with pineapple wedges and thinly sliced lime. Serves 2

Chill those glasses in readiness for a drink with a

## tropical rum blend

Put 280 g (10 oz/2 cups) roughly chopped honeydew melon into a blender. Add 3 tablespoons white rum, 3 tablespoons Malibu, 3 tablespoons Midori and 400 ml (14 fl oz) grapefruit juice and blend until smooth. Pour into four glasses over ice and garnish with wedges of honeydew. Serves 4

## lychee and rum blast

Put 10 seeded tinned lychees, 3 tablespoons chilled lychee syrup, 4 tablespoons chilled coconut milk, 3 tablespoons dark rum and 10 mint leaves into a blender. Blend until smooth and then pour into two chilled cocktail glasses and serve immediately. Serves 2

smooth kick or an icy swirl of fruit-tinged alcohol.

# classic party cocktails

## pimm's with ginger syrup

Put 125 ml (4 fl oz/$1/2$ cup) pineapple juice, 3 tablespoons Pimm's and 1$1/2$ tablespoons ginger syrup (page 244) into a tall glass with ice. Top with soda water and garnish with lime and pineapple. Serves 1

## watermelon, mint and vodka

First make some watermelon ice cubes. Remove the seeds from a large piece of watermelon and juice the flesh. Pour into an ice cube tray and freeze overnight. To make the drink, put 2 sprigs of mint and 5 watermelon ice cubes in a tall glass. Add 125 ml (4 fl oz/$1/2$ cup) watermelon juice, $1/2$ teaspoon lime juice and 1$1/2$ tablespoons vodka and stir well. Serves 1

## mojito

Put 4 sprigs of mint and 2 teaspoons sugar in a glass. Quarter half a lime, add it to the glass and crush well with a muddler or the back of a wooden spoon. Add 3 tablespoons white rum and 4 ice cubes and top with soda water. Serves 1

## peach tree

Fill a small tumbler with ice and pour over 3 tablespoons peach syrup and 3 tablespoons dark Jamaican rum. Stir well and garnish with a wedge of lime, if you like. (The syrup from poached stone fruit makes an ideal base for this drink, see page 346.) Serves 1

# classic dips

## eggplant

Preheat the oven to 200°C (400°F/Gas 6). Put 2 tablespoons oil in a small roasting tin. Cut 1 bulb of garlic across the middle so that the cloves are cut in half. Put each half bulb of garlic cut-side down in the oiled dish and add 1 large whole eggplant (aubergine). Bake for 20 minutes, or until the garlic halves are golden brown and the eggplant is soft. Remove from the oven and allow to cool. With the tip of a small sharp knife, separate the garlic cloves from the bulb and put them in a blender or food processor. Cut the eggplant in half, scoop out the soft flesh and add it to the garlic. Blend to a purée. Transfer to a bowl and fold through 4 tablespoons tahini and 2 tablespoons lemon juice. Season with sea salt. Just before serving, fold through 2 tablespoons finely chopped flat-leaf (Italian) parsley and garnish with a sprinkle of cayenne pepper. Serve with bread. Serves 6–8

## beetroot

Preheat the oven to 200°C (400°F/Gas 6). Put 4 beetroot in a roasting tin with 250 ml (9 fl oz/1 cup) water. Cover with aluminium foil and bake for 1 hour, or until fully cooked. Carefully rub the skin off the beetroot — wear rubber gloves to prevent your hands from getting stained. Put the beetroot into a food processor and blend to a smooth paste. Transfer to a bowl and stir in 250 g (9 oz/1 cup) plain yoghurt and 1 teaspoon pomegranate molasses. Season to taste with sea salt and freshly ground black pepper. Garnish with finely chopped mint and 1 tablespoon roughly chopped walnuts. Serve with toasted ciabatta or Turkish bread. Serves 6–8

## taramasalata

Soak 4 thick slices of sourdough bread in some water. Squeeze any excess moisture from the bread and tear it into pieces. Put the bread into a food processor with 100 g (3$^1$/$_2$ oz) tin tarama (sea mullet roe), 1 crushed garlic clove, 1 tablespoon diced red onion and 3 tablespoons lemon juice. Process until smooth and then slowly drizzle in 250 ml (9 fl oz/1 cup) vegetable oil until it thickens to the consistency of sour cream. Serve with warm pitta bread. Serves 8

## guacamole

Put 1 seeded and finely chopped red chilli into a bowl. Add the juice of 2 limes, 3 tablespoons olive oil, 2 finely sliced spring onions (scallions), 3 tablespoons finely chopped coriander (cilantro) leaves and 1 finely diced Lebanese (short) cucumber. Cut 1 ripe tomato in half, scoop out the seeds and finely dice the flesh. Add the tomato flesh to the bowl and stir the ingredients together. Cut 2 avocados in half and remove the stones. With a small sharp knife, cut the flesh into a fine dice with crisscrossing lines. Run a large spoon between the skin and the flesh and scoop out the diced avocado. Add to the bowl and lightly fold to combine. Serve with corn chips or toasted tortilla triangles. Serves 4–6

# steamed prawn wonton basics

1 Lightly whisk 2 egg whites in a large bowl. Add 300 g (10$^1$/$_2$ oz) minced (ground) prawn (shrimp) meat, $^1$/$_2$ teaspoon sea salt, $^1$/$_4$ teaspoon Chinese five-spice powder, 30 g (1 oz/$^1$/$_2$ cup) finely sliced spring onions (scallions) and 1 teaspoon finely grated fresh ginger. Stir to combine.

2 Put 1 square wonton wrapper onto a clean surface and moisten the edges with a little water. Put 1 heaped teaspoon of the filling mixture into the centre of the wrapper and then bring the four corners together, sealing the sides. Set aside the wonton and repeat with the remaining mixture.

3 Put the wontons into a bamboo steamer basket lined with oiled greaseproof paper. Set the basket over a large saucepan of boiling water and steam for 10–12 minutes. Serve with a lemon dipping sauce. Makes 24

## hints & tips

- Steamed and fried wontons are often served with a dipping sauce, whether something simple like Chinese black vinegar or complex such as plum sauce, sweet chilli sauce and sweet lemon sauce.

- To make plum sauce, put 1 tablespoon Chinese black vinegar into a small jug or bowl with 1 tablespoon rice wine, 2 tablespoons sugar, 1 teaspoon light soy sauce and 125 ml (4 fl oz/$^1$/$_2$ cup) water. Heat 1 tablespoon vegetable oil in a small saucepan over medium heat and add 1$^1$/$_2$ teaspoons very finely chopped garlic and 2 teaspoons finely grated fresh ginger. Fry for 1 minute and then add the flesh of 4 blood plums. Cook until the plums are beginning to disintegrate, then add the liquid ingredients. Reduce the heat and simmer for 15 minutes, then remove from the heat and cool.

- To make a sweet lemon dipping sauce, put the juice of 2 lemons into a small saucepan with 2 star anise, 3 cardamom pods, 3 tablespoons sugar and 2 teaspoons light soy sauce. Simmer over medium heat for 5 minutes, stirring to dissolve the sugar. Cool before serving.

# classic wontons

## spinach, black bean and orange

Blanch 1 kg (2 lb 4 oz/2 bunches) English spinach until emerald green. Drain and set aside to cool. Finely chop the spinach leaves and put them in a bowl with the grated zest of 1 orange and 3 tablespoons Chinese salted black beans. Put 1 tablespoon grated palm sugar, 1 tablespoon Chinese rice wine and 1/2 teaspoon sesame oil into a small bowl. Stir until the sugar has dissolved and then pour the sauce over the spinach. Stir to combine the filling ingredients. Put 1 square wonton wrapper on a clean surface and moisten the edge with a little water. Put 1 heaped teaspoon of the filling mixture in the centre, bring the four corners together and pinch to seal the edges. Put onto a tray lined with baking paper. Repeat with the remaining mixture. Steam for 10–12 minutes and serve with sweet chilli sauce. Makes 24

## chicken and mushroom

Soak 4 dried shiitake mushrooms in hot water for 30 minutes. Drain the mushrooms, squeeze out any excess moisture and cut off the tough stalks. Finely chop the mushrooms and put them into a bowl with 250 g (9 oz) minced (ground) chicken, 4 tablespoons finely chopped bamboo shoots, 2 tablespoons light soy sauce, 1 teaspoon finely grated fresh ginger and 1/2 teaspoon sesame oil. Gently stir to combine the filling ingredients. Put 1 square wonton wrapper on a clean surface and moisten the edge with water. Put 1 heaped teaspoon of the filling mixture into the centre and draw all the edges together. Pinch the edges together to form little bags. Put onto a tray lined with baking paper and repeat with the remaining mixture. Steam for 15 minutes and serve with plum sauce (page 252). Makes 24

## sweet pork

Put 300 g (10$^{1/2}$ oz) minced (ground) pork, $^{1/2}$ teaspoon sea salt, 1 teaspoon light soy sauce, 1 tablespoon Chinese rice wine, 3 finely sliced spring onions (scallions), $^{1/2}$ teaspoon Chinese five-spice powder and 1 teaspoon finely grated fresh ginger in a bowl. Stir to combine. Put 1 square wonton wrapper on a clean surface and moisten the edges with a little water. Put 1 heaped teaspoon of the filling mixture in the centre of the wrapper and then fold the wrapper in half to form a triangle. Press to seal the edges, then bring the two pointy ends together over the top of the filling to form a bundle. Repeat with the remaining mixture. Put the wontons onto a tray lined with baking paper. To cook, deep-fry in peanut oil and serve with a small dipping bowl of Chinese black vinegar. Makes 24

## citrus scallop

Dice 300 g (10$^{1/2}$ oz) white scallop meat and put it into a bowl with $^{1/2}$ teaspoon grated orange zest, 3 tablespoons finely chopped coriander (cilantro) leaves, 3 tablespoons finely sliced spring onions (scallions), $^{1/4}$ teaspoon sesame oil, 1 seeded and finely chopped large red chilli, 1 teaspoon fish sauce, 1 finely shredded kaffir lime (makrut) leaf and $^{1/4}$ teaspoon finely grated fresh ginger. Stir to combine, then sprinkle over 2 tablespoons plain (all-purpose) flour and stir again. Put 1 square wonton wrapper on a clean surface and moisten the edges with a little water. Put 1 teaspoon of the filling in the centre, then bring the four corners together, sealing the sides. Repeat with the remaining mixture. Put the wontons on a tray lined with baking paper. To cook, deep-fry in peanut oil and serve with fresh lime wedges. Makes 30

# nori roll basics

1 First make the rice dressing. Put 4 tablespoons rice vinegar into a small saucepan with 4 tablespoons sugar and 1 tablespoon sea salt. Heat over medium heat, stirring until the sugar has dissolved. Remove from the heat and allow to cool. Cook the sushi rice (see hints & tips below) and then spoon the cooked rice onto a tray. Pour over the rice dressing and allow to cool. Prepare the filling ingredients. Thinly slice 2 Lebanese (short) cucumbers, 1 avocado and 1 daikon into long, thin lengths. Put pickled ginger and wasabi into small bowls.

2 You will need 4 nori sheets. Lay the first sheet onto a sushi mat. Put several spoonfuls of the rice onto the nori sheet. Dip your hands in water and then press out the rice until it covers three-quarters of the nori sheet, leaving one edge clear of rice. Lay the filling ingredients and pickled ginger across the rice.

3 Dab a little of the wasabi along the edge of the nori sheet where there is no rice. Using the sushi mat, tightly roll the nori and rice, starting from the rice-covered end. Once rolled, set aside and continue with the remaining three nori sheets and ingredients. Using a sharp knife, cut the sushi roll into six rounds, approximately 1.5 cm ($^5$/$_8$ in) wide. Makes 24 slices

## hints & tips

- To cook sushi rice, put 325 g (11$^1$/$_2$ oz/1$^1$/$_2$ cups) sushi or short-grain rice into a large bowl and cover with plenty of water. Stir vigorously, then drain away the cloudy water. Repeat several times until the water is clear. Drain the rice. Put the rice into a saucepan with 500 ml (17 fl oz/2 cups) water. Put over medium heat and stir once or twice while it comes to the boil. When the water has come to the boil, stir again, then cover. Boil for a further 1 minute, then reduce the heat to low and simmer for 20 minutes. Remove from the heat and allow to stand, covered, for 5 minutes before using.

- Sushi rolls can be filled with a range of ingredients — avocado, thinly sliced carrot, tinned tuna mixed with a little mayonnaise, snowpea (mangetout) shoots, smoked salmon or roe, sashimi-quality raw fish or finely chopped prawn (shrimp) meat — but always include pickled ginger.

# classic bites

## thai fish cakes

Put 450 g (1 lb) red snapper fillets into a food processor with 2 tablespoons fish sauce, 1 tablespoon red curry paste, 1 egg, 1 teaspoon grated palm sugar and 3 finely sliced kaffir lime (makrut) leaves. Process until smooth. Finely slice 70 g (2¹/₂ oz) French beans into rounds. Remove the seeds from 1 large red chilli and finely chop the chilli. Stir the beans and chilli into the puréed fish. Roll 1 heaped tablespoon of mixture into a ball and then flatten it a little. Set aside and repeat with the remaining mixture. Heat sunflower oil in a large frying pan over medium to high heat and fry the fish cakes, a few at a time, until golden brown on both sides. Drain on paper towels and serve with sweet chilli sauce. Makes 20

## whitebait fritters

Put 125 g (4¹/₂ oz/1 cup) plain (all-purpose) flour into a food processor. Add ¹/₂ teaspoon cayenne pepper, 1 teaspoon grated lemon zest, 1 egg, 1 tablespoon melted butter, ¹/₂ teaspoon salt and 3 tablespoons milk. Process to form a thick batter. Spoon into a bowl and stir in 250 g (9 oz) small whitebait and 3 tablespoons finely chopped flat-leaf (Italian) parsley. Heat some vegetable oil in a deep heavy-based frying pan over medium heat. To test if the oil is sizzling hot, drop in a little batter, then drop small spoonfuls of the batter into the oil and fry on each side until golden brown. Remove and drain on paper towels. Serve while still warm, with lime wedges. Makes 20

## fish cakes

Put 250 ml (9 fl oz/1 cup) water and 2 kaffir lime (makrut) leaves in a frying pan over high heat. Bring to the boil, then add 500 g (1 lb 2 oz) salmon fillet and cover. Reduce the heat and simmer for 5 minutes. Remove from the heat. Using a fork, break up the cooled salmon and put in a large bowl with 150 g (5 1/2 oz/2 cups) fresh breadcrumbs, 2 eggs, 2 very finely sliced kaffir lime leaves, 30 g (1 oz/1/2 cup) finely sliced spring onions (scallions), 2 tablespoons finely chopped lemongrass, 2 tablespoons finely chopped coriander (cilantro) leaves, 2 seeded and finely chopped large red chillies, 1 tablespoon lime juice, 1 teaspoon fish sauce and 1/2 teaspoon white pepper. Stir to combine and then shape into 24 small patties. Heat some vegetable oil in a nonstick frying pan over medium heat. Cook the fish cakes, in batches, until golden. Serve with lemon wedges. Makes 24

## chilli corn cakes

Remove the kernels from 2 fresh corn cobs. Put 90 g (3 1/4 oz/ 3/4 cup) plain (all-purpose) flour, 1 teaspoon baking powder, 1 egg, 1 tablespoon melted butter and 1/2 teaspoon salt into a mixing bowl. Stir to combine. Add 3 tablespoons milk and 1 teaspoon Tabasco sauce to form a thick batter, then add the corn and stir through. Heat some vegetable oil in a deep heavy-based frying pan over medium heat. To test if the oil is sizzling hot, drop in a little batter, then drop small spoonfuls of the batter into the oil and fry on each side until golden brown. Remove and drain on paper towels. Serve while still warm. Makes 24

# cocktail recipes
## savoury tarts
seared scallops
## mean martinis and
## asian-style pancakes
pick your mood, dim the lights
and invite friends over
to celebrate life

scallops with ginger and lemongrass

lime and coconut pancakes with chicken and mint

## scallops with ginger and lemongrass

2 tablespoons finely chopped lemongrass
2 teaspoons grated fresh ginger
1/2 red chilli, seeded and finely chopped
1 tablespoon sesame oil
2 tablespoons mirin
1 tablespoon fish sauce
juice of 1 lime
12 scallops on the shell, cleaned
coriander (cilantro) leaves, to serve
lime wedges, to serve

Mix together the lemongrass, ginger, chilli, sesame oil, mirin, fish sauce and lime juice in a bowl. Leave to infuse for a few minutes.

Spoon a little of the marinade over each of the scallops and arrange them, still in their shells, in one or two steamer baskets. Put the steamer baskets over a large saucepan of simmering water, cover and steam for 4 minutes, swapping the baskets after 2 minutes.

Remove the scallops from the baskets without letting any of the juices escape from the shells, and serve them with a sprinkle of coriander and lime wedges. Makes 12

## lime and coconut pancakes with chicken and mint

170 ml (51/2 fl oz/2/3 cup) lime juice
2 teaspoons sesame oil
2 tablespoons grated palm sugar
2 teaspoons fish sauce
1 teaspoon red chilli, seeded and finely chopped
400 g (14 oz) chicken, poached and shredded
125 g (41/2 oz/1 cup) plain (all-purpose) flour
1 egg, lightly beaten
grated zest and juice of 1 lime
250 ml (9 fl oz/1 cup) coconut milk
1 large handful mint
1 large handful coriander (cilantro) leaves

Combine the lime juice, sesame oil, sugar, fish sauce and chilli in a bowl and stir to dissolve the sugar. Add the chicken.

Make the pancakes by sifting the flour and 1/4 teaspoon salt into a bowl. Make a well in the centre and stir in the egg, zest, juice and coconut milk. Whisk to form a smooth batter. Grease a large nonstick frying pan and heat over low heat. Drizzle in the batter in a cobweb of lines, making a circle

10 cm (4 in) in diameter. Cook for 2 minutes, then flip and cook for a further 1–2 minutes, or until golden. Transfer to a plate and repeat with the remaining pancake mixture.

Just prior to serving, toss the mint and coriander leaves through the chicken. Fill each pancake with some of the chicken mixture, roll up and serve immediately. Makes 20

## spicy nut biscuits

1 tablespoon grated fresh ginger
1 green chilli, seeded and finely chopped
200 g (7 oz/11/3 cups) raw cashew nuts
100 g (31/2 oz/2/3 cup) pistachio kernels
200 g (7 oz/scant 11/4 cups) rice flour
11/2 teaspoons ground cumin
2 tablespoons roughly chopped coriander (cilantro) leaves
1 tablespoon black sesame seeds
1 tablespoon butter
2 eggs, beaten
150 ml (5 fl oz) vegetable oil

Put the ginger, chilli, cashew nuts, pistachios, rice flour, cumin, coriander, sesame seeds, butter and 2 teaspoons salt in a food processor. Pulse a few times to grind the nuts, then transfer to a large bowl. Add the eggs and 3 tablespoons water and stir until the mixture is combined and slightly sticky.

Take 1 heaped teaspoon of the mixture, roll into a ball and flatten slightly. Heat the oil in a deep frying pan or wok over low heat. Put a few of the flattened balls into the oil. Cook for 5 minutes, turning once, until golden brown. Drain on paper towels. Repeat with the remaining mixture. Makes 50

These nutty little biscuits, full of Asian flavours, are the perfect foil to serious cocktails like martinis, gin and tonics and straight vodka shots.

spicy nut biscuits

## artichoke tartlets

115 g (4 oz) jar artichoke hearts in oil, drained
15 garlic cloves, roasted until soft
3 tablespoons olive oil
1/2 teaspoon truffle oil
24 prebaked mini shortcrust tart cases (page 78)
3 tablespoons shaved Parmesan cheese

Put the artichoke hearts, roasted garlic, olive oil and truffle oil in a blender or food processor and blend until smooth. Season according to taste with salt and freshly ground black pepper. Put 1 teaspoon of the mixture into each of the tart cases and top with the shaved Parmesan cheese. Makes 24

## gravlax with dill dressing on pumpernickel

1 egg yolk
1 teaspoon wholegrain mustard
1 tablespoon lemon juice
1/2 teaspoon sugar
3 tablespoons olive oil
185 ml (6 fl oz/3/4 cup) light olive oil
3 teaspoons finely chopped dill
150 g (51/2 oz) gravlax (page 118) or smoked salmon
30 small slices pumpernickel bread

Whisk together the egg yolk, mustard, lemon juice, sugar and 1/2 teaspoon salt in a bowl. Mix the oils together in a jug and slowly pour into the egg yolk mixture, whisking continuously until all the oil is incorporated and the dressing thickens. Fold through the finely chopped dill and set aside.

Divide the gravlax or salmon among the sliced bread and spoon a little of the dressing over. Season with freshly ground black pepper and serve. Makes 30 pieces

## tartlets with white bean purée and cherry tomatoes

100 g (31/2 oz/1/2 cup) white beans, soaked overnight
2 garlic cloves
24 cherry tomatoes
11/2 tablespoons lemon thyme leaves
125 ml (4 fl oz/1/2 cup) olive oil
24 prebaked mini shortcrust tart cases (page 78)

Drain the beans and put them with the garlic cloves in a saucepan filled with water. Bring to the boil, then reduce the heat and simmer for 30 minutes. Meanwhile, preheat the oven to 180°C (350°F/Gas 4) and put the tomatoes in a roasting tin with 3 tablespoons olive oil, 2 teaspoons lemon thyme leaves and 1/2 teaspoon salt. Bake for 30 minutes. Add 2 teaspoons salt to the white beans in the last 5 minutes of their cooking time. Check that the beans are soft, then drain. Mash by hand or in a food processor with the remaining olive oil and thyme leaves. Season to taste with salt and freshly ground black pepper.

Fill each of the tart cases with 1 teaspoon of the white bean mash and top with 1 roasted cherry tomato. Serve immediately. Makes 24

## coconut prawns

4 egg whites
125 g (41/2 oz/1 cup) plain (all-purpose) flour
100 g (31/2 oz/12/3 cups) shredded coconut
170 ml (51/2 fl oz/2/3 cup) oil
20 raw prawns (shrimp), peeled and deveined, tails intact
sweet chilli and ginger sauce, to serve
lime wedges, to serve

Whisk the egg whites in a bowl until light and fluffy. Put the flour and coconut onto two separate plates. Heat a deep pan or wok and add the oil. While the oil is heating, toss one prawn in the flour, dip it into the egg white and roll it in the coconut. Set it aside. Repeat with the remaining prawns.

Once the oil has reached frying point (if you drop a coconut shred into the oil it will sizzle), carefully lower the prawns into the oil in batches of five. When the coconut has turned light brown on one side, turn over the prawns and cook until they are crisp and golden on both sides. Remove the prawns and drain them on paper towels. Serve with sweet chilli and ginger sauce and a squeeze of fresh lime. Makes 20

lemongrass prawns

crab with lemon, parsley and chilli

## lemongrass prawns

20 small bamboo skewers
2 lemongrass stalks, trimmed and roughly chopped
1 handful coriander (cilantro) leaves
4 tablespoons ground rice
1 tablespoon grated palm sugar
2 tablespoons lime juice
20 raw king prawns (shrimp), peeled and deveined, tails intact
lime wedges, to serve

Put the bamboo skewers into a bowl of cold water to soak. Put the lemongrass, coriander, ground rice, palm sugar and lime juice into a food processor. Process to form a thick paste. Set aside.

With a sharp knife, slice the prawns along the back. Remove the dark vein and open out the prawn along this incision by lightly flattening it with the palm of your hand. Press 1 teaspoon of the lemongrass paste along this surface, then skewer the prawn around the paste so that the paste is held in place. When all the prawns are ready, lightly grill them on a barbecue or cook in a frying pan. Cook the prawns on each side for a few minutes or until they are orange and the flesh is no longer opaque. Serve with lime wedges. Makes 20

## crab with lemon, parsley and chilli

10 slices white bread, crusts removed
2¹/₂ tablespoons olive oil
250 g (9 oz) crab meat, shredded
2 tablespoons grated lemon zest
1 tablespoon virgin olive oil
1 small red chilli, seeded and finely chopped
3 tablespoons finely chopped flat-leaf (Italian) parsley
2 teaspoons lemon juice
40 English spinach leaves, to serve

Preheat the oven to 150°C (300°F/Gas 2). Cut each slice of bread into four circles using a small round biscuit cutter. Put the bread on a baking tray, lightly brush with olive oil and bake until golden brown. Allow to cool. Put the crab meat in a bowl, add the remaining ingredients and stir well to combine. Top each toast with an English spinach leaf and put 1 heaped teaspoon of the crab mixture on top, then serve immediately. Makes 40

## chilli pumpkin quesadillas

4 tablespoons pitted and chopped black olives
1 large red chilli, seeded and chopped
125 ml (4 fl oz/¹/₂ cup) olive oil
500 g (1 lb 2 oz) pumpkin
1 teaspoon smoky paprika
300 g (10¹/₂ oz/2 cups) grated mozzarella cheese
150 g (5¹/₂ oz/1 cup) crumbled feta cheese
ten 16 cm (6¹/₄ in) white corn tortillas
90 g (3¹/₄ oz/1 bunch) coriander (cilantro)

Preheat the oven to 180°C (350°F/Gas 4). Put the olives, chilli and oil into a blender and blend to form a flavoured oil. Dice the pumpkin into small pieces and put onto a baking tray. Brush with a little of the chilli oil and sprinkle with the paprika. Bake for 30 minutes, or until golden brown and soft. Put the cheeses into a bowl and toss to combine.

Put one tortilla onto a clean board. Sprinkle with a liberal coating of the mixed cheeses, some of the roast pumpkin and a scattering of coriander leaves. Cover with a second tortilla, brush well with the flavoured oil and set aside. Repeat with the remaining ingredients. Put the quesadillas onto an oiled baking tray and bake for 7 minutes. Turn over the tortillas and cook for a further 7–8 minutes. Remove from the oven and slice into quarters. Serve immediately. Makes 20

Lemongrass-flavoured prawns, zesty crab on toast and gooey cheesy quesadillas... definitely pass-the-daiquiri food.

chilli pumpkin quesadillas

# lime and cashew blue-eye cod rolls with black vinegar

115 g (4 oz/3/4 cup) salted and roasted cashews
1 large red chilli, seeded and roughly chopped
1 handful coriander (cilantro) leaves
1 teaspoon finely grated lime zest
1 tablespoon lime juice
500 g (1 lb 2 oz) blue-eye cod fillets, divided into 12 portions
12 small rice paper wrappers
2 tablespoons peanut oil
2 tablespoons Chinese black vinegar or balsamic vinegar, to serve

Put the cashews, chilli, coriander, lime zest and juice into a food processor or blender and process to form a paste. Put 1 tablespoon of cashew paste on the top of each fish piece and set aside. Dip one of the rice paper wrappers in a bowl of water until it has softened. Lay the wrapper on a dry surface and put the fish on top. Fold the wrapper around to form a neat parcel. Set aside and repeat with the remaining fish.

Heat half the oil in a nonstick frying pan over medium heat and add the fish parcels. Cook for 3 minutes on each side, or until golden brown. You may wish to add more oil when necessary. Serve with the vinegar as a dipping sauce.
Makes 12

# salmon in pastry

300 g (10 1/2 oz) salmon fillet, skin removed and boned
2 teaspoons sumac
1 teaspoon grated fresh ginger
100 g (3 1/2 oz) unsalted butter, cut into cubes and softened
1 tablespoon glacé ginger, finely chopped
1 tablespoon currants
1 kaffir lime (makrut) leaf, finely sliced
2 sheets ready-made puff pastry, thawed
2 tablespoons milk

Preheat the oven to 200°C (400°F/Gas 6). Cut the salmon fillet lengthways into four 2 cm (3/4 in) wide strips. Put the sumac, ginger, butter, glacé ginger, currants and lime leaf in a bowl and mix until soft and well combined. Cut the pastry sheets in half and put a piece of salmon along the centre of each one. Top each with a quarter of the flavoured butter and fold the pastry around the fish, pressing the edges together at the top to form a seal. Put the salmon parcels on a baking tray lined with baking paper, ensure that the pastry is well sealed, and brush with a little milk. Bake for 20–25 minutes, or until golden brown. Remove and allow to cool until just warm. Slice into 2.5 cm (1 in) portions and serve. Makes 30

# salt and pepper tofu with cucumber sauce

1 egg white
2 garlic cloves, crushed
1 teaspoon grated fresh ginger
500 g (1 lb 2 oz) firm tofu, cut into 2 cm (3/4 in) cubes
3 tablespoons sugar
2 teaspoons lime juice
1 teaspoon finely chopped red chilli
3 tablespoons finely diced cucumber
2 tablespoons finely chopped fresh coriander (cilantro) leaves
60 g (2 1/4 oz/1/2 cup) cornflour (cornstarch)
1 tablespoon ground Sichuan peppercorns
1 teaspoon caster (superfine) sugar
1 small red chilli, extra, seeded and finely chopped
1 teaspoon each of sea salt, ground white pepper and ground black pepper
300 ml (10 1/2 fl oz) peanut oil, for frying

Lightly whisk the egg white in a bowl, then add the garlic, ginger and tofu. Stir to coat the tofu, then cover and refrigerate overnight.

To make a cucumber sauce, put the sugar and 4 tablespoons water in a small saucepan and bring to the boil. Cool, then add the lime juice, chilli, cucumber and coriander. Set aside.

In a shallow bowl, mix together the cornflour, peppercorns, sugar, extra chilli, the sea salt and peppers.

Heat the oil in a deep frying pan or saucepan over medium heat. Coat the tofu in the flour mixture, shake off any excess and deep-fry in batches for about 1 minute, or until the tofu is lightly coloured. Drain on paper towels. Serve immediately, accompanied by the sauce. Serves 6–8 as a starter

# prosciutto and mozzarella wraps

2 Roma (egg) tomatoes
20 slices prosciutto, thinly sliced
200 g (7 oz) mozzarella cheese, thinly sliced

Slice each tomato into ten vertical slices, then cut the slices in half horizontally. Lay a slice of prosciutto on the work surface and put one halved slice of tomato on it, followed by a slice of mozzarella, then another slice of tomato. Season with freshly ground black pepper and roll up firmly to make a little parcel. Repeat with the remaining ingredients. Heat a greased frying pan over medium heat and cook the prosciutto parcels for 2–3 minutes, or until golden brown. Makes 20

coconut and ginger pancakes with five-spice duck

goat's cheese tartlets

## coconut and ginger pancakes with five-spice duck

1 Chinese roasted duck, skin and flesh shredded
2 teaspoons Chinese five-spice powder
175 g (6 oz/1 cup) rice flour
425 ml (15 fl oz) coconut milk
1 egg, beaten
1 tablespoon grated palm sugar
1 teaspoon grated fresh ginger
1–2 tablespoons peanut oil
1 large handful coriander (cilantro) leaves
hoisin or plum sauce, to serve

Put the duck skin on a baking tray and grill (broil) for 1–2 minutes, or until crisp. Put the skin in a bowl and add the shredded duck meat and any meat juices. Stir in the five-spice powder.

To make the pancakes, sift the rice flour and 1/4 teaspoon salt into a bowl. Make a well in the centre of the dry ingredients and stir in the coconut milk, egg, sugar and ginger. Whisk to form a smooth batter.

Heat the oil in a frying pan over medium heat. Put two to three coriander leaves in the centre and drizzle 2 tablespoons of the batter over them to form a pancake 10 cm (4 in) in diameter. Cook until the edges start to crisp. Turn and cook the other side, then remove and set aside. Repeat with the remaining batter. Put some of the duck mixture along one end of each pancake and top with hoisin or plum sauce. Roll up and serve. Makes 20

## goat's cheese tartlets

2 sheets of filo pastry
50 g (1³/4 oz) butter, melted
a few thyme leaves
150 g (5¹/2 oz) goat's cheese
250 ml (9 fl oz/1 cup) cream
1 egg, beaten
3 egg yolks

Preheat the oven to 180°C (350°F/Gas 4). Cut the filo sheets into small squares, approximately 5 x 7 cm (2 x 2³/4 in) in size. Lightly butter three 12-hole shallow muffin tins. Line each of the holes with one square of filo, pressing the pastry well into the sides. Brush with melted butter and scatter some thyme leaves on top. Cover with a second piece of filo, brush with more butter and bake for a few minutes until the pastry is lightly golden.

Crumble the goat's cheese into a bowl. Slowly add the cream, mashing with a fork until the mixture is smooth and creamy. Fold in the egg and egg yolks and season well with sea salt and freshly ground black pepper. Spoon the mixture into the tart cases and bake for 12 minutes, or until puffed and golden. Makes 36

## bread sticks

2 teaspoons dried yeast or 15 g (¹/2 oz) fresh yeast
¹/2 teaspoon sugar
300 g (10¹/2 oz/2¹/2 cups) plain (all-purpose) flour
2 tablespoons black sesame seeds
1 tablespoon ground cumin seeds
2 tablespoons chopped thyme
1 egg
1 tablespoon olive oil

In a small bowl, mix the yeast with 250 ml (9 fl oz/1 cup) warm water and the sugar. Set aside for 5–10 minutes, or until the surface begins to froth. Put the flour, sesame seeds, cumin seeds, thyme and ¹/2 teaspoon salt in a large bowl and make a well in the centre. Pour in the yeast mixture and mix to form a soft dough. Gather into a ball, turn out onto a lightly floured surface and knead for 8–10 minutes, or until the dough is smooth and elastic. Put the dough in an oiled bowl and cover with plastic wrap. Leave for 3 hours in a warm place.

When the dough has doubled in size, punch down and turn out onto a floured surface, then knead lightly for 1–2 minutes. Roll out the dough to a thickness of 5 mm (¹/4 in) and cut into strips approximately 25 cm (10 in) long and 1 cm (¹/2 in) wide. Roll lightly and put onto baking trays lined with baking paper. Cover and allow to rise for a further 30 minutes.

Preheat the oven to 180°C (350°F/Gas 4). In a small bowl, beat the egg with 3 tablespoons water. Brush the top of the dough with the egg wash, then bake for 15 minutes, or until golden. Remove from the oven, brush the bread sticks all over with the olive oil and sprinkle with sea salt. Return to the oven for a further 4–5 minutes, or until golden brown. Remove from the oven and transfer the bread sticks to a wire rack to cool. Store in an airtight container until ready to use. Makes 30–35

These golden bread sticks are the ideal nibble, bringing a salty, crisp crunch to pre-dinner drinks.

bread sticks

# dinner

There is nothing more glorious than a bowl of the best mash, a platter of thick good-quality sausages and a rich onion sauce. Dinner comes into its own during the cooler months, and a meal like this reminds us that the simple things in life are often the best.

# dinner inspiration
pots and baking trays
roasting tins full of sticky vegetables
soups and sauce
creamy mash
golden roasted chicken
cool nights and warm food

# chicken stock basics

1 Fill a large heavy-based saucepan with 3 litres (105 fl oz/12 cups) cold water. Cut a fresh chicken into several large pieces and put them into the pan.

2 Bring just to the boil, then reduce the heat to a simmer. Skim any fat from the surface, then add 1 sliced onion, 2 sliced celery stalks, 1 roughly chopped leek, 1 bay leaf, a few flat-leaf (Italian) parsley stalks and 6 peppercorns. Maintain the heat at a low simmer for 2 hours.

3 Strain the stock into a bowl and allow to cool. Using a large spoon, remove any fat that has risen to the surface. If a more concentrated flavour is required, return the stock to a saucepan and simmer over low heat. If you are not using the stock immediately, cover and refrigerate or freeze it. Makes about 2 litres (70 fl oz/8 cups)

## hints & tips

● If you've made a large amount of stock, store it in small containers in the freezer so that it can be used for risottos and sauces as well as for soups. Stocks will keep in the refrigerator for two to three days.

● The leftovers of a roasted chicken make a great stock. Have the stockpot ready after dinner and put the carcass in along with some stock vegetables. If there is quite a bit of flesh left on the chicken, shred it and make a wonderful roasted chicken soup the following day. This is especially worthwhile if you've spent money on an organic chicken. Simply add the shredded chicken flesh to the strained stock along with 2 finely diced zucchini (courgettes), 1 grated carrot, 3 tablespoons rice or barley, 2 finely sliced spring onions (scallions) and some roughly chopped flat-leaf (Italian) parsley leaves. Simmer until the rice or barley is cooked through.

# classic stocks

## veal

Preheat the oven to 200°C (400°F/Gas 6). Put 1 kg (2 lb 4 oz) veal bones and 2 tablespoons olive oil into a large roasting tin, rub the oil over the bones and bake for 30 minutes. Add 2 chopped onions, 3 garlic cloves, 2 roughly chopped leeks, 2 sliced celery stalks and 2 roughly chopped large tomatoes to the tin. Continue baking for about 1 hour, or until the bones are well browned. Transfer the roasted bones and vegetables to a large heavy-based saucepan and cover with plenty of cold water. Bring to the boil over medium heat, then reduce the heat to a simmer. Skim any fat from the surface, then add 1 bay leaf and 6 black peppercorns. Cook at a low simmer for 4 hours. Strain the stock into a bowl and allow to cool. Using a large spoon, remove any fat on the surface. Return the stock to a saucepan and simmer over low heat to reduce and concentrate the flavour. Makes about 2 litres (70 fl oz/8 cups)

## vegetable

Put 2 tablespoons unsalted butter, 2 crushed garlic cloves and 2 roughly chopped onions into a large, heavy-based saucepan. Put the pan over medium heat and stir until the onion is soft and transparent. Add 4 coarsely chopped leeks, 3 coarsely chopped carrots, 3 thickly sliced celery stalks, 1 coarsely chopped fennel bulb, 1 handful flat-leaf (Italian) parsley, 2 sprigs of thyme and 2 black peppercorns. Add 4 litres (140 fl oz/16 cups) water and bring to the boil. Reduce the heat and simmer for 2 hours. Allow to cool. Strain into another saucepan, using the back of a large spoon to press the liquid from the vegetables. Bring the stock to the boil, then reduce the heat to a rolling boil until the stock is reduced by half. Makes about 2 litres (70 fl oz/ 8 cups)

## dashi

Put 2 litres (70 fl oz/8 cups) cold water and 30 g (1 oz) dried kombu into a large heavy-based saucepan and slowly bring to the boil over medium heat. Regulate the heat so that the water takes around 10 minutes to come to the boil. As it nears boiling point, test the thickest part of the kombu. If it is soft to the touch and your thumbnail passes easily into the surface, remove from the water. Once the water is boiling, add 125 ml (4 fl oz/$1/2$ cup) cold water and 20 g ($3/4$ oz) bonito flakes. When the stock returns to the boil, remove the pan from the heat and skim the surface of the stock to remove any muddy froth. When the bonito flakes sink to the bottom, strain the stock into a bowl through muslin cloth or a very fine sieve. The finished stock should be clear and free of bonito flakes. Makes about 2 litres (70 fl oz/8 cups)

## fish

Put 1 kg (2 lb 4 oz) fish bones into a large saucepan with 2 litres (70 fl oz/8 cups) water. Bring just to the boil, then reduce the heat and simmer for 20 minutes. Strain the liquid through a fine sieve into another saucepan to remove the bones and then add 1 chopped onion, 1 chopped carrot, 1 sliced fennel bulb, 2 sliced celery stalks, a few sprigs of thyme and parsley and 4 black peppercorns. Bring back to the boil, then reduce the heat and simmer for a further 35 minutes. Strain into a bowl and allow to cool. Makes about 1 litre (35 fl oz/4 cups)

# classic soups

## tomato and basil

Put 3 tablespoons olive oil, 2 finely sliced red onions and 2 finely chopped garlic cloves into a large saucepan over medium heat. Sauté until the onion is transparent, then add 1 kg (2 lb 4 oz) roughly chopped ripe tomatoes and cook for 5 minutes. Add 1 litre (35 fl oz/4 cups) vegetable stock (page 284). Bring almost to the boil, then reduce the heat and simmer for 20 minutes. Remove from the heat and allow to cool. Add 15 large basil leaves and 1 tablespoon soy sauce. Transfer to a blender and blend until smooth. Return the soup to the saucepan, season to taste with sea salt and freshly ground black pepper and heat to serve. Serves 4

## winter chicken

Put 2 tablespoons olive oil, 2 finely chopped rashers of bacon and 2 finely diced white onions into a large saucepan. Sauté over medium heat until the bacon is nicely browned. Add 1 grated carrot, 1 bay leaf, 2 peeled and diced large potatoes and 3 finely sliced celery stalks. Stir for 1 minute, then add 2 chicken breast fillets, cut into small cubes, and 1.5 litres (52 fl oz/6 cups) chicken stock (page 282). Simmer for 30 minutes. Season according to taste with sea salt and white pepper. Add 1 roughly chopped handful flat-leaf (Italian) parsley just prior to serving. For a richer version garnish each serve with 1 tablespoon sour cream. Serves 4

## duck and noodle

Trim and reserve the excess fat from 2 duck breasts. Finely slice the meat across the breast in 5 mm (1/4 in) thick slices. Slice 8 spring onions (scallions) into 3 cm (11/4 in) lengths. Heat the duck fat in a frying pan, add the spring onions and sauté lightly, then set aside. Cook 250 g (9 oz) soba noodles in boiling water, drain and set aside. Combine 1.5 litres (52 fl oz/6 cups) dashi stock (page 285), 4 tablespoons soy sauce and 1 tablespoon sugar in a saucepan and bring to the boil. Reduce the heat and simmer for 10 minutes. Add the sliced duck and cook for a further 1 minute. Divide the noodles among four warmed bowls. Top the noodles with the duck meat and sautéed spring onion. Ladle the hot duck broth into each bowl and serve. Serves 4

## fisherman's soup

Heat 2 tablespoons olive oil in a large saucepan and add 1 finely sliced onion, 2 crushed garlic cloves and a generous pinch of saffron threads. Cook over low to medium heat until the onion is soft but not brown. Add 1 finely diced fennel bulb and cook for a couple of minutes before adding 3 finely chopped ripe tomatoes. Add 1.5 litres (52 fl oz/6 cups) fish stock (page 285) and simmer for 10 minutes. Add 500 g (1 lb 2 oz) ling fillets, cut into bite-sized pieces, and simmer for a further few minutes, or until the fish is cooked through. Season to taste with sea salt and freshly ground black pepper and serve with some lemon, a drizzle of extra virgin olive oil and warm crusty bread. Serves 4

# roasted chicken basics

1 Preheat the oven to 200°C (400°F/Gas 6). Rinse a 1.8 kg (4 lb) chicken under cold running water and pat dry with paper towels. Scatter most of 1 handful lemon thyme over the base of a roasting tin. Generously rub the chicken skin with salt and put the chicken on top of the herbs, breast-side up.

2 Halve 1 lemon and cut 1 white onion into quarters. Put the onion and lemon inside the chicken cavity along with a few sprigs of lemon thyme. Place your finger under the skin that covers the breast and slightly pull it away from the flesh. Put 1 tablespoon chilled butter under the skin. Repeat on the other side.

3 Bake the chicken for 1 hour 15 minutes, or until it is cooked through. To test if the chicken is cooked, pull a leg away from the body — the juices that run out should be clear and not pink. When the chicken is cooked, squeeze 2 lemons over it and bake for a further 5 minutes. Remove from the oven and allow the chicken to rest for 10 minutes before carving. Arrange the chicken pieces on a serving platter and pour some of the lemony pan juices over them. Serves 4

## hints & tips

● The great thing about chicken is that it will carry so many flavours. If you like the idea of roasted chicken with a twist, rub it with Chinese five-spice for an instant taste of Asia or use sumac for a peppery-lemon flavour. Alternatively, drizzle the chicken with honey near the end of the cooking time or brush with a little soy sauce. You can also rub finely chopped ginger and lemongrass into the skin and put larger pieces in the cavity before cooking; when the chicken is nearly cooked, drizzle it with a little lime juice.

● When roasting a chicken, it's a nice idea to roast an extra chicken at the same time, if you can. It's wonderful to have a cold cooked chicken in the refrigerator for quick meals, especially during summer when so many simple and Asian-style salads can be made with the chopped or shredded flesh.

# classic roasts

## beef

Preheat the oven to 220°C (425°F/Gas 7). Stand a 2 kg (4 lb 8 oz) rib joint of beef in a roasting tin and allow to come to room temperature. Rub the beef all over with olive oil and season with 1 teaspoon sea salt and 1 teaspoon freshly ground black pepper. Roast for 20 minutes, then reduce the heat to 180°C (350°F/Gas 4) and roast for a further 1 hour. Transfer the beef to a warm platter, cover with aluminium foil and rest it for 15 minutes before carving. Serve with roasted vegetables, mustard and horseradish and/or Yorkshire puddings (page 292). Serves 6–8

## lamb

Preheat the oven to 200°C (400°F/Gas 6). With the point of a small sharp knife, make several incisions into the skin of a leg of lamb weighing about 1.5 kg (3 lb 5 oz). Rub the surface of the lamb with a little olive oil and then rub salt and pepper into the skin. Peel and halve 5 garlic cloves and press them into the incisions. Scatter 35 g (1 oz/1 bunch) of rosemary over the base of a roasting tin and put the lamb on top of it. Bake for 30 minutes, then spoon some of the juices from the tin over the lamb. Bake for a further 40 minutes. Transfer the lamb to a warm platter, cover with aluminium foil and rest it for 15 minutes before carving. Serve with roasted vegetables and fresh mint sauce (page 292). Serves 6

## pork

For roasting pork, ask your butcher to score the skin of a piece of pork shoulder, weighing about 1.5 kg (3 lb 5 oz). Preheat the oven to 220°C (425°F/Gas 7). Pat the pork dry with paper towels and rub the scored skin well with salt. Season with freshly ground black pepper. Put several sprigs of sage in the base of a roasting tin and put the pork on top, skin-side up. Bake for 25 minutes, then reduce the heat to 180°C (350°F/Gas 4) and cook for a further 1 hour. To test if cooked, insert a sharp knife or skewer into the centre of the pork — the juice should run clear. Transfer the pork to a warm platter and cover with aluminium foil. If the skin needs further cooking, remove it with a sharp knife, then put it in the roasting tin on the top shelf of the oven for a few minutes. Rest the pork for 15 minutes before carving. Serve with apple sauce or baked apples (page 293). Serves 6

## fish

Put 2 roughly chopped lemongrass stalks, 1 thickly sliced large piece of fresh ginger and 3 spring onions (scallions) cut into 4 cm (1½ in) lengths in a roasting tin. Pour over 250 ml (9 fl oz/1 cup) white wine. Rinse a 1.5 kg (3 lb 5 oz) whole snapper under cold running water and pat dry with paper towels. Using a sharp knife, cut the fish skin in a crisscross pattern. Rub the fish with a little sea salt and put on top of the lemongrass. Put 1 finely sliced lemongrass stalk and 1 thickly sliced lemon into the fish cavity. Lightly drizzle the fish with 2 tablespoons olive oil and bake for 35–40 minutes. Serve with lemon wedges or chilli-lime sauce (page 293) and coriander (cilantro) leaves. Serves 4

## classic sides

### Yorkshire puddings

Sift 125 g (4$^{1}/_{2}$ oz/1 cup) plain (all-purpose) flour into a bowl with $^{1}/_{2}$ teaspoon salt. Make a well in the centre and break 2 eggs into it. Whisk the mixture, while slowly adding 250 ml (9 fl oz/1 cup) milk, to form a smooth batter. Transfer the batter into a pouring jug. Liberally oil two 6-hole muffin tins (or, for mini puddings, two 12-hole muffin tins) and heat the tins in a 200°C (400°F/Gas 6) oven for 15 minutes. Remove from the oven and quickly pour in the batter to half-fill each individual hole. Immediately return to the oven and bake for 25 minutes. Makes 12, or 24 mini puddings

### fresh mint sauce

Put 1 handful fresh mint leaves on a chopping board, scatter with 1 teaspoon sugar, then finely chop. Transfer the sugared mint to a serving bowl or jug and stir in 1 teaspoon sugar, 2 tablespoons boiling water and 4 tablespoons apple cider vinegar. Makes 7 tablespoons

There is something about a roast dinner which

## baked apples

Preheat the oven to 180°C (350°F/Gas 4). Put 2 tablespoons balsamic vinegar into a small bowl with 1 tablespoon honey, 1 tablespoon melted butter and a generous amount of freshly ground black pepper. Quarter and core 3 apples and toss in the balsamic marinade. Put them skin-side down in a small baking tray and drizzle with the remaining marinade. Bake for 30 minutes, then turn the apples over and bake for a further 15 minutes. Serves 6

## chilli-lime sauce

Combine 125 g (4$^{1}$/$_{2}$ oz/$^{2}$/$_{3}$ cup) grated palm sugar with 170 ml (5$^{1}$/$_{2}$ fl oz/$^{2}$/$_{3}$ cup) water in a heavy-based saucepan. Bring to the boil and boil for 3 minutes. Add 1 tablespoon dried red chilli flakes, stir through, then remove the sauce from the heat. Allow to cool before stirring in 2 tablespoons lime juice. Makes 200 ml (7 fl oz)

calls for a groaning table, so here are a few extras.

# classic stuffings

## olive and basil stuffing for lamb

Put 85 g (3 oz/$^1$/$_2$ cup) pitted Kalamata olives, 15 basil leaves, 1 handful flat-leaf (Italian) parsley leaves, 2 garlic cloves and 100 g (3$^1$/$_2$ oz/1 cup) ground almonds into a food processor. Pulse once or twice to form a rough paste. Press the paste into a boned leg of lamb and use a skewer to keep the opening closed. Roast the lamb immediately. Makes enough for 1 leg of lamb

## apple and sage stuffing for pork

Put 1 finely diced onion, 2 tablespoons olive oil, 2 finely chopped garlic cloves, 3 finely sliced sage leaves and 3 finely chopped prosciutto slices in a frying pan over medium heat. Sauté until the onion is soft and transparent, then transfer the onion mixture to a bowl. Add 100 g (3$^1$/$_2$ oz/1$^1$/$_4$ cups) fresh breadcrumbs, 50 g (1$^3$/$_4$ oz/$^1$/$_2$ cup) finely chopped dried apple and 2 tablespoons apple juice. Stir to combine and then season with $^1$/$_4$ teaspoon ground white pepper. Using a large knife, make an incision through a loin of pork, press the stuffing into it and then roast. Makes enough for 1 pork loin

Baked stuffings such as these are so easy to make

## thyme and bacon stuffing for chicken

Put 1 finely diced large onion, 2 finely chopped rashers of bacon, 2 tablespoons butter and 1 tablespoon thyme leaves in a frying pan. Sauté over medium heat until the onion is transparent, then transfer the onion and bacon mixture to a bowl. Add 125 g (4 1/2 oz/1 1/2 cups) fresh breadcrumbs and the finely grated zest and juice of 1 lemon. Add 1 roughly chopped handful flat-leaf (Italian) parsley and 1 egg and stir to combine. Spoon the stuffing into the cavity of a chicken and then roast. Makes enough for 1 chicken

## spinach and walnut stuffing for beef

Wash 500 g (1 lb 2 oz/1 bunch) English spinach. Drain the leaves well and roughly chop them, removing the lower part of the stalks. Sauté 1 finely diced onion and 2 very finely chopped garlic cloves in 1 tablespoon butter in a frying pan over medium heat until the onion is soft and transparent. Add the spinach, cover and cook for 2 minutes, then remove from the heat and allow the spinach mixture to cool. Process 100 g (3 1/2 oz/heaped 3/4 cup) walnuts in a food processor. Stir the walnuts through the spinach mixture and season with a little sea salt and freshly ground black pepper. Using a large knife, make an incision through the centre of a beef fillet. Press the spinach into the incision and roast the fillet until medium-rare. Makes enough for 1 beef fillet

and will bring a roast to life with their rich flavourings.

# salt-baked fish basics

1 For salt-baking, you'll need a 1.5 kg (3 lb 5 oz) whole snapper, gutted but not scaled, and 1.5 kg (3 lb 5 oz) coarse-grained sea salt. Rinse the fish and pat dry with paper towels. Put a few sprigs of dill in the cavity and set aside.

2 Preheat the oven to 200°C (400°F/Gas 6). Put approximately one-third of the salt on the bottom of a roasting tin to just cover the metal. Put the fish on the salt and then pack the remaining salt around it. Using your hands, sprinkle some water over the salt, just enough to lightly dampen the salt. Press the damp salt with your hands to firm the packing around the fish.

3 Bake the fish for 30 minutes. Remove the tin from the oven and crack the salt encasing the fish. Carefully remove the salt from the fish, using a pastry brush to brush off any loose salt. Using a sharp knife, cut the skin down the centre of the fish and pull it away from the flesh. With a spatula or large knife, gently remove the flesh from the fish and place on a serving platter. Serve with a baby leaf salad, lemon wedges and lemon sauce or lemon mayonnaise.

## hints & tips

- The beauty of cooking fish by this method, apart from the spectacle and drama of the salt casing, is that it results in wonderfully succulent flesh. The scales prevent the fish from absorbing the salt so it's essential that your fish isn't scaled when you purchase it.

- If coarse-grained sea salt isn't available, substitute cooking salt. And if you have an excess of salt, use it to make salt-baked potatoes. Par-boil whole desiree potatoes in their skins until almost cooked through. Transfer them to a small baking tray, cover with salt and bake for 30 minutes. For fun, present the potatoes in the baking tray and get your guests to dig for them; otherwise remove the potatoes from the salt and serve alongside the fish.

# classic sauces

## bread

Press 2 cloves into 1 small white onion and put it into a heavy-based saucepan with 500 ml (17 fl oz/2 cups) milk, 60 g (2¼ oz) butter and 1 bay leaf. Stir over medium heat until the butter melts. Remove from the heat and allow to sit for 10 minutes so that the flavours infuse the milk. Remove the onion and bay leaf. Put the pan over medium heat and bring the milk almost to the boil. Gradually stir in 100 g (3¼ oz/1¼ cups) fresh breadcrumbs, pressing them against the side of the pan until the sauce is smooth. Stir in 1 tablespoon butter and season with ½ teaspoon salt and ¼ teaspoon ground white pepper. Serve with roasted chicken. Serves 4–6

## onion

Put 4 finely sliced onions, ¼ teaspoon finely chopped rosemary and 1 tablespoon butter in a saucepan over medium heat. Cook until the onion is soft and transparent, then cover, reduce the heat to low and cook for 15 minutes. Add 250 ml (9 fl oz/1 cup) veal stock (page 284). Bring almost to the boil, then reduce the heat and simmer, uncovered, for a further 10 minutes. Season to taste with sea salt and freshly ground black pepper. Serve with grilled (broiled) sausages or roasted or grilled beef. Serves 4

## lemon

Put 3 finely sliced spring onions (scallions) into a small heavy-based saucepan with the juice of 1 lemon and 250 ml (9 fl oz/1 cup) fish stock (page 285). Bring to the boil, then reduce the heat and simmer for 15 minutes, or until the liquid has been reduced by half. Whisk in 2 tablespoons diced cold butter. Serve the sauce spooned over fish. Serves 4–6

## red wine

Put 1 tablespoon finely diced red onion, 1 chopped garlic clove, 2 tablespoons finely chopped celery, 2 tablespoons grated carrot and 250 ml (9 fl oz/1 cup) red wine in a small saucepan over low heat. Simmer for 10 minutes, then strain into another saucepan and add 250 ml (9 fl oz/1 cup) veal stock (page 284). Bring to the boil, then reduce the heat and simmer for 15 minutes, or until the liquid has been reduced by half. Just before serving, stir or whisk in 2 tablespoons chilled diced butter. Serve with lamb or beef. Serves 4

# vegetable essentials

When it comes to vegetables, there really is only one hard and fast rule and that is to choose what is seasonal. Apart from that you can be as simple or creative as you like. However, as always, my advice is to keep things as easy as possible. If the produce is fresh, then all you have to do is cook it, add a little oil or butter and sprinkle with spice or seasoning.

Roasting vegetables is easy and the cooking process brings out the natural sweetness of most vegetables, resulting in a crisp, slightly caramelized exterior. Add a few extra ingredients and you can raise Sunday roast favourites to fairly spectacular heights. For example, you can spruce up pumpkin pieces with lime juice, olive oil, a little soy sauce and some finely chopped lemongrass. Bake until golden brown and serve with roast chicken — delicious. Similarly, sweet potato tossed in olive oil, ground cumin and a little ground red chilli, and baked until golden brown, is not to be missed. And when roasting vegetables with meat, try to include parsnips in the mix — sticky with pan juices and sweet at the centre, a roasted parsnip is a wonderful thing. Or fill a tray with tomatoes still on the vine, season with sea salt, fresh thyme and a drizzle of oil, and bake until the skins begin to split.

The beauty of roasting vegetables is not only the wonderful flavours they bring to the table but the fact that once they are in the oven you really don't have to do anything else apart from turning them once. This frees you up to relax and be adventurous with the rest of the meal.

## on the side

- Good-for-you greens like broccoli, English spinach, zucchini (courgette) and beans don't have to be boring. You can enliven them simply with a drizzle of herb-infused olive oil, savoury-sweet kecap manis, lime juice and chilli flakes, oyster sauce, toasted sesame seeds, butter and mustard or a scattering of toasted pine nuts or almonds.

- There really is nothing nicer than classic, minted green peas. To make, simply add some fresh mint to the peas' cooking water, reserving a few lovely looking mint leaves. Drain the cooked peas, then fold through the reserved mint, olive oil and freshly ground black pepper.

- For perfectly green beans, simply blanch in boiling water until they turn emerald in colour. Quickly drain them and put into a serving bowl. Drizzle with extra virgin olive oil and a splash of lemon juice or balsamic vinegar, then season with sea salt and freshly ground black pepper.

- For a really easy side dish, toss a selection of green beans in extra virgin olive oil, lemon juice and thyme leaves. Pile them onto a serving plate, crumble over some creamy feta cheese and season with freshly ground black pepper.

- Add a luscious smoky sweetness to any dish with grilled (broiled) red capsicums (peppers). You can marinate them in oil, garlic, fresh herbs and, depending on the recipe, a sprinkle of ground cumin or paprika, then store them in the refrigerator ready for use. Cut into thick strips, they can be added to a warm salad; or cut into pieces, they can be tossed with herbs and served with grilled (broiled) meat.

- Barbecue fresh corn cobs and serve them with the charred husks pulled back, accompanied by a bowl of chipotle chilli or Tabasco-flavoured mayonnaise. Or flavour butter with coriander (cilantro) leaves, finely chopped black olives and a little ground cumin and paprika and serve melted over the hot corn cobs.

- Sauté sliced zucchini (courgettes) with a little garlic and olive oil. Season with sea salt and freshly ground black pepper and spoon into a roasting tin. Cover with finely grated Parmesan cheese and a sprinkle of paprika and grill (broil) until lightly golden. Serve with grilled (broiled) sausages or lamb cutlets.

- Put finely sliced fennel bulbs in a roasting tin and toss with a little olive oil, lemon juice and finely chopped flat-leaf (Italian) parsley, then season with salt and freshly ground black pepper. Cover and bake in a preheated 200°C (400°F/Gas 6) oven for 30 minutes. Serve with pork sausages and mustard.

- Bake 2 eggplants (aubergines) in a preheated 200°C (400°F/Gas 6) oven until the flesh is soft. Scoop out the flesh and roughly chop into large pieces, then toss with a little tahini, lemon juice and flat-leaf (Italian) parsley. Season generously with ground cumin, sea salt and freshly ground black pepper. Serve with grilled (broiled) lamb cutlets.

- Drizzle steamed baby carrots with melted butter that has been flavoured with a dash of honey and thyme leaves.

# potato essentials

As far as I know, I have no Irish ancestors, but I have to say, when it comes to potatoes, I can be a little on the greedy side. I'm the first to order house-speciality potatoes in restaurants, whether thin crispy fries, thick wedges all salty and ready for dipping in sour cream, or a magnificent pile of buttery mash. However, I'm not the only one with a passion for the simple spud — I've noticed that my fellow diners who have virtuously chosen the green salad are quick to dive into my potatoes. Fried, mashed, roasted, tossed in oil, awash with butter, puréed with cream, coated in spices or layered with flavours, the potato really is one of our most versatile, and most loved, vegetables.

## the perfect potato

- For creamy mashes, always use floury potatoes like bison, Pontiac or King Edward and always mash the potatoes as soon as you've cooked and drained them. If you like your mash to be fine textured, then use a food mill or a small handheld ricer. Never purée potato in a food processor as you'll end up with a gluey mess. And never skimp on the butter. There's nothing worse than milky mash, so if you're watching your waistline, serve a bowl of boiled new potatoes instead, scattered with fresh herbs and a light drizzle of extra virgin olive oil.

- For perfectly boiled potatoes, always use waxy varieties like kipfler, Nicola, pink-eye or bintje. A simple way to boil small potatoes without the potato breaking up is to put the whole potatoes in a large pot of salted cold water. Bring to the boil and then cover with a lid and allow to simmer for a few minutes. Turn off the heat and leave the potatoes to sit in the boiling water, with the lid on, for 40 minutes. The potatoes should be cooked through and still hot enough to serve.

- Toss warm boiled potatoes in olive oil and lots of fresh herbs such as dill, mint, parsley and chives. Slightly smash them up and then pile them into a warm serving bowl.

## everyone's favourite

A roast potato is a magnificent thing and here are a few of my favourite approaches to roasting:

- For perfect roasts, peel and cut floury potatoes into large chunks. (I always advise making more than you think you'll need because there never seems to be enough roasted potato.) Boil the potato chunks in salted water until almost cooked through. Transfer to a roasting tin and run the tines of a fork over the potato chunks to give the surface a little texture. Drizzle with olive oil and bake in a preheated 200°C (400°F/Gas 6) oven for about 1 hour, or until golden and crispy, turning at least once during baking.

- Put wedges of desiree potatoes in a roasting tin and pour over enough water to cover the base to a depth of 5 mm (1/4 in). Add some big chunks of butter and scatter over rosemary or thyme. Cover with aluminium foil and bake in a preheated 200°C (400°F/Gas 6) oven for 30 minutes, then remove the foil and continue baking until the potatoes are cooked through and golden brown.

- Put bite-sized chunks of potato into a roasting tin with whole garlic cloves. Drizzle with olive oil and season with a little cinnamon and paprika. Rub the oil and spices over the potato and bake in a preheated 200°C (400°F/ Gas 6) oven until golden and crunchy.

- Layer thinly sliced, peeled potatoes in a small ovenproof frying pan or roasting tin and brush each layer with melted butter. Add a layer of very finely chopped fresh herbs or sautéed onions and then top with more layers of potato. Bake in a preheated 200°C (400°F/Gas 6) oven until the potato is cooked through and the top is golden brown. Serve sliced into warm wedges.

- Rinse kipfler potatoes under cold running water. Slice them in half lengthways and put them in a roasting tin. Drizzle with olive oil, squeeze over the juice of 2 lemons and sprinkle with some sea salt and sprigs of fresh rosemary. Bake in a preheated 200°C (400°F/Gas 6) oven for 1–11/2 hours.

# classic mash

## white bean

Soak 200 g (7 oz/1 cup) cannellini beans overnight. Drain the beans and put them into a saucepan with 4 garlic cloves. Cover generously with cold water and bring to the boil. Reduce the heat and simmer for 1 hour, or until the beans are soft. Stir in 2 teaspoons salt in the last 5 minutes of cooking time. Once the beans are cooked, drain and roughly mash them by hand or in a food processor with 125 ml (4 fl oz/$\frac{1}{2}$ cup) olive oil and 1 tablespoon thyme leaves. Season to taste with sea salt and freshly ground black pepper. Spoon into a warm serving bowl and serve immediately. Serve with grilled (broiled) sausages or lamb. Serves 4

## celeriac

Peel 1 kg (2 lb 4 oz) celeriac and 2 potatoes and cut them into chunks. Put the vegetables into a large saucepan of salted cold water with 1 teaspoon lemon juice and 2 garlic cloves. Bring to the boil and cook for 25 minutes, or until the celeriac is soft and you can easily push a knife through it. Drain the vegetables and return them to the saucepan. Add 2 tablespoons butter and $\frac{1}{4}$ finely diced white onion. Mash while still warm, slowly adding 125 ml (4 fl oz/$\frac{1}{2}$ cup) cream until the mixture is smooth and creamy. Season to taste and serve immediately. Serve with grilled (broiled) steak or seared lamb. Serves 4

Who can say no to a warm bowl of creamy mash?

## pumpkin

Peel 1 kg (2 lb 4 oz) pumpkin and cut it into chunks. Put the pumpkin into a large pot of salted cold water and bring to the boil. Boil for 10–12 minutes, or until the pumpkin is cooked through. Drain and return the pumpkin to the pot. Mash while the pumpkin is still warm, then whisk in 100 g (3¹/2 oz) butter, ¹/4 teaspoon ground white pepper and a sprinkle of ground cumin. Season with sea salt according to taste. Spoon into a warm serving bowl and drizzle with extra virgin olive oil. Serve with grilled (broiled) lamb or steak. Serves 4

## potato

Peel 1 kg (2 lb 4 oz) floury potatoes and cut into chunks. Put the potatoes into a large pot of cold salted water and bring to the boil. Cook for about 30 minutes. Put 125 ml (4 fl oz/¹/2 cup) milk with 100 g (3¹/2 oz) butter into a small saucepan. Warm over low heat until the butter has melted. When the potato is cooked through, drain and return it to the warm pot. Mash while still warm, then whisk in the buttery milk until the potato is soft and creamy. Season according to taste. Spoon into a warm serving bowl and serve immediately. Serve with roasted chicken or grilled (broiled) sausages. Serves 4

# risotto basics

1 Heat 1 litre (35 fl oz/4 cups) chicken or vegetable stock (page 282 and 284) in a saucepan over high heat. When almost boiling, reduce the heat to a gentle simmer. Melt 50 g (1³/₄ oz) butter in a large heavy-based saucepan over medium heat. Add 1 finely diced onion and 15 saffron threads and sauté until the onion is soft and transparent.

2 Add 275 g (9³/₄ oz/1¹/₄ cups) risotto rice and stir for 1 minute, or until the grains are glossy and well coated in the buttery saffron. Add 250 ml (9 fl oz/ 1 cup) of the hot stock, simmer and stir until it is absorbed. Continue to add the stock, a bit at a time, stirring continuously, until the stock is absorbed and the rice is al dente — cooked through but still a little firm to the bite.

3 Bring a saucepan of water quickly to the boil and blanch 175 g (6 oz/1 bunch) asparagus until it is bright green. Drain and slice into bite-sized pieces. Fold 2 tablespoons lemon juice and 85 g (3 oz/heaped ³/₄ cup) grated Parmesan cheese through the risotto and season with sea salt and freshly ground black pepper. Spoon onto warm serving plates and top with the asparagus. Serves 4

## hints & tips

- There are a couple of things to consider when aiming for the perfect creamy risotto. Make sure your stock is kept warm and close at hand on the stove. Always use a good-quality risotto rice such as arborio or carnaroli. If you must, you can substitute with a short-grain rice but it won't have the same creaminess or texture.

- To partly prepare risotto in advance, follow the recipe until the first 250 ml (9 fl oz/1 cup) stock is added. Stir until the stock is absorbed then remove from the heat. When needed, return the pot to the heat and add the remaining stock as per the recipe. Reheating completely cooked risotto results in a stodgy mess so it is much better to follow this method.

- The saffron adds a slight flavour and a fabulous golden colour but if you can't buy it, don't worry, as it can easily be omitted from this recipe without compromising the risotto flavour.

# classic risottos

## tomato

Heat 1 litre (35 fl oz/4 cups) chicken stock in a saucepan. Halve 8 ripe tomatoes, remove the seeds and then cut into bite-sized chunks. Put 2 tablespoons butter and 1 tablespoon olive oil in a large heavy-based saucepan over medium heat. Add 1 diced red onion and sauté until soft and transparent. Add 225 g (8 oz/1 cup) risotto rice and stir for 1 minute, or until the grains are coated and glossy. Add 125 ml (4 fl oz/ 1/2 cup) white wine, simmer and stir until absorbed. Add 250 ml (9 fl oz/1 cup) stock and stir until absorbed. Add the tomato and 250 ml (9 fl oz/1 cup) stock and stir until the stock is absorbed. Stir in 250 ml (9 fl oz/1 cup) stock. When absorbed, test if the rice is al dente. If undercooked, add the remaining stock and simmer until the stock has reduced and the rice is coated in a creamy sauce. Fold 100 g (31/2 oz/ 1 cup) grated Parmesan cheese through, then put into bowls. Serve with a drizzle of olive oil and basil leaves. Serves 4

## pancetta and pea

Heat 1 litre (35 fl oz/4 cups) chicken stock in a saucepan. Heat 2 tablespoons butter in a large heavy-based saucepan over medium heat and add 1 finely diced onion, 8 finely chopped pancetta slices and 4 finely sliced sage leaves. Sauté until the onion is soft and transparent. Add 225 g (8 oz/1 cup) risotto rice and stir for 1 minute, or until the grains are well coated and glossy. Add 250 ml (9 fl oz/1 cup) stock, simmer and stir until absorbed. Add another 250 ml (9 fl oz/1 cup) stock and stir until absorbed. Add 150 g (51/2 oz/1 cup) frozen peas and 250 ml (9 fl oz/1 cup) stock, stirring until absorbed. Test if the rice is al dente. If not fully cooked, add the remaining stock and simmer until the stock has reduced and the rice is coated in a creamy sauce. Fold 70 g (21/2 oz/3/4 cup) grated Parmesan cheese and 1 small handful flat-leaf (Italian) parsley through the risotto. Spoon into warmed bowls. Serve with a drizzle of olive oil. Serves 4

## leek and pumpkin

Heat 1 litre (35 fl oz/4 cups) chicken or vegetable stock in
a saucepan. Peel and finely dice 800 g (1 lb 12 oz) Jap
pumpkin. Finely slice 2 leeks. Heat 2 tablespoons butter in a
large heavy-based saucepan over medium heat. Add 2 finely
chopped garlic cloves and the sliced leeks. Sauté until the
leek is soft. Add 225 g (8 oz/1 cup) risotto rice and stir for
1 minute, or until the grains are well coated and glossy. Add
250 ml (9 fl oz/1 cup) stock, simmer and stir until absorbed.
Add the diced pumpkin and another 250 ml (9 fl oz/1 cup)
stock and stir until absorbed. Add 250 ml (9 fl oz/1 cup)
stock, stir until absorbed, then test if the rice is al dente. If
undercooked, add the remaining stock and simmer until the
stock has reduced and the rice is coated in a creamy sauce.
Fold 4 tablespoons grated Parmesan cheese through. Spoon
into bowls and sprinkle with more cheese. Garnish with a
drizzle of olive oil. Serves 4

## zucchini and thyme

Heat 1 litre (35 fl oz/4 cups) chicken or vegetable stock in
a saucepan. Heat 1 tablespoon butter in a large frying pan
over medium heat. Add 2 chopped garlic cloves, 1 finely
diced onion and 3 finely diced zucchini (courgettes). Sauté
until soft, then set aside. Heat 2 tablespoons butter and
1 tablespoon thyme in a large heavy-based saucepan over
medium heat. Add 225 g (8 oz/1 cup) risotto rice and stir for
1 minute, or until the grains are coated. Add 250 ml (9 fl oz/
1 cup) white wine, simmer and stir until absorbed. Add 250 ml
(9 fl oz/1 cup) stock and stir until absorbed. Stir in another
250 ml (9 fl oz/1 cup) stock. When nearly all absorbed, stir in
the zucchini. Test if the rice is al dente. If undercooked, add
the remaining stock and simmer until the stock has reduced
and the rice is coated with the sauce. Fold 70 g (2$^1$/$_2$ oz/
$^3$/$_4$ cup) grated Parmesan cheese through. Spoon into bowls.
Garnish with goat's cheese and a drizzle of olive oil. Serves 4

# noodle essentials

There are enough versions of the simple noodle in Asian cuisine to suit every occasion and mood. From the refined elegance of the soba noodle to the clean flavours of the quickly cooked rice noodle or the gutsy hokkien (egg) noodle being flipped around a wok, all noodles are both filling and very flavoursome.

While some noodles can be bought fresh, most are available in a dried form, making them perfect pantry items. The shapes and textures are so varied — from thin and threadlike to fat and slippery — and it's also worth keeping in mind that each cuisine has its own preferred noodle. When buying, choose dried noodles that have been made in the country that uses them most frequently. Both fresh and dried noodles are perfect for quickly tossing through a stir-fry, or forming the base of a salad or soup.

## using your noodle

- Egg noodles feature prominently in Chinese cuisine where their rich flavour and dense texture are well suited to the cuisine's intense sauces and rich flavours. They can be bought in their dried form and occasionally as fresh noodles from large Asian supermarkets. Hokkien (egg) noodles are thick egg noodles that are commonly sold fresh in the refrigerator section of large supermarkets. Simply cover the hokkien noodles with hot water and soak for 1 minute to separate the noodles before adding to your favourite stir-fry.

- Also commonly used in Chinese cooking are the wonderful glass-like noodles known as bean starch or cellophane noodles. Unless cooking for a large number, buy cellophane noodles that are packaged as small individual bundles. When cooked, these noodles can be tossed through salads or stir-fries: simply pour boiling water over them and stand for 15 minutes before draining. Otherwise you can deep-fry them straight from the packet and they'll bring a wonderful crunch to Asian salads or seafood dishes.

- The soba noodles of Japan are made from buckwheat flour and are mostly available in dried form. This highly nutritious noodle comes into its own when served in chilled soups or as the base for a light and refreshing noodle salad. The best way to cook them is to put the noodles in boiling water and allow the water to come back to the boil. Add 125 ml (4 fl oz/$1/2$ cup) cold water and allow to come to the boil again. Repeat the process of adding cold water twice more. This should all take about 5–6 minutes only. After this time, check the noodles — they should be nicely al dente.

- Udon and somen noodles are also from Japan. They are usually sold in their dried form and are both wheat based. With their snowy-white colour and velvety texture, these noodles are a great base for salads and soups. Somen noodles are thin and need only be boiled for 3–4 minutes. The thicker udon can occasionally be bought fresh from Japanese food stores, but in their dried form they should be boiled for 4–5 minutes. These noodles in particular have a wonderful chewy texture and are perfect for soups and slurping.

- Rice noodles come in an array of styles, both dried and fresh. They are most commonly used in Vietnamese and Thai cuisines. The fresh noodles are often sold in sheets, which can be wrapped around food or cut into strips to form hand-made noodles. Cutting noodles this way brings a lovely rustic feel to any stir-fry or Asian dish. Simply cover the fresh noodles with hot water for several minutes to soften them before using. Dried rice noodles range in style from thin threads to thick flat noodles. They cook quickly, making them perfect for that fast meal, soup or stir-fry. The thin vermicelli style needs only to be soaked for 5 minutes in boiling water, while the larger flat noodles need to be boiled for 3–4 minutes.

- Unlike pasta, Asian-style noodles require a relatively short cooking time. For this reason it is vital not to overcook them as it is often the texture that they are bringing to a meal that is important. When adding noodles to stir-fries, add them at the end to ensure that they retain their texture and absorb the flavours of the sauce.

The beauty of stir-fries is their
tofu turns this simple vegetable

## stir-fry basics

1 Prepare the stir-fry ingredients. Soak 4 dried shiitake mushrooms in 125 ml (4 fl oz/1/2 cup) hot water. Cut 200 g (7 oz) firm tofu into 2 cm (3/4 in) cubes. Finely chop 2 garlic cloves. Finely slice 3 spring onions (scallions). Seed and finely chop a large red chilli. Trim 125 g (41/2 oz) snowpeas (mangetout) and chop 100 g (31/2 oz) oyster mushrooms. Remove the sprigs from 500 g (1 lb 2 oz/1 bunch) watercress. Drain the shiitake mushrooms, reserving the soaking water, then remove the tough stalks and finely slice the mushrooms.

2 Heat 3 tablespoons vegetable oil in a wok and fry the tofu over medium to high heat until golden. Remove and drain on paper towels. Wipe the wok clean and heat 1 tablespoon vegetable oil and 1 teaspoon sesame oil over medium heat. Add the garlic, spring onions and chilli and stir-fry for 1 minute. Add the remaining vegetables a handful at a time, stirring constantly.

3 Add 1 tablespoon light soy sauce, 2 tablespoons hoisin sauce, 1 tablespoon fish sauce and the reserved mushroom soaking water to the wok and stir to combine. Cover and simmer for 3 minutes. Stir in the fried tofu, gently toss the stir-fry and serve with steamed rice or fried noodles. Serves 4

### hints & tips

● The secret to a successful stir-fry is preparation. Since the actual cooking process is dependent on speed, it is essential to have everything laid out and ready to go. Marinate your meat, prepare the vegetables and have all the seasonings and sauces close at hand.

● If preparing a dish with a large amount of meat or vegetables, it is essential to cook the stir-fry in small batches. The worst thing you can do to a stir-fry is overfill your wok. This results in a drop in temperature, the meat will stew and the vegetables will cook unevenly.

versatility. The addition of Chinese mushrooms and stir-fry into a hearty bowl of Asian flavours.

# classic stir-fries

## chilli pork with sugarsnap peas

Thinly slice 400 g (14 oz) pork fillet. Combine 3 tablespoons
hoisin sauce, 2 tablespoons shaoxing wine, 1 tablespoon finely
grated fresh ginger, 1/2 teaspoon red chilli flakes, 2 teaspoons
sesame oil and 1 crushed garlic clove in a large bowl. Stir to
blend, then add the sliced pork. Stir several times to coat the
pork well, cover and refrigerate for several hours or overnight.
Remove the pork and reserve the marinade. Heat 1 tablespoon
peanut oil in a hot wok. Stir-fry 1 finely sliced red capsicum
(pepper) and 300 g (10 1/2 oz) trimmed sugarsnap peas until the
capsicum is beginning to soften. Remove from the pan and set
aside. Stir-fry the pork, in batches, until brown. Return all of the
pork and vegetables to the wok along with 90 g (3 1/4 oz/1 cup)
bean sprouts and the reserved marinade. Continue to stir-fry until
the sauce begins to bubble. Garnish with basil leaves and serve
with steamed rice or warm noodles. Serves 4

## king prawns

Peel and devein 800 g (1 lb 12 oz) raw king prawns (shrimp),
leaving the tails intact. Peel and julienne a 3 cm (1 1/4 in)
piece of fresh ginger. Thinly slice 2 red capsicums (peppers)
and 2 yellow capsicums (peppers). Thinly slice 2 zucchini
(courgettes) lengthways, then slice them diagonally to form
thin strips. Heat 3 tablespoons peanut oil in a hot wok and
stir-fry the prawns for 1 minute. Add the ginger, capsicum and
zucchini and stir-fry for a further 1 minute. Add 4 tablespoons
shaoxing wine and simmer for 1 minute. Add 2 tablespoons
soy sauce and 1 teaspoon sesame oil. Toss for a further
1 minute and then remove from the heat. Garnish with fresh
lime wedges and garlic chives. Serves 4 as a starter

## sesame beef

Thinly slice 500 g (1 lb 2 oz) rump steak and put it into a bowl with 1 tablespoon peanut oil, 1 teaspoon sesame oil and 2 finely chopped garlic cloves. Stir to coat the beef well, cover and refrigerate for a few hours or overnight. Finely slice 250 g (9 oz/1 cup) bamboo shoots. Slice 500 g (1 lb 2 oz/1 bunch) washed English spinach. Seed and chop 2 large red chillies. Combine 3 tablespoons hoisin sauce, 3 tablespoons shaoxing wine and 1 tablespoon grated palm or soft brown sugar in a small bowl. Stir until the sugar has dissolved, then set aside. Add the beef mixture, in batches, to a hot wok and stir-fry until browned. Remove and set aside. Stir-fry 2 tablespoons sesame seeds for 1 minute, then add the beef, bamboo shoots, spinach and chilli. Toss for 1 minute, then add the blended sauce. As the sauce begins to bubble, toss a few times, then add 1 tablespoon lemon juice. Toss once more. Serve with fresh rice noodles or steamed rice. Serves 4

## hokkien noodle

Rinse 550 g (1 lb 4 oz/1 bunch) bok choy (pak choi) and slice it into halves or quarters depending on its size. Peel 1 telegraph cucumber, slice it in half lengthways and, using a teaspoon, remove the seeds, then cut the cucumber into thick slices on the diagonal. Finely slice 1 red capsicum (pepper). Heat 1 tablespoon peanut oil in a wok over medium heat and add 2 finely chopped garlic cloves, 2 seeded and finely sliced large red chillies, 1 tablespoon grated fresh ginger and 1 sliced red onion. Stir-fry until the onion is soft, then remove and set aside. Add the bok choy, cucumber and capsicum to the wok and stir-fry until the bok choy is soft and wilted. Remove and set aside. Add 450 g (1 lb) fresh hokkien (egg) noodles and 3 tablespoons kecap manis and stir-fry until the noodles are heated through. Return the vegetables to the wok and stir-fry for 1 minute. Divide among four plates and sprinkle with 1 tablespoon black sesame seeds to serve. Serves 4

# dinner recipes
fill the kitchen with rich aromas
warming winter soups
roasted meats
slow-baked fish
golden vegetables
and heady spices
a comforting end to a busy day

## roasted capsicum soup

4 red capsicums (peppers)
4 ripe vine-ripened tomatoes, stems removed
1 tablespoon olive oil
750 ml (26 fl oz/3 cups) vegetable stock (page 284)
1 teaspoon finely chopped tinned chipotle chilli
1 teaspoon ground cumin
4 tablespoons plain yoghurt
1 tablespoon finely chopped mint
corn tortillas, to serve

Preheat the oven to 200°C (400°F/Gas 6). Put the capsicums and tomatoes onto a baking tray and rub with a little oil. Bake for 30 minutes, or until both the capsicums and tomatoes are slightly blackened and blistered. Remove from the oven and allow to cool. Remove the skins and seeds from the capsicums and put them with the tomatoes into a blender or food processor. Blend to a smooth purée.

Put the purée into a saucepan with the vegetable stock, chilli and cumin. Bring to the boil, then reduce the heat to low. Simmer the soup for 10 minutes and season to taste with sea salt and freshly ground black pepper.

In a small bowl, blend together the yoghurt and mint. Ladle the soup into four warmed bowls and add a spoonful of the yoghurt. Serve with grilled (broiled) corn tortillas. Serves 4

## miso broth with somen noodles, shiitake and pumpkin

6 dried shiitake mushrooms
1 teaspoon dashi granules
3 tablespoons miso paste
2 tablespoons soy sauce
300 g (10 1/2 oz) pumpkin, peeled and cut into 2 cm (3/4 in) cubes
200 g (7 oz) somen noodles
2 spring onions (scallions), sliced diagonally

Cover the mushrooms with 500 ml (17 fl oz/2 cups) hot water and soak for about 30 minutes. Remove and finely slice the mushrooms, reserving the soaking liquid.

Put the dashi granules, 1 litre (35 fl oz/4 cups) water, the reserved mushroom liquid, miso paste, soy sauce, sliced mushrooms and pumpkin into a large saucepan and bring to the boil. Reduce the heat and simmer for 10 minutes.

Bring a large pot of water to the boil and cook the somen noodles for 3 minutes. Drain, rinse and divide among four warm bowls. Spoon the miso soup over the noodles and top with the sliced spring onion. Serves 4

## tomato and tofu broth

1 litre (35 fl oz/4 cups) dashi stock (page 285)
2 teaspoons mirin
4 tablespoons white miso paste
1 tablespoon grated fresh ginger
4 Roma (plum) tomatoes
300 g (10 1/2 oz) silken firm tofu
115 g (4 oz) baby English spinach leaves
1 tablespoon soy sauce

Put the stock, mirin, miso paste and ginger into a saucepan and bring to the boil, then reduce the heat to a simmer. Slice the tomatoes in half and scoop out the seeds using a spoon. Discard the seeds, dice the tomato flesh and add the tomatoes to the broth, simmering for a further 10 minutes.

Cut the tofu into cubes and put it into four soup bowls. Add the spinach leaves and soy sauce to the broth and cook for 1 minute, or until the leaves have just wilted. Ladle the soup over the tofu and serve immediately. Serves 4

## prawn and lemongrass soup

12 raw king prawns (shrimp)
3 lemongrass stalks
100 g (3 1/2 oz) oyster mushrooms
100 g (3 1/2 oz) enoki mushrooms
6 kaffir lime (makrut) leaves
2 spring onions (scallions), finely sliced
150 g (5 1/2 oz/1 2/3 cups) bean sprouts
juice of 3 limes
2 small red chillies
4 tablespoons fish sauce
coriander (cilantro) leaves and mint leaves, to garnish

Peel and devein the prawns and set aside the shells. Cut off the white part of the lemongrass stalks, reserving the tops. Cut the lemongrass stalks into 2 cm (3/4 in) lengths and flatten with a cleaver or the end of a heavy-handled knife.

Heat 1 litre (35 fl oz/4 cups) water in a saucepan, add the prawn shells and the lemongrass tops. Bring the water to the boil, then strain into a large bowl and return the prawn stock to the saucepan. Add the crushed lemongrass, mushrooms and kaffir lime leaves. Return to the boil, then reduce the heat to a simmer and cook for 3–4 minutes. Add the prawns and as they start to turn pink, add the spring onion, bean sprouts, lime juice, chillies and fish sauce. Stir well, then season.

Ladle into four warmed bowls and serve with a sprinkle of coriander and mint. Serves 4

# chilli, corn and black bean soup

6 corn cobs
1 tablespoon olive oil
2 red onions, diced
2 garlic cloves, very finely chopped
1 red chilli, seeded and finely chopped
2 tablespoons tomato paste (purée)
1 teaspoon smoky paprika
1 litre (35 fl oz/4 cups) chicken or vegetable stock (page 282 and page 284)
200 g (7 oz/1 cup) cooked black beans
4 tablespoons sour cream
extra paprika and coriander (cilantro) leaves, to serve

With a sharp knife, slice away the kernels from the corn cobs and set aside.

Put a large saucepan over medium heat and add the olive oil, diced onion, garlic and chilli. Cook for 5 minutes, or until the onion is soft and transparent. Add the corn kernels, tomato paste, paprika and stock. Bring to the boil, then reduce the heat to a simmer and cook for 15 minutes. Add the cooked black beans just prior to serving, then garnish the soup with sour cream, extra paprika and coriander. Serves 4

# bean salad

3 tablespoons extra virgin olive oil
1 tablespoon lemon juice
1 teaspoon walnut oil
1/2 teaspoon caster (superfine) sugar
1/2 teaspoon Dijon mustard
400 g (14 oz) green beans, trimmed
400 g (14 oz) tin butterbeans (lima beans), rinsed and drained
1 handful flat-leaf (Italian) parsley, chopped

Put the extra virgin olive oil, lemon juice, walnut oil, sugar and mustard into a large bowl and season liberally with freshly ground black pepper and sea salt. Whisk with a fork until combined. Blanch the green beans in boiling water until they begin to turn bright green, then quickly drain and add to the bowl. Toss the green beans until they are well coated in the dressing. Allow to cool, then add the butterbeans and parsley and toss again. Serves 4 as a side dish

# snapper fillets with a pink peppercorn dressing

4 tablespoons olive oil
2 tablespoons lime juice
1 teaspoon pink peppercorns
1 tablespoon finely chopped pickled ginger
1 handful coriander (cilantro) leaves
1 tablespoon finely chopped lemongrass
4 x 200 g (7 oz) snapper fillets
2 tablespoons oil
steamed green beans, sliced on the diagonal, to serve

To make the pink peppercorn dressing, put the olive oil, lime juice, pink peppercorns, pickled ginger, coriander and lemongrass into a small bowl and stir to combine.

Rinse the snapper fillets under cold running water and pat them dry with paper towels. Season both sides of the fillets with sea salt. Heat the oil in a frying pan over high heat and add the snapper skin-side down. Using a spatula, press the surface of the fish into the hot pan and cook for 1 minute, or until the skin is crispy. Turn over the fillets, reduce the heat to medium and cook for a further 8 minutes.

Put the fillets onto warm serving plates. Spoon the pink peppercorn dressing over the fish and serve with steamed green beans. Serves 4

# leek and chickpea soup

2 tablespoons butter
15 saffron threads
3 leeks, cleaned and finely diced
1 lemon, zest peeled into thick strips
1 carrot, peeled and grated
3 tablespoons roughly chopped flat-leaf (Italian) parsley
1 litre (35 fl oz/4 cups) chicken stock (page 282)
400 g (14 oz) tin chickpeas, drained and rinsed

Heat the butter and saffron threads in a large saucepan over medium heat. Add the leek when the butter begins to bubble, and cook until it is soft and transparent. Add the lemon zest, carrot and parsley and cook for a further 1 minute before adding the stock and chickpeas. Bring to the boil, then reduce the heat and simmer for 15 minutes. Serves 4

lamb shank with white beans

lemon and thyme lamb cutlets

## lamb shank with white beans

125 g (4¹/2 oz/1 cup) plain (all-purpose) flour
4 trimmed lamb shanks (about 1.5 kg/2 lb 12 oz)
170 ml (5¹/2 fl oz/²/3 cup) olive oil
1 large red onion, finely sliced
2 garlic cloves, crushed
1 teaspoon rosemary leaves
1 celery stalk, diced
2 carrots, thinly sliced into rounds
200 g (7 oz/1 cup) dried haricot beans, soaked overnight
500 ml (17 fl oz/2 cups) veal stock (page 284)
125 ml (4 fl oz/¹/2 cup) dry Marsala
lemon zest, horseradish and flat-leaf (Italian) parsley, to garnish

Preheat the oven to 200°C (400°F/Gas 6). Put the flour in a plastic bag, add the shanks and toss until well coated. Heat half the olive oil in a casserole dish. Add the shanks and turn until they are browned on all sides. Set aside.

Heat the remaining oil in a frying pan over medium heat. Add the onion, garlic and rosemary and cook until the onion is soft and lightly golden. Spoon the cooked onion, celery, carrot and drained beans over the lamb shanks, then add the stock and Marsala. Cover and bake for 2 hours, moving the shanks around in the liquid halfway through. Remove from the oven and sprinkle with finely grated lemon zest, fresh horseradish and finely chopped fresh parsley. Serves 4

## lemon and thyme lamb cutlets

20 g (³/4 oz/1 bunch) lemon thyme
12 lamb cutlets, French trimmed
3 tablespoons lemon juice
125 ml (4 fl oz/¹/2 cup) olive oil
550 g (1 lb 4 oz) kipfler or salad potatoes
85 g (3 oz/²/3 cup) pitted black olives
1 handful flat-leaf (Italian) parsley, chopped

Put half the lemon thyme into a nonmetallic container and lay the lamb cutlets on top. Cover with the remaining thyme, the lemon juice and half the olive oil, making sure the cutlets are well coated in the marinade. Marinate for at least 1 hour, or preferably overnight in the refrigerator.

Cut the potatoes into big chunks, put them in a large saucepan of salted cold water and bring to the boil over high heat. When the water has reached boiling point, cover the pan with a lid and remove it from the heat. Leave the potatoes to sit for 30 minutes.

Take the cutlets out of the marinade and barbecue or grill (broil) them for 2–3 minutes on each side, then set aside.

Drain the potatoes and return them to the pan along with the olives, parsley and remaining olive oil, stirring vigorously so that the potatoes are well coated and begin to break up a little. Season to taste. Serve the cutlets with the warm potatoes and a green salad, if you wish. Serves 4

## grilled polenta with mushrooms

5 g (¹/8 oz) dried porcini mushrooms
350 g (12 oz/2¹/3 cups) polenta
70 g (2¹/2 oz/²/3 cup) grated Parmesan cheese
1 tablespoon butter
1 garlic clove, finely chopped
100 g (3¹/2 oz) Swiss brown mushrooms, finely sliced
100 g (3¹/2 oz) fresh shiitake mushrooms, finely sliced
100 g (3¹/2 oz) oyster mushrooms
150 g (5¹/2 oz/1 bunch) rocket (arugula), stalks removed
2 tablespoons extra virgin olive oil

Put the dried porcini mushrooms into a small bowl and cover with 250 ml (9 fl oz/1 cup) warm water.

Put the polenta into a jug so that it can be poured easily. Put 1.5 litres (52 fl oz/6 cups) water and 1 teaspoon sea salt into a large saucepan and bring to the boil. Lower the heat to a simmer and slowly pour in the polenta, stirring with a whisk until completely blended. When the polenta starts to bubble, reduce the heat to low and cook, stirring occasionally with a wooden spoon for about 40 minutes. The polenta is ready when it is thick and beginning to pull away from the side of the pan. Stir in the Parmesan cheese, then pour the polenta into a flat tray and smooth down with the back of the wooden spoon. Set aside.

Meanwhile, squeeze any excess liquid from the porcini mushrooms, reserving their soaking liquid, and finely slice. Put them into a deep frying pan with the butter and garlic and cook over low heat until the garlic is lightly golden. Add the reserved soaking liquid from the porcini mushrooms and the sliced Swiss brown and shiitake mushrooms. Cover with a lid and simmer for 10 minutes. If the mixture becomes a little dry, then add some more water to give the mushrooms a nice wet texture. At the end of cooking time, add the whole oyster mushrooms and cook for a further 3 minutes. Season with sea salt and freshly cracked black pepper. Set aside.

With a sharp knife, mark out the polenta into large triangles. Cook the polenta under a grill (broiler) until the top is golden brown or sear each side on a chargrill pan. Pile the warm polenta triangles onto a bed of rocket leaves on four warmed plates and top with the mushrooms. Drizzle with a little extra virgin olive oil. Serves 4

grilled polenta with mushrooms

## shiitake mushroom, pumpkin and tofu

300 g (10$^1$/2 oz) silken firm tofu
6 dried shiitake mushrooms
2 cm ($^3$/4 in) fresh ginger, peeled and cut into thin strips
250 g (9 oz) daikon, peeled and cut into 1 cm ($^1$/2 in) rounds
100 g (3$^1$/2 oz) carrot, peeled and cut into 1 cm ($^1$/2 in) rounds
500 g (1 lb 2 oz) pumpkin, peeled and cut into large chunks

Remove the tofu from the refrigerator and allow it to come to room temperature.

Put the shiitake mushrooms into 500 ml (17 fl oz/2 cups) hot water to soak for 30 minutes. Remove the mushrooms and trim off any tough stems. Put the mushrooms in a saucepan along with the strained soaking liquid and add the ginger, daikon and carrot. Bring to the boil, then reduce the heat and simmer for 10 minutes. Add the pumpkin pieces and allow to gently simmer, covered for a further 20–25 minutes.

Cut the tofu into large chunks and divide between two warmed bowls. Check that the pumpkin is cooked through with the point of a sharp knife, then spoon the hot ingredients and stock into the bowls. Serve immediately. Serves 2

## spiced barramundi

12 whole macadamia nuts
$^1$/4 white onion, finely diced
4 garlic cloves
2 red chillies, seeded and finely chopped
2 teaspoons finely grated fresh ginger
1 teaspoon ground turmeric
4 tablespoons tamarind water
1 teaspoon soy sauce
4 x 200 g (7 oz) barramundi fillets (or other firm, white-fleshed fish)
125 ml (4 fl oz/$^1$/2 cup) coconut milk
steamed Asian greens, to serve

Preheat the oven to 200°C (400°F/Gas 6). Put the nuts, onion, garlic, chilli, ginger, turmeric, tamarind water and soy sauce in a blender or food processor and blend to a paste. Rinse the barramundi fillets in cold water and pat dry with paper towels. Rub half the paste over the fish, put it on a baking tray and bake for 12 minutes.

Put the remaining half of the paste into a small saucepan and add the coconut milk. Stir over medium heat. When the fish is cooked, serve with steamed Asian greens and some of the coconut sauce. Serves 4

## sage and parmesan veal cutlets

4 sage leaves
85 g (3 oz/1 cup) fresh breadcrumbs
4 tablespoons grated Parmesan cheese
2 tablespoons roughly chopped flat-leaf (Italian) parsley
2 eggs
4 x 200 g (7 oz) veal cutlets
2 tablespoons butter
2 tablespoons olive oil
lemon wedges, to serve
green salad, to serve

Preheat the oven to 200°C (400°F/Gas 6). Put the sage, breadcrumbs, Parmesan and parsley into a food processor. Season with $^1$/2 teaspoon sea salt and some freshly ground black pepper, then process until fine breadcrumbs form. Beat the eggs in a bowl. Dip each cutlet into the egg mixture, then press firmly into the breadcrumbs.

Heat the butter and olive oil in a large frying pan over medium to high heat. Cook the cutlets for 2 minutes on each side, then bake for 12 minutes. Serve with lemon wedges and a green salad. Serves 4

## cajun-roasted turkey

1 kg (2 lb 4 oz/2 bunches) English spinach
1 boned single turkey breast (about 1.5 kg/2 lb 12 oz)
1 tablespoon olive oil
2 tablespoons sweet Cajun spice mix
20 g ($^3$/4 oz/1 bunch) thyme
cranberry sauce, to serve

Preheat the oven to 180°C (350°F/Gas 4). Blanch the spinach in boiling water and then drain. Cut into the turkey breast to ensure there is a pocket for the spinach, then rub it with the oil and spice mix. Put the breast onto a sheet of baking paper large enough to wrap around it. Squeeze any excess moisture from the spinach and stuff it into the middle of the breast. Season with sea salt and freshly ground black pepper and cover with a sprinkling of thyme sprigs. Wrap the paper around the breast and secure with cooking twine. Put the turkey onto a baking tray and bake for 40 minutes.

Remove the turkey from the oven to rest and reserve any of the juices. Slice the turkey, put on four warm serving plates and pour over the reserved liquid. Serve with cranberry sauce. Serves 4

Bring a little sunshine to a winter evening with a

potato, capsicum and zucchini curry

ginger-spiked curry or a citrus-roasted chicken.

roasted chicken with lime pickle

## potato, capsicum and zucchini curry

500 g (1 lb 2 oz) new potatoes, halved
3 tablespoons olive oil
2 large red onions, halved and then sliced into eighths
2 garlic cloves, crushed
1 teaspoon ground turmeric powder
1 tablespoon grated fresh ginger
1 teaspoon fennel seeds, lightly crushed
3 red chillies, seeded and finely chopped
400 ml (14 fl oz) coconut milk
1 red capsicum (pepper), cut into thick strips
5 kaffir lime (makrut) leaves
500 g (1 lb 2 oz) small zucchini (courgettes), sliced
4 tablespoons lime juice
2 teaspoons fish sauce
3 handfuls coriander (cilantro) leaves

Put the potatoes in a saucepan and cover with cold water. Bring to the boil, cover and remove from the heat. Meanwhile, heat the olive oil in a saucepan over medium heat and add the onion, garlic, turmeric, ginger, fennel seeds and chilli. Cook until the onion is soft, then add the coconut milk, capsicum and kaffir lime leaves. Add the strained potatoes, cover and simmer for 15 minutes. Add the zucchini and cook for a further 5 minutes. When ready to serve, add the lime juice and fish sauce. Garnish with coriander leaves. Serves 4

## roasted chicken with lime pickle

1.8 kg (4 lb) chicken
1 lemon, halved
1 onion, quartered
2 tablespoons butter
3 tablespoons Indian lime pickle, finely chopped
1 handful watercress sprigs
mashed potato (page 305)

Preheat the oven to 200°C (400°F/Gas 6). Rinse the chicken and pat it dry with paper towels. Put the chicken on a baking tray, breast-side up, and stuff with the lemon and onion. Push the butter under the skin of the chicken breast. Rub the lime pickle over the chicken and lightly season with sea salt. Bake

for 1 hour 15 minutes, or until cooked through. Check the chicken is cooked by pulling a leg away from the body — the juices that run out should be clear and not pink.

Allow the chicken to rest for 15 minutes before carving and serving on a platter. Drizzle with some of the pan juices and garnish with watercress sprigs. Serve with mashed potato or rice with tomatoes and spinach (page 333). Serves 4

## spiced duck breast

4 duck breast fillets, skin on
2 tablespoons soft brown sugar
$1/2$ teaspoon Sichuan peppercorns
1 star anise
1 tablespoon sea salt
125 ml (4 fl oz/$1/2$ cup) brandy
4 dried shiitake mushrooms
2 thin leeks, cut into 5 cm (2 in) lengths
400 g (14 oz) Jap or butternut pumpkin (squash), cubed
2 tablespoons light olive oil

Preheat the oven to 180°C (350°F/Gas 4). Score the duck skin in a crisscross pattern. Put the sugar, peppercorns, star anise and sea salt into a spice grinder or mortar and pestle and grind them together. Rub the spice mixture into the duck skin. Put the brandy in a small nonmetallic container, add the duck breasts, skin-side up, cover and marinate for at least 1 hour, or overnight in the refrigerator.

Soak the dried mushrooms in 500 ml (17 fl oz/2 cups) boiling water for 30 minutes, then strain the liquid into a roasting tin and finely slice the mushrooms. Put the mushroom slices in the roasting tin with the leek and pumpkin, season, cover with aluminium foil and bake for 30 minutes, or until the pumpkin is soft. Increase the oven temperature to 200°C (400°F/Gas 6).

Heat a frying pan over high heat and sear the duck, skin-side down, until lightly browned. Put the duck breasts onto a rack set over a baking tray, this time skin-side up, and drizzle with the brandy marinade. Roast them for 15 minutes. (If the duck skin hasn't completely crisped up in your oven, put the duck breast under a hot grill (broiler) for 1 minute.) Arrange the pumpkin, leek and mushrooms on four warmed plates and top with a thinly sliced duck breast. Serves 4

Remember that much of the duck flavour is in the crisp fatty skin so, just for tonight, forget the diet.

spiced duck breast

# saffron mash with roasted beets and mushrooms

8 baby beets
300 g (10$^1$/$_2$ oz) mixed pine, oyster and fresh shiitake mushrooms
3 tablespoons extra virgin olive oil
2 garlic cloves, finely sliced
8 sprigs of thyme
1 kg (2 lb 4 oz) desiree potatoes, peeled and cut into chunks
125 ml (4 fl oz/$^1$/$_2$ cup) milk
15 saffron threads
100 g (3$^1$/$_2$ oz) butter
4 tablespoons toasted pumpkin seeds (pepitas)

Preheat the oven to 200°C (400°F/Gas 6). Put the beets in a roasting tin with 125 ml (4 fl oz/$^1$/$_2$ cup) water. Cover with aluminium foil and bake for 1 hour, or until cooked. Rub the skin off the beets, then slice in half and wrap in foil. Put the mushrooms, olive oil, garlic and thyme in a roasting tin, cover with foil and bake for 30 minutes. Return the mushrooms and beets to the oven just prior to serving to warm.

Meanwhile, cook the potato in a pot of salted water. Heat the milk, saffron and butter in a saucepan over low to medium heat until the saffron begins to colour the milk. Mash the potato while still warm, then whisk in the saffron milk. Season with sea salt. Cut the warmed beet into quarters and serve with the mash and mushrooms. Sprinkle with toasted pumpkin seeds and some thyme sprigs from the roasting tin. Serves 4

# peppered beef with pumpkin mash

1.5 kg (3 lb 5 oz) beef eye fillet
2 tablespoons freshly ground black pepper
pumpkin mash (page 305), flavoured with chives, to serve

Trim the fillet, then rub the pepper into the surface. Put it on a tray and leave it in the refrigerator, uncovered, overnight.

Preheat the oven to 200°C (400°F/Gas 6). Put the fillet on a baking tray and roast for 10 minutes before turning the meat and cooking for a further 5 minutes. Remove from the oven and season the fillet with sea salt. Cover with some aluminium foil and rest for 15 minutes. Drain any juices from the tray and retain them to pour over the meat later.

Return the fillet to the oven for a further 15 minutes. Serve in thick slices with a drizzle of pan juices and a large spoonful of mashed pumpkin flavoured with finely chopped chives stirred through. Serves 6

# rice with tomatoes and spinach

1 tablespoon butter
500 g (1 lb 2 oz/1 bunch) English spinach, washed and drained
400 g (14 oz/2 cups) basmati rice
3 tablespoons light olive oil
$^1$/$_2$ teaspoon ground turmeric
1 teaspoon ground cumin
1 red onion, finely sliced
2 vine-ripened tomatoes, finely chopped
750 ml (26 fl oz/3 cups) vegetable stock (page 284)

Melt the butter in a frying pan over medium heat. Finely chop the spinach and add it to the hot butter. Cover and cook until the spinach is dark green and softly wilted. Remove the pan from the heat and set aside.

Wash the rice several times until the water runs clear, then drain. Heat the olive oil in a large saucepan over medium heat and add the turmeric, cumin and onion. Cook for 6 minutes, or until the onion is golden and slightly caramelized. Add the rice and stir together for 1 minute. Squeeze any excess moisture from the spinach, then add it to the rice along with the tomato and stock. Stir once and bring to the boil. Cover, reduce the heat to the lowest setting, and cook for 25 minutes.

Serve with yoghurt, grilled (broiled) fish and a wedge of fresh lime. Serves 6 as a side dish

# seaside risoni

200 g (7 oz/1 cup) risoni
2 tablespoons butter
12 saffron threads
2 garlic cloves, finely chopped
400 g (14 oz) tin chopped tomatoes
500 ml (17 fl oz/2 cups) white wine
12 large raw prawns (shrimp), peeled and deveined, tails intact
16 black mussels, cleaned
2 tablespoons finely chopped preserved lemon rind
1 handful flat-leaf (Italian) parsley

Bring a large pot of salted water to the boil. Cook the risoni until al dente, then drain and set aside. In a deep wide frying pan or wok, heat the butter, saffron and garlic until the butter begins to bubble. Add the tomato and white wine and simmer for 2 minutes. Add the risoni, prawns and mussels and cover the pan with a lid. Simmer until the mussels have opened, discarding any that don't. Divide the mixture among four warmed pasta bowls. Garnish with preserved lemon rind and parsley leaves. Serves 4

fish tagine

slow-baked tuna with kaffir lime leaves

# fish tagine

4 tablespoons olive oil
1 large red onion, roughly chopped
10 saffron threads
1 teaspoon ground cumin
4 large potatoes, sliced into bite-sized pieces
    (about 750 g/1 lb 10 oz)
2 celery stalks, roughly chopped
400 g (14 oz) tin chopped tomatoes
1 small cinnamon stick
600 g (1 lb 5 oz) thick snapper fillets, cut into
    4 cm (1 1/2 in) chunks
1 handful flat-leaf (Italian) parsley
2 tablespoons finely chopped preserved lemon rind
crusty bread, to serve

Heat the olive oil in a large deep-based frying pan or flame-proof casserole over medium heat. Add the onion, saffron and cumin and cook until the onion is soft and caramelized. Add the potato, celery, tomato, cinnamon and 250 ml (9 fl oz/ 1 cup) water. Bring to the boil, then reduce the heat to a simmer and cook for 10 minutes. When the potato is soft, season the fish fillets with sea salt and add them to the stew. Simmer for a further 10 minutes, then season with freshly ground black pepper. Garnish with the parsley leaves and preserved lemon and serve with warm crusty bread. Serves 4

# slow-baked tuna with kaffir lime leaves

600 g (1 lb 5 oz) piece tuna fillet
15 kaffir lime (makrut) leaves
2 tablespoons pink peppercorns
250–500 ml (9–17 fl oz/1–2 cups) light olive oil
mayonnaise (page 64), to serve
lime wedges, to serve

Preheat the oven to 130°C (250°F/Gas 1). Trim the tuna fillet, removing any of the dark flesh, and if the fillet is particularly thick, slice it in half lengthways. Put the tuna in a loaf tin or small casserole dish. Season with some sea salt and scatter over the kaffir lime leaves and peppercorns. Pour over enough oil to cover the fillet, then seal the dish with a lid or aluminium foil. Bake the tuna for 45 minutes.

Lift the tuna out of the oil and serve it in thick slices with steamed potatoes, mayonnaise and wedges of fresh lime. Serves 4

# spiced pork with warm greens

2 tablespoons soy sauce
2 tablespoons mirin
1 tablespoon sesame oil
2 garlic cloves, finely chopped
1 tablespoon soft brown sugar
1 teaspoon Chinese five-spice powder
4 star anise
1 tablespoon finely grated fresh ginger
2 small pork loin fillets (about 500 g/1 lb 2 oz)
1.6 kg (3 lb 8 oz/4 bunches) choy sum, washed
steamed rice, to serve

Put the soy sauce, mirin, sesame oil, garlic, brown sugar, Chinese five-spice powder, star anise and ginger in a large bowl and stir until the sugar has dissolved and the ingredients are well combined. Add the pork and marinate for at least 1 hour, or cover and put in the refrigerator overnight.

Preheat the oven to 180°C (350°F/Gas 4). Heat a nonstick frying pan over high heat and add the pork. Sear on both sides until golden, then transfer to a baking tray and bake for 10 minutes. Pour the remaining marinade into the frying pan with 125 ml (4 fl oz/1/2 cup) water, bring to the boil, then reduce the heat and simmer for 3 minutes.

Meanwhile, steam or stir-fry the choy sum until bright green. Remove the pork from the oven and allow it to rest for a few minutes. Serve thin slices of pork with the warm choy sum, steamed rice and a spoonful of the sauce. Serves 4

This pork fillet is flavoured with ginger, star anise and five-spice, bringing the aromas of the east to your table.

spiced pork with warm greens

moroccan lamb

chilli mussels

## moroccan lamb

125 ml (4 fl oz/$1/2$ cup) lemon juice
3 tablespoons olive oil
1 teaspoon ground cinnamon
3 garlic cloves, sliced
1 teaspoon ground cumin
finely grated zest of 1 orange
2 lamb backstraps, trimmed (about 500 g/1 lb 2 oz)
1 handful flat-leaf (Italian) parsley
20 mint leaves, roughly chopped
20 oregano leaves
2 vine-ripened tomatoes, roughly chopped
couscous, to serve

Put the lemon juice, olive oil, cinnamon, garlic, cumin and orange zest in a glass or ceramic bowl and stir to combine. Add the lamb, toss to coat, then cover and marinate in the refrigerator for 3 hours, or overnight.

Remove the lamb from the marinade and put it in a nonstick frying pan over high heat. Sear until the uncooked side is beginning to look a little bloody, then turn over the lamb, reduce the heat and cook for a further 5 minutes. Remove the lamb from the heat and rest it for a few minutes.

Toss the fresh herbs and tomato together in a bowl and divide among four plates. Slice the lamb across the grain and arrange over the tomato. Serve with warm couscous. Serves 4

## chilli mussels

2 kg (4 lb 8 oz) black mussels
3 tablespoons olive oil
1 teaspoon chilli flakes
3 garlic cloves, finely chopped
15 saffron threads
1 kg (2 lb 4 oz) tin peeled tomatoes
3 tablespoons tomato paste (purée)
185 ml (6 fl oz/$3/4$ cup) white wine
1 handful flat-leaf (Italian) parsley, roughly chopped
crusty bread, to serve

Scrub the mussels and remove the beards. Rinse well in cold water and set aside.

Heat the olive oil in a large saucepan over medium heat and sauté the chilli, garlic and saffron for 1 minute. Add the tomatoes, breaking them up as you stir. Mix in the tomato paste and cook for 10 minutes. Bring to the boil and add the mussels. Cover and cook for 3 minutes, or until all the mussels have opened, discarding any that don't.

Reduce the heat to a simmer and remove the mussels to four warmed bowls. Add the white wine to the pan and cook for another 2 minutes before ladling the hot liquid over the mussels. Garnish with the parsley and serve with warm crusty bread. Serves 4

## steak with onion salsa

2 large red onions, thickly sliced
2 ripe tomatoes
2 handfuls flat-leaf (Italian) parsley
10 oregano leaves
1 tablespoon balsamic vinegar
3 tablespoons extra virgin olive oil
4 x 175 g (6 oz) fillet steaks

Preheat a barbecue. To make the onion salsa, barbecue the onion slices until they are blackened on both sides. Remove and put on a chopping board. Put the tomatoes on the barbecue and, while they are cooking, begin to roughly chop the cooked onion. Transfer the onion to a bowl. Once the tomatoes begin to blacken, turn them over and cook for a further 1 minute. Put them in the bowl with the onion and roughly chop with a sharp knife or a pair of kitchen scissors. Add the parsley, oregano, vinegar and extra virgin olive oil. Season with sea salt and cracked black pepper to taste and toss all the salsa ingredients together.

Meanwhile, put the steaks on the barbecue and sear for 2–3 minutes. Turn over and cook for a further 1 minute. Remove from the barbecue and set aside to rest. Serve with the onion salsa. Serves 4

steak with onion salsa

# desserts

At their best, desserts can finish a meal with a bold flourish or they can consist of nothing more than a bowl of raspberries and ice cream, eaten late at night in front of the television. Whether the statement is simple or spectacular, it should always feel indulgent.

# dessert inspiration
the magical alchemy
of eggs, sugar, fruit and cream
whisked whites
crunchy meringues
melting chocolate
the season's best fruit
and big dollops of cream

# fruit poaching basics

1 Put 350 g (12 oz/1¹/2 cups) caster (superfine) sugar into a heavy-based saucepan with 1 litre (35 fl oz/4 cups) water, 1 split vanilla bean and 2 pieces of lemon zest. Bring to the boil over high heat, stirring until the sugar has dissolved. Remove from the heat.

2 Peel 4 pears, leaving the stems on. With the point of a small sharp knife, remove the core with one circular movement.

3 Cut a piece of baking paper slightly larger than the size of the saucepan and screw it up. Stand the pears upright in the syrup and cover with the baking paper. Feel for where the stems are and cut the paper with small scissors so that the stems can stick through. Press the paper down. Cover the saucepan with a lid, put over low heat and gently simmer for 1¹/2 hours. Remove the saucepan from the heat and allow the pears to cool in the syrup. Serves 4

## hints & tips

- If you wish to serve a sauce with the pears, reduce the poaching liquid by simmering over low heat until it forms a thick syrup. The lemon zest, if left in the simmering syrup, will form candied zest. Finely slice it and serve sprinkled over the pears.

- For a different flavour, substitute 250 ml (9 fl oz/1 cup) water in the poaching syrup with white or red wine.

- To poach stone fruit, make the poaching syrup as in step 1. Bring the syrup to a simmer and lower the fruit into the syrup. Depending on the amount of fruit, you may need to do this in batches — all of the fruit should be covered in syrup. Cover with baking paper and gently simmer the submerged fruit for 5 minutes before testing with a skewer or small sharp knife to see if it is cooked through. When cooked, remove with a slotted spoon. When all the fruit is poached, raise the heat and boil the syrup until it reduces to a thick consistency. Pour over the poached fruit.

# berry essentials

If I only had one more meal left on earth, it would have to be a big bowl of perfect berries, eaten slowly, one by one. Wild strawberries, luscious raspberries, juicy mulberries, fat blueberries, tart red currants — each mouthful celebrating the tangy sweetness and varied textures of berries. While most varieties are available throughout the year, berries are really summertime fruits and for this reason they always make me think of sunny days. So, to complete the scenario, I'll put myself on a verandah overlooking a blue ocean with the sun on my face. And given that it is going to be my last meal, I'm adding some rich dark chocolate ice cream and several glasses of sublime dessert wine.

That's the wonderful thing about berries. They can be served quite simply and still seem perfectly indulgent. Pile them into a bowl, sprinkle with a little sugar or dollop with some rich cream — desserts don't come much easier.

## berry care

Berries are by their very nature delicate so take care when buying and preparing them. Here are a few tips:

- When buying berries, always check punnets for any signs of mould or mush. Never buy a punnet which is seeping liquid or if the berries look slightly damaged. If the top row of berries are looking a little battered, then things are only going to be worse at the bottom of the punnet.

- Prepare berries well before you need them. Carefully remove the berries from their punnets and check them for any signs of damage or mould. Put the undamaged fruit onto a large plate and either return to the refrigerator or set aside until ready to serve. If you want to wash the berries, do it close to serving time. Put them in a colander and rinse lightly under water, being careful not to bruise them. Allow to drain before serving. Strawberries are best rinsed before removing their stems as hulled strawberries will absorb water and lose much of their flavour.

- Berries are more flavoursome when at room temperature so take the prepared berries out of the refrigerator before you serve the main meal. If serving strawberries, prepare them by removing the stems and green leaves and slicing them in half. Put them into a bowl, sprinkle with a little caster (superfine) sugar and set aside. By the time you're ready to serve dessert, the strawberries will be at room temperature and will have made their own sweet sauce with the sugar.

- Although berries are in season in summer, they fortunately freeze well. So, for a taste of summer in the cooler months invest in some frozen berries. Berry syrup makes a great sauce for puddings or over ice cream. To make a raspberry or strawberry sauce simply cook frozen raspberries and strawberries with some sugar over low heat until the sugar has dissolved. Transfer to a blender or food processor, blend and then strain through a fine sieve. Frozen raspberries can be scattered over a bread and butter pudding before baking, while frozen blueberries can be folded through cake batters. Or you can simmer frozen blueberries with a little sugar, test for sweetness (if too sweet add a dash of lemon juice), then allow to cool. Spoon over toasted Madeira cake and drizzle with plenty of warm custard.

## simple but superb

Here are some great ideas for easy ways to serve berries:

- Berries and cream are a combination made in taste heaven. Serve strawberries in a bowl with whipped cream and broken meringue, or mash the berries with a little sugar and liqueur and pour the mixture over vanilla ice cream.

- Put pouring cream into a jug and add 1 split vanilla bean or a few drops of good-quality natural vanilla extract. Fill a bowl with mixed berries and toasted almonds and serve with the vanilla-tinged cream. Or, infuse custard with vanilla and pour over a bowl of berries that have been drizzled with a sweet liqueur.

- Cut strawberries into quarters and put in a bowl with a dash of balsamic vinegar. Gently fold the vinegar through the berries. Spoon the strawberries over a dollop of mascarpone cheese and drizzle with Ligurian honey.

- Lightly roast hazelnuts, then rub off the bitter dark skin and roughly chop. Finely dice several pieces of Turkish delight and put into a bowl with the hazelnuts. Stir in softened chocolate ice cream. Refreeze the ice cream and then serve with fresh strawberries.

- Blend raspberries, white peaches, orange juice and crushed ice for the perfect summer afternoon drink.

- Fill sweet pastry cases with a little mascarpone cheese and top with berries that have been dipped in caster (superfine) sugar. Drizzle with sweet liqueur or cardamom and rosewater syrup (page 355) before serving.

- Blend raw sugar with 1 vanilla bean to form a fine powder, then sprinkle the vanilla sugar over a bowl of blueberries. Toss with a dash of Cointreau and serve the blueberry mixture layered with whipped cream and raspberries in chilled glasses.

# Crème anglaise forms the base

## crème anglaise basics

1 Put 250 ml (9 fl oz/1 cup) milk and 250 ml (9 fl oz/1 cup) cream into a heavy-based saucepan. Lightly rub 1 vanilla bean between your fingers to soften it. With the point of a small sharp knife, cut the pod in half lengthways and put it into the saucepan. Put the saucepan over medium heat and bring the milk and cream just to simmering point. Remove the saucepan from the heat.

2 Whisk 5 egg yolks with 4 tablespoons caster (superfine) sugar in a bowl until light and foamy. Whisk a little of the warm milk and cream into the eggs. Add the remaining liquid, reserving the vanilla bean, and whisk to combine. Rinse the saucepan and return the mixture to the clean saucepan.

3 Cook over medium heat, stirring constantly with a wooden spoon, until the mixture thickens and coats the back of the spoon. Strain into a bowl, then scrape the vanilla seeds from the split pod into the custard. Stir the specks of vanilla through the custard and then pour into a serving jug. Serves 6–8

### hints & tips

- The most important thing about making a cooked custard is not to rush the process. If the custard comes to the boil or if it is cooked over too high a heat, it will overcook and curdle or split.

- Once the custard has thickened, remove it immediately from the heat and strain it into a bowl to prevent if from continuing to cook in the hot pan. If you fear overcooking the custard, then put a large metal bowl into a sink or larger bowl filled with ice. Strain the finished custard into the chilled metal bowl in the sink and stir so that the heat quickly diminishes.

- Crème anglaise can be made in advance. Allow to cool before covering and storing in the refrigerator. It will keep for two to three days.

of most ice creams and is also delicious as custard.

# classic ice creams

## chocolate

Put 375 ml (13 fl oz/1¹/₂ cups) milk, 250 ml (9 fl oz/1 cup) cream and 100 g (3¹/₂ oz/²/₃ cup) roughly chopped dark chocolate in a heavy-based saucepan over medium heat. Bring the milk and cream just to simmering point, stirring to help the chocolate to melt. Remove the saucepan from the heat. Put 4 egg yolks and 4 tablespoons caster (superfine) sugar in a mixing bowl and whisk until light and foamy. Add 2 tablespoons cocoa powder and whisk again. Whisk in a little of the warm chocolate mixture. Add the remaining liquid and whisk to combine. Return the mixture to the cleaned saucepan. Cook over medium heat, stirring constantly with a wooden spoon, until the mixture thickens and coats the back of the spoon. Strain into a bowl and allow to cool. Churn in an ice-cream machine according to the manufacturer's instructions. Serves 4

## lemon sorbet

Put 225 g (8 oz/1 cup) sugar and 250 ml (9 fl oz/1 cup) water into a saucepan over high heat. Stir until the sugar has dissolved, then remove from the heat. Stir in the finely grated zest of 2 lemons and the juice of 5 lemons. Allow to cool, then transfer to a container, cover and refrigerate for 1 hour. Churn the chilled liquid in an ice-cream machine according to the manufacturer's instructions. Whisk 1 egg white in a bowl until light and frothy. After 30 minutes of churning, add the egg white to the sorbet mixture in the ice-cream machine and continue to churn until the sorbet is firm. Serve or store in a covered container in the freezer. Serves 4

## coffee granita

Put 115 g (4 oz/$^1$/$_2$ cup) sugar and 125 ml (4 fl oz/$^1$/$_2$ cup) water in a saucepan over high heat. Stir until the sugar has dissolved. Remove from the heat and stir in 1 teaspoon finely grated lemon zest, 1 tablespoon lemon juice and 500 ml (17 fl oz/2 cups) strong coffee. Allow to cool, then cover and put in the refrigerator. Pour the chilled mixture into a cake tin or large shallow metal container. The mixture must freeze quickly and a shallow metal container chills the liquid faster. Cover and put in the freezer. After 1 hour, use a fork to drag the icy crystals from the edges of the container into the centre. Return to the freezer and repeat this process every 30 minutes until the mixture is completely frozen and icy. Ideally, serve the granita at this point; however, if making in advance, remove from the freezer 1 hour before serving, thaw slightly, then break up the crystals again and return to the freezer for a further 30 minutes before serving. Serves 4

## vanilla

Put 375 ml (13 fl oz/1$^1$/$_2$ cups) milk and 250 ml (9 fl oz/1 cup) cream in a heavy-based saucepan. Lightly rub 2 vanilla beans between your fingers to soften them. Cut the pods in half lengthways and put them in the saucepan. Put the saucepan over medium heat and bring the milk and cream just to simmering point. Remove from the heat. Whisk 5 egg yolks with 125 g (4$^1$/$_2$ oz/heaped $^1$/$_2$ cup) caster (superfine) sugar in a bowl until light and foamy. Whisk in a little of the warm milk and cream. Add the remaining liquid, reserving the vanilla beans, and whisk to combine. Return the mixture to the cleaned saucepan. Cook over medium heat, stirring constantly with a wooden spoon, until the mixture thickens and coats the back of the spoon. Strain into a bowl. Scrape the vanilla seeds from the split pods into the mixture and stir through. Allow to cool before churning in an ice-cream machine according to the manufacturer's instructions. Serves 4

In summertime, serve platters of ripe figs or sliced mango cheeks, big bowls of cherries and stone fruit or large wedges of juicy pineapple.

# sweet fruit essentials

Dessert doesn't have to mean hours spent in the kitchen baking when there are so many wonderful seasonal fruits available. In summer particularly, when the fruit is so inviting, there really is nothing easier than a scatter of berries or a few slices of golden sunshine, be it pineapple, mango, peach or apricot, served with your own or a shop-bought icy treat. Especially after a rich meal, there's no better way to finish than with the freshness and lightness of fruit.

If you have a large freezer, stock up on great ice creams and sorbets (home-made or bought), fill the fruit bowl and keep some mascarpone, thick (double/heavy) cream and home-made spiced syrups in the refrigerator. With a few of these ingredients at hand, dessert is simply a matter of slicing, scooping and drizzling.

## sweet syrups

Here are a couple of versatile syrups to get you started. Both will keep in the refrigerator for a few weeks:

- To make a cardamom and rosewater syrup, put 115 g (4 oz/1/2 cup) sugar, 1 teaspoon lemon juice and 5 lightly crushed cardamom pods into a heavy-based saucepan with 250 ml (9 fl oz/1 cup) water. Bring slowly to the boil, stirring to ensure that the sugar dissolves completely, then reduce the heat and simmer for 5 minutes. Remove from the heat and stir in 1/2 teaspoon rosewater. Pour into a sterilized glass jar. This is a beautiful syrup to pour over fresh figs, pitted cherries, mixed berries or to simply drizzle over chocolate ice cream.

- To make a lemongrass and passionfruit syrup, put 225 g (8 oz/1 cup) sugar into a heavy-based saucepan with 2 bruised stalks of lemongrass and 250 ml (9 fl oz/1 cup) water. Bring to the boil, then reduce the heat and simmer for 10 minutes, or until the liquid has reduced by half. Add 125 g (4 1/2 oz/1/2 cup) passionfruit pulp to the hot mixture and stir for 1 minute before removing from the heat and allowing to cool. Remove the lemongrass and pour the syrup into a sterilized glass jar. Spoon the syrup over tropical fruit or any fruit-based ice creams or sorbets.

## desserts in a flash

Here are a few great ideas using everyday ingredients that are quick and easy to make:

- Serve wedges of chilled ripe pineapple with some finely sliced mint leaves and lemon or lime sorbet.

- Slice a banana in half lengthways, top with a large scoop of vanilla ice cream and drizzle with lemongrass and passionfruit syrup.

- A classic summertime favourite is fruit salad with freshly sliced yellow peaches, sliced bananas, passionfruit and the juice of an orange or lime. Serve with ice cream. Or, combine diced red papaya and yellow peaches with passionfruit and lime juice. Sweeten with grated palm sugar if desired and serve with lime sorbet.

- Put finely diced mango into a bowl with finely sliced strawberries, halved blueberries and finely sliced mint leaves. Spoon the fruit salsa over lime sorbet.

- Marinate thickly sliced white peaches in Sauternes with a pinch of ground cloves. Serve with a little crème anglaise (page 350) or sweetened mascarpone cheese.

- Sometimes there is nothing finer than slices of crisp green apple and slivers of strong bitey Cheddar cheese. Serve with some freshly cracked walnuts or almonds.

- For a great winter fruit salad, remove the segments from 4–6 oranges using a sharp knife and put them into a bowl. Squeeze the remaining flesh of the oranges over the bowl to release any juice. Add thin slices of banana and red apple, the juice of 1 lemon and soft brown sugar to taste. Serve with vanilla ice cream or creamy yoghurt.

- Toss thickly sliced bananas in a little lime juice and ground cinnamon, or in lemon and Cointreau syrup, then serve with spiced yoghurt (page 52).

- Finely slice 10 dried figs and put into a bowl with the juice and zest of 1 orange, 1/4 teaspoon ground cinnamon, 1 teaspoon rosewater and enough hot water to cover. Allow the figs to soak overnight. Remove, then serve the marinated figs spooned over ice cream.

It may be some remnant of my
their manifestations irresistible.

# meringue basics

1 Preheat the oven to 150°C (300°F/Gas 2). Separate 3 eggs, discarding the yolks. Line a large baking tray with baking paper.

2 Put the egg whites and 175 g (6 oz/³/₄ cup) raw caster (superfine) sugar in a small bowl over a saucepan of simmering water and stir until the sugar has dissolved and the mixture is warm. Remove the bowl from the heat and beat the mixture with electric beaters until it is thick and cool. This will take about 10–12 minutes. Add ¹/₄ teaspoon natural vanilla extract and beat for a further 1 minute.

3 Spoon large dollops of the meringue mixture onto the prepared tray and bake for 45 minutes. Turn off the oven and leave the door slightly ajar, allowing the meringues to cool slowly. When completely cool, store the meringues in an airtight container. Makes 6 large meringues

## hints & tips

● Meringues are a great way to utilize leftover egg whites after making custard or mayonnaise. If stored in an airtight container, they will stay fresh for several days. Serve with whipped cream and fresh berries or passionfruit.

● To make a pavlova, preheat the oven to 180°C (350°F/Gas 4). Line a baking tray with baking paper and draw a circle on it, approximately 30 cm (12 in) in diameter. Beat 4 egg whites with a pinch of salt until the whites are firm. Then, while continuing to beat, slowly add 250 g (9 oz/heaped 1 cup) caster (superfine) sugar. Fold in 1 tablespoon cornflour (cornstarch) and 1 teaspoon white wine vinegar. Spoon the mixture onto the baking tray, keeping within the circle and building up the meringue into a smooth flat-topped mound. Bake for 5 minutes, then reduce the oven temperature to 150°C (300°F/Gas 2) and bake for a further 1 hour. Turn off the oven and, with the door ajar, allow the meringue to cool completely — ideally, leave it to cool in the oven overnight. Serve topped with whipped cream and covered with freshly sliced banana, strawberries and passionfruit.

childhood sweet tooth, but I find meringues in all
Crispy swirls, whipped cream, fresh berries...yum.

# classic puddings

## lemon delicious

Preheat the oven to 180°C (350°F/Gas 4). Butter a large ovenproof dish. Finely grate the zest of 2 lemons, then juice them. Separate 3 eggs. In a bowl, beat 70 g (2½ oz) unsalted butter with 175 g (6 oz/¾ cup) caster (superfine) sugar and the grated lemon zest until pale and creamy. Add the egg yolks and whisk to combine. Whisk in 3 tablespoons sifted plain (all-purpose) flour and 185 ml (6 fl oz/¾ cup) milk, adding them alternately to make a smooth batter. Add the lemon juice and stir to ensure it is well combined. In a separate bowl, whisk the egg whites until they form stiff peaks and then lightly fold them through the batter. Pour the mixture into the prepared dish and put the dish into a large roasting tin. Fill the tray with enough hot water to reach halfway up the side of the dish. Bake for 1 hour. Serves 8

## sticky date

Preheat the oven to 180°C (350°F/Gas 4). Butter four 300 ml (10½ fl oz) ramekins. Put 150 g (5½ oz/scant 1 cup) pitted and finely chopped dates in a bowl with 1½ teaspoons bicarbonate of soda. Pour over 150 ml (5 fl oz) boiling water and set aside for 10 minutes. Beat 2½ tablespoons unsalted butter with 125 g (4½ oz/⅔ cup) soft brown sugar in a bowl until pale and creamy. Whisk in 2 eggs. Stir in 1 teaspoon natural vanilla extract and add 1 tablespoon finely chopped glacé ginger. Add 125 g (4½ oz/1 cup) sifted self-raising flour and lightly fold it through the batter. Fold the date mixture through. Spoon the batter into the ramekins and carefully put the ramekins onto a baking tray. Bake for 20–25 minutes, or until the puddings are firm. Serve with butterscotch sauce (page 363) and whipped cream. Serves 4

## bread and butter

Preheat the oven to 180°C (350°F/Gas 4). Lightly butter a ceramic baking dish. Remove the crusts from a 450 g (1 lb) loaf of brioche, slice the brioche, then cut the slices into triangles. Arrange the triangles over the base of the baking dish and sprinkle with 1 teaspoon ground cinnamon. Put 3 eggs, 3 tablespoons caster (superfine) sugar and 500 ml (17 fl oz/2 cups) cream into a bowl and whisk together. Pour the cream mixture over the brioche and drizzle 4 tablespoons golden syrup over the pudding. Bake for 25 minutes, or until the pudding is set and nicely golden brown. Serve with fresh berries. Serves 6

## chocolate

Preheat the oven to 180°C (350°F/Gas 4). Lightly butter six 300 ml (10$^1$/$_2$ fl oz) ramekins. Put 4 tablespoons cocoa powder, 90 g (3$^1$/$_4$ oz/$^1$/$_2$ cup) brown sugar and 300 ml (10$^1$/$_2$ fl oz) boiling water in a large jug. Put 2 eggs and 150 g (5$^1$/$_2$ oz/$^2$/$_3$ cup) caster (superfine) sugar in a large bowl and lightly beat together. Put 2$^1$/$_2$ tablespoons chopped unsalted butter, 100 g (3$^1$/$_2$ oz/$^2$/$_3$ cup) chopped dark chocolate and 125 ml (4 fl oz/$^1$/$_2$ cup) milk in a small saucepan over medium heat for 3 minutes, or until the butter and chocolate have melted. Remove from the heat and cool slightly. Add 125 g (4$^1$/$_2$ oz/1 cup) sifted self-raising flour and 2 tablespoons cocoa powder to the beaten egg mixture and then stir in the melted chocolate. Divide the batter among the ramekins and spoon the hot water mixture over the puddings. Transfer to a baking tray and bake for 30 minutes, or until firm. Dust with cocoa and serve with cream or warm custard. Serves 6

Once mastered, soufflés are the
with passionfruit because the

# baked soufflé basics

1 Preheat the oven to 200°C (400°F/Gas 6). Lightly butter six 300 ml (10$^1$/$_2$ fl oz) ramekins. Sprinkle the ramekin bases with caster (superfine) sugar and shake and tilt the ramekins so that the bottoms and sides are covered before tipping out any excess sugar. Separate 7 eggs, discarding 2 egg yolks. Put 5 egg yolks into a metal bowl with 115 g (4 oz/$^1$/$_2$ cup) sugar and whisk until very thick and pale yellow.

2 Put the bowl over a saucepan of simmering water and stir gently until the mixture thickens and becomes quite hot to touch. Remove from the heat and put the bowl into a large basin or sink filled with iced water. Stir the mixture until it cools. Fold in 4 tablespoons passionfruit pulp. In a separate bowl, beat the 7 egg whites until soft peaks form. Add 1 teaspoon cornflour (cornstarch) and beat for a further 1 minute. Fold half the beaten egg whites through the passionfruit mixture until well blended and then lightly fold in the remaining egg whites.

3 Spoon the batter into the prepared ramekins, filling to within 1 cm ($^1$/$_2$ in) of the top. Smooth the top with a spatula, then run your finger around the inside of the rim, making a groove in the soufflé mix. Bake for 5 minutes, then reduce the temperature to 180°C (350°F/Gas 4) and bake for a further 12 minutes, or until the soufflés have risen and the tops are golden brown. Remove from the oven, sprinkle with icing (confectioners') sugar and serve immediately. Serves 6

## hints & tips

● When making soufflés, make sure the oven is hot and ready for baking. It's the combination of the whipped eggs and the hot oven that makes a soufflé light. And remember it's also essential to eat the soufflé as soon as it's baked.

● Since soufflés are highly reliant on the oven temperature, it's a good idea to test the timing of this recipe in your oven before making the soufflés for a dinner party.

● For a classically flavoured soufflé, add 3 tablespoons Grand Marnier and 1 teaspoon finely grated orange zest instead of the passionfruit.

perfect finish to a heavy meal. I love mine flavoured
fruit brings a lovely tang to the sugary cloud.

# cooked dessert essentials

Hot and gooey, pastries leaking caramel juices, baked fruits collapsing under the weight of their warm sweet juices...there's nothing more heartwarming than desserts that come straight from the oven to the table. But don't panic, I'm not talking rolling pins and baking weights. There are many easy options that will give you the flavour bonus from time spent in the oven but that don't involve too much preparation. Here are a few of my favourites:

## apple delicious

- Make a simple apple pudding by putting peeled and cored wedges of green apple into a roasting tin. Rub enough unsalted butter into 150 g (5 1/2 oz/scant 2 cups) fresh breadcrumbs to make them slightly sticky. Sprinkle the breadcrumbs over the apple, drizzle with golden syrup and bake in a preheated 180°C (350°F/Gas 4) oven for about 30 minutes, or until the breadcrumbs are golden brown. Serve with ice cream and a spoonful of golden syrup.

- For the easiest of apple tarts, melt together 100 g (3 1/2 oz) unsalted butter and 115 g (4 oz/1/2 cup) sugar. Put into a bowl with 1 teaspoon ground cinnamon, 2 grated green apples, 1 teaspoon lemon juice and 2 eggs and fold together. Pour into a prebaked tart case and bake in a preheated 180°C (350°F/Gas 4) oven for 30 minutes, or until golden brown.

- For simple apple turnovers, toss thin slices of apple with a little sugar, ground cinnamon and lemon zest. Cut out 12 cm (4 1/2 in) rounds of butter puff pastry and spoon a little of the apple mixture into the centre of each circle. Fold over each pastry circle to form a half moon, then seal the edges. Put the turnovers on a baking tray, sprinkle with sugar and prick the pastry surface with a fork. Bake in a preheated 180°C (350°F/Gas 4) oven for 30 minutes until golden brown. Serve hot.

- Simpler still, cut out rounds of butter puff pastry and put them on a baking tray. Top with finely sliced green apple, a sprinkle of sugar and a dab of butter. Bake in a preheated 180°C (350°F/Gas 4) oven for 15 minutes until golden. Serve with a scoop of vanilla ice cream

## warm summer fruits

- Slice figs in half and sprinkle with finely grated ginger and a little ground cinnamon. Drizzle with maple syrup and bake in a preheated 220°C (425°F/Gas 7) oven for 10 minutes. Serve with vanilla ice cream and almond bread.

- Sprinkle nectarine halves with sugar and cook under a hot grill (broiler) until the sugar has melted. Serve in a pile with pistachio ice cream.

- Poach plums in orange juice with a cinnamon stick or vanilla bean and serve chilled with whipped cream and plain chocolate biscuits. Or, poach nectarines in a light syrup spiced with ground cinnamon and cardamom and star anise and serve with caramel ice cream.

- Poach plums in red wine until just soft. Remove with a slotted spoon and serve with Greek-style yoghurt, a drizzle of honey and cardamom and rosewater syrup (page 355).

- Put halved and stoned peaches on a baking tray. Mix a little softened unsalted butter with finely chopped glacé ginger and soft brown sugar and put a little in the centre of each peach half. Grill (broil) for a few minutes until the butter is bubbling and golden. Serve with vanilla ice cream.

## something exotic

- Simmer rhubarb stalks with sugar to taste (enough to balance the tartness) and serve with cinnamon toast. Or, for a luscious dessert, put roughly chopped rhubarb stalks in an ovenproof dish, toss with soft brown sugar, orange juice, grated orange zest and a split vanilla bean, then cover and bake in a preheated 180°C (350°F/Gas 4) oven for 30 minutes.

- Peel and core 4 quinces, slice them into thick wedges and put them in a roasting tin. Add 250 ml (9 fl oz/1 cup) water, 2 tablespoons butter and 3 tablespoons sugar. Cover the dish with foil and bake in a preheated 150°C (300°F/Gas 2) oven for 3–4 hours. The longer you bake the quinces, the richer their colour will be. You can add a cinnamon stick, vanilla bean or a little grated ginger to the roasting tin for extra flavour. Serve the quinces piled over chocolate brownies with a dollop of cream or with liqueur-tinged mascarpone or simply with vanilla ice cream.

- Stir any extra syrup from baked quinces into thick (double/heavy) cream or custard — it adds a sweet, perfumed tang. Or, make a syrup from the discarded skins by simmering them in a sugar syrup (page 229) with a vanilla bean or cinnamon stick. Strain and use the syrup to poach pears or to pour over a basic sponge or chocolate cake.

- To make a butterscotch sauce, combine 4 tablespoons cream with 70 g (2 1/2 oz/heaped 1/3 cup) soft brown sugar and 1 1/2 tablespoons unsalted butter in a small heavy-based saucepan. Bring to the boil, reduce the heat to a simmer and whisk to combine. Remove from the heat and cool. Pour over puddings, poached fruit or toasted cinnamon brioche for a winter treat.

# sweet and lavish essentials

Every now and then, it's easiest just to head down to the local delicatessen or your favourite speciality shop and pick up a few sweet somethings or a great cheese. After all, the simplest treat, and one of the best desserts in the world, is nothing more than a large block of good-quality chocolate shared amongst friends.

A few soft and flavoursome cheeses and an array of crispbreads and crackers requires but a few moments at the delicatessen counter. Or if you want to spend a little more time, here are a few quick suggestions for serving cheese and fruit simply:

- The richness of quince is perfectly suited to blue cheeses, as well as fresh cheeses such as ricotta. For a dessert that isn't overly sweet, serve thin slices of quince or quince paste with a bowl of ricotta cheese and thin crackers.
- Serve biscotti or almond bread with mascarpone cheese and finely sliced white peaches seasoned with a little ground black pepper.
- Serve a glass of sweet dessert wine or liqueur with a small bowl of mascarpone and biscotti. Dip the biscuits in the sweet wine and then spoon over a little mascarpone.
- Drizzle chocolate brownies with Grand Marnier and top with a scoop of chocolate or vanilla ice cream.
- Offer a selection of figs, pears and purple grapes with cheeses such as creamy rich dolcelatte or a runny brie. Accompany with seeded lavash or crisp crackers and a good dessert wine, then sit back and enjoy.
- Sprinkle finely sliced oranges with ground cinnamon and serve with honey-laced mascarpone cheese and brandy snap biscuits.
- Serve a platter of black pepper-seasoned peaches with a bowl of mascarpone cheese and a pile of almond bread.
- Marinate quarters of fig in Grand Marnier or your favourite liqueur and serve with a scoop of vanilla-bean ice cream.
- Stir quince paste through soft goat's curd with a splash of Grand Marnier. Spoon onto a serving plate and cover with toasted flaked almonds. Serve with fresh whole berries or sliced nectarines.
- Smash up a square of honeycomb and pile the sticky golden shards onto a plate with fresh figs. Split the figs in half, cover with splintered honeycomb and enjoy the sweet crunch and soft flesh.

- Stir mashed honeycomb through mascarpone or thick (double/heavy) cream and serve dolloped over fresh peach slices.
- Serve chewy squares of nougat, flavoured with almonds and citrus zest, with a bowl of strawberries or cherries.
- Finely slice nougat and layer it in parfait glasses with vanilla ice cream. Drizzle with a little melted chocolate or coffee liqueur.
- Offer piles of dusty pink Turkish delight with roasted pistachio nuts, or cut it into tiny squares and serve it tumbled over vanilla ice cream in individual bowls.

## late night indulgences

- As a late night feast or a simple solution to dessert, invest in some pre-made biscuits, confectionery or pastries and add a twist of your own or simply pile a plate with rich indulgence and tempt your friends with a little sweet sin.
- If you want to end the night with a little more fun, then return to your childhood with a midnight feast of everyone's favourite sweets ... honeycomb, nougat, Turkish delight and a big bowl of colourful mixed lollies.
- Middle Eastern pastries are an Arabian Nights adventure for the tastebuds, and though richly sweet, can be cut into small bite-sized pieces. Serve piled onto a platter with tiny cups of rich dark coffee — who could resist such spiced ground nuts, glistening pastry and rosewater-tinged syrup? They are available from speciality Middle Eastern pastry shops.
- Everyone's late-night favourite is affogato. To whip up this coffee with a kick, simply put a small spoonful of vanilla, chocolate or hazelnut ice cream into a glass and add a spoonful of coffee liqueur. Pour espresso coffee over the ice cream and serve with a spoon.

# dessert recipes
## sweet puddings
### berries and whipped cream
## chocolate anything
## crunchy meringues
### wobbly jellies
impress friends and family

and save some for leftovers

## chocolate parfait

125 g (4¹/2 oz/heaped ¹/2 cup) sugar
125 g (4¹/2 oz) dark chocolate, broken into pieces
4 egg yolks
300 ml (10¹/2 fl oz) cream, whipped
1 tablespoon Frangelico
50 g (1³/4 oz/¹/2 cup) toasted flaked almonds
fresh berries and raspberry sauce (page 349), to serve

Line a terrine or loaf tin with baking paper and set aside. Put the sugar and 150 ml (5 fl oz) water in a saucepan and bring to the boil, stirring until the sugar has dissolved. Boil for 3 minutes. Remove from the heat and add the chocolate, stirring until the chocolate has melted and the syrup is smooth.

Whisk the egg yolks in a bowl until they are pale. Slowly pour in the sugar syrup and continue to whisk until the mixture has cooled. Fold in the whipped cream, Frangelico and almonds and pour the mixture into a terrine mould. Cover and put in the freezer overnight.

To serve, turn out the parfait from the terrine or tin and with a large warm knife cut into six thick slices. Serve with fresh berries and raspberry sauce. Serves 6

## berry granita

175 g (6 oz/³/4 cup) caster (superfine) sugar
625 ml (21 fl oz/2¹/2 cups) Earl Grey tea
250 g (9 oz/1²/3 cups) strawberries
juice of 1 orange
150 g (5¹/2 oz/1¹/4 cups) raspberries, to serve

Dissolve the sugar in the hot tea and set aside to cool. In a blender or food processor, blend the strawberries with the orange juice to a purée. Stir the puréed strawberries into the cool tea and pour into a plastic container about 15 x 20 cm (6 x 8 in). Cover and put in the freezer for 2 hours.

Remove from the freezer and use a fork to break up the ice crystals, mixing them back into the chilled liquid. Repeat this process every 40 minutes until you have a container filled with flavoured crushed ice. If freezing overnight, remove from the freezer and allow it to soften for 30 minutes before breaking up the crystals and returning to the freezer. To serve, layer the granita with the raspberries in tall glasses. Serves 4–6

## rhubarb jelly

1 kg (2 lb 4 oz/2 bunches) rhubarb
350 g (12 oz/1¹/2 cups) caster (superfine) sugar
grated zest and juice of 1 orange
1 teaspoon ground cinnamon
300 ml (10¹/2 fl oz) orange juice
8 gelatine leaves

Preheat the oven to 180°C (350°F/Gas 4). Chop the rhubarb into 3 cm (1¹/4 in) lengths and put into a large ovenproof glass or ceramic dish. Add the sugar, orange zest and juice, cinnamon and 500 ml (17 fl oz/2 cups) water. Cover with a lid or aluminium foil and bake for 1 hour. Strain the cooked rhubarb through a fine sieve into a measuring jug. Add enough orange juice to make up to 900 ml (31 fl oz) of liquid.

Soak the gelatine leaves in a bowl of cold water until softened. Meanwhile, lightly oil a jelly mould or glass bowl with vegetable oil or any other flavourless oil, then set aside upturned so that any excess oil will drain out.

Put 250 ml (9 fl oz/1 cup) of the rhubarb liquid into a saucepan and bring almost to the boil. Remove from the heat. Squeeze the softened gelatine leaves to remove any excess water and add them to the hot liquid. Swirl them around until they have completely dissolved, then add the liquid to the remaining rhubarb juice. Stir to combine, then pour the jelly into the mould and refrigerate for 5 hours to chill and set.

To turn out, lightly warm the outside of the mould with a cloth rinsed in hot water, cover with a plate, then turn it over. Give the mould a good shake. It may take a couple of attempts. Delicious with pouring cream or vanilla ice cream. Serves 8

## apple vanilla ice with grapefruit

4 tablespoons sugar
1 vanilla bean, halved lengthways
1 green apple, grated
200 ml (7 fl oz) cloudy apple juice
2 ruby grapefruits, segmented, to serve

Put the sugar, vanilla and 170 ml (5¹/2 fl oz/²/3 cup) water into a saucepan and bring to the boil. Stir until the sugar has dissolved, then reduce the heat and stir in the grated apple. Remove from the heat and allow to cool.

Add the apple juice, stir, and put the mixture into a plastic container. Put in the freezer for 1 hour. Remove and stir the mixture with a fork to break up the ice crystals. Return to the freezer for another 1–2 hours. Before serving, stir again with a fork. Serve with the grapefruit segments. Serves 4

honey-spiced figs

peach and blueberry shortcake

## honey-spiced figs

8 figs
juice and zest of 1 orange
12 small mint leaves, torn
1 tablespoon honey
200 ml (7 fl oz) thick (double/heavy) cream
1/2 teaspoon caster (superfine) sugar
1 tablespoon ground walnuts

Slice the figs and put them, overlapping, onto a serving plate. Pour over the orange juice, then scatter with the orange zest and mint leaves and drizzle with the honey. Set aside. Put the cream, sugar and walnuts into a small bowl, and stir to combine. Serve the cream with the honeyed figs. Serves 4

## peach and blueberry shortcake

60 g (2¼ oz/½ cup) plain (all-purpose) flour
3 tablespoons cornflour (cornstarch)
3 tablespoons soft brown sugar
1/2 teaspoon ground ginger
1/2 teaspoon baking powder
1¹/2 tablespoons unsalted butter, softened
1 egg yolk
150 g (5½ oz) blueberries
2 tablespoons caster (superfine) sugar
2 peaches, peeled and sliced
icing (confectioners') sugar, to serve
thick (double/heavy) cream, to serve

Preheat the oven to 180°C (350°F/Gas 4). Sift the flours, sugar, ginger and baking powder into a bowl, then work in the butter and the egg yolk to form a soft dough. If the dough is too stiff, add a splash of cold water. Roll out the pastry and cut it into four 8 cm (3¼ in) rounds. Put the pastry on a baking tray lined with baking paper. Bake for 12 minutes, or until golden brown. Leave to cool.

Heat a nonstick pan over medium heat and add the blueberries, 2 tablespoons water and the caster sugar. Heat until the sugar has melted and the berries look glossy and their skins start to split. Arrange the shortcakes on four plates with the peaches on top, spoon over the berries and dust with icing sugar. Serve with thick cream. Serves 4

## hazelnut meringue with berries

2 egg whites
115 g (4 oz/1/2 cup) caster (superfine) sugar
4 tablespoons ground hazelnuts
290 ml (10 fl oz) cream
1 teaspoon natural vanilla extract
450 g (1 lb) mixed strawberries, raspberries and blackberries, with the strawberries quartered

Preheat the oven to 150°C (300°F/Gas 2). Whisk the egg whites in a mixing bowl until they form soft peaks, then slowly add the sugar, continuing to beat until the mixture is stiff. Fold in the ground hazelnuts.

Line two baking trays with baking paper and divide the meringue between them, putting a big dollop in the middle of each tray. Using the back of a spoon, spread out the mixture until you have two 20 cm (8 in) circles of meringue. Bake for 40 minutes. Turn off the oven, but leave the meringues in the oven, with the door ajar, for 30 minutes.

Whip the cream and fold in the vanilla. When the meringues are cool, put one of the rounds on a serving plate and top with some of the cream and half the berries, arranging them so that they make a flat surface for the next meringue layer. Put the other meringue on top and decorate with the remaining berries and cream. Allow to sit for 15 minutes before serving. Serves 6

It will come as no surprise to anyone that this dish is an all-time favourite of mine, combining as it does nutty meringue, cream and fresh berries.

hazelnut meringue with berries

## white peach ice cream

3 large white peaches, peeled and stoned
3 tablespoons Cointreau
2 tablespoons lemon juice
1 teaspoon rosewater
4–6 tablespoons caster (superfine) sugar
290 ml (10 fl oz) cream, whipped
50 g (1³/4 oz/¹/2 cup) toasted flaked almonds

Cut the peaches into small cubes and mix them in a bowl with the Cointreau, lemon juice, rosewater and sugar, stirring until the sugar has dissolved.

Gently fold the fruit mixture into the whipped cream, then stir in the almonds. Pour the mixture into a 22 x 8 x 7 cm (8¹/2 x 3¹/4 x 2³/4 in) terrine or mould and freeze it overnight.

Unmould the terrine by dipping it briefly into hot water before turning it out. Serve the ice cream in slices on chilled plates. Serves 6

## chocolate pots

200 g (7 oz) dark chocolate, chopped
300 ml (10¹/2 fl oz) cream
¹/2 teaspoon natural vanilla extract
1 egg
fresh strawberries or almond biscotti, to serve

Put the chocolate and cream in a double boiler or in a saucepan over low heat. Allow the chocolate to melt, stirring occasionally. Add a pinch of salt and the vanilla, then whisk in the egg. Continue to whisk over low heat until smooth.

Pour the mixture into six individual pots and chill for 3 hours. Serve with fresh strawberries or almond biscotti. Serves 6

## chocolate samosas

1 egg yolk
12 wonton wrappers
125 g (4¹/2 oz) milk chocolate, finely chopped
70 g (2¹/2 oz/¹/2 cup) toasted hazelnuts, roughly chopped
2 sugar bananas, sliced
500 ml (17 fl oz/2 cups) vegetable oil
icing (confectioners') sugar, to serve
thick (double/heavy) cream, to serve

Whisk the egg yolk with 2 tablespoons water in a bowl. Lay 12 wonton wrappers on a dry, clean surface and put some chocolate, hazelnuts and banana slices in the centre of each one. Brush the edges of the wonton wrappers with a little of the egg wash and twist the edges together. Put the wontons onto a dry plate, cover and refrigerate until needed.

Heat the oil in a deep-based frying pan or saucepan until it is beginning to shimmer. Put the wontons into the hot oil, a few at a time, and cook until golden. Remove and drain on paper towels. Repeat until all the wontons are cooked. Sprinkle with icing sugar and serve hot with a generous dollop of thick cream. Serves 4

## blackberry fool

300 g (10¹/2 oz/2¹/2 cups) blackberries
3 tablespoons caster (superfine) sugar
2 tablespoons crème de framboise (optional)
1 teaspoon orange flower water
325 ml (11 fl oz) cream, whipped
almond bread or biscotti, to serve

Put the blackberries, sugar, liqueur and orange flower water into a blender or food processor and blend to a purée (if you don't like seeds, sieve the purée at this point).

Fold the puréed berries into the cream and spoon the mixture into four chilled glasses or small bowls. Serve with almond bread or biscotti. Serves 4

figs in sauternes with crème fraîche parfait

strawberries with nutty filo

## figs in sauternes with crème fraîche parfait

12 figs, halved
400 ml (14 fl oz) Sauternes
1 teaspoon honey
5 egg yolks
125 g (4$^1/_2$ oz/heaped $^1/_2$ cup) caster (superfine) sugar
1 teaspoon natural vanilla extract
500 ml (17 fl oz/2 cups) crème fraîche

Put the figs in a bowl and cover with the Sauternes. Drizzle with honey then cover and refrigerate for 12 hours or overnight.

Whisk the egg yolks, sugar and vanilla extract in a large bowl until the mixture is thick and very pale. Gently fold through the crème fraîche, then spoon into an 8 x 22 cm (3$^1/_4$ x 8$^1/_2$ in) tin lined with baking paper. Freeze until firm. Slice the parfait into six thick slices and serve on chilled plates with the halved figs and a spoonful of the Sauternes. Serves 6

## strawberries with nutty filo

4 tablespoons flaked almonds
3 tablespoons pistachio kernels
2 tablespoons honey
1 teaspoon grated lemon zest
1 tablespoon lemon juice
4 sheets filo pastry
2 tablespoons unsalted butter, melted
1 teaspoon ground cinnamon
icing (confectioners') sugar, to serve
250 g (9 oz) strawberries, hulled and halved
cardamom and rosewater syrup (page 355), to serve

Preheat the oven to 180°C (350°F/Gas 4). Finely chop the almonds and pistachios and put them in a small bowl along with the honey, lemon zest and juice. Put a piece of baking paper on a greased baking tray. Lay one of the filo sheets on top, brush the sheet with a little melted butter and then lay another sheet on top. Brush the top sheet with butter and sprinkle on the cinnamon and the nut mixture. Top with two more buttered sheets of pastry. Bake the pastry for 15 minutes, or until it is golden brown.

Remove the pastry from the oven and liberally cover the top with sifted icing sugar, then break it into rough pieces. Divide the strawberries among four plates. Top with the pastry and drizzle with some rosewater syrup. Serves 4

## baked apples

2 small panettone (about 100 g/3$^1/_2$ oz each) or 1 large one
4 large green apples
2 tablespoons soft brown sugar
2 tablespoons unsalted butter
icing (confectioners') sugar, to serve
thick (double/heavy) cream or vanilla custard, to serve

Preheat the oven to 180°C (350°F/Gas 4). Line a baking tray with baking paper. Trim off the rounded top of one of the small panettone and slice the cake into four rounds, or cut four rounds from four slices of a large panettone. Put the rounds on the baking tray and lightly butter them.

Core the apples with an apple corer or a small sharp knife, making sure that you remove all the tough core pieces. Slice and butter the other small panettone, or some of the large one, before tearing it into small pieces. Stuff the panettone pieces into the centre of the apples, alternating the pieces with a little brown sugar. Top with 1 teaspoon brown sugar per apple and a dob of butter. Put one apple onto each panettone round and bake them for 40 minutes.

Serve warm, dusted with icing sugar and accompanied with thick (double/heavy) cream or vanilla custard. Serves 4

This is a baked apple with personality, and no wonder, with its base of sticky sweet panettone.

baked apples

# rhubarb fool

500 g (1 lb 2 oz/1 bunch) rhubarb
2 tablespoons sugar
juice of 2 oranges
90 g (3¼ oz/½ cup) dark brown sugar
300 ml (10½ fl oz) cream, whipped

Trim and rinse the rhubarb before chopping it into 2 cm (³/₄ in) lengths. Put the rhubarb into a saucepan over low heat with the sugar and orange juice. Cover and simmer for about 15 minutes. Remove the pan from the heat and allow the rhubarb to cool.

Spoon a little of the rhubarb into the base of four glass serving bowls. Sprinkle with brown sugar and top with the whipped cream. Spoon another layer of rhubarb over the cream and lightly sprinkle with more brown sugar. Serves 4

# rose-tinged rice pudding

500 ml (17 fl oz/2 cups) milk
3 tablespoons sugar
2 teaspoons finely grated orange zest
70 g (2½ oz/⅓ cup) short-grain rice
125 ml (4 fl oz/½ cup) cream, whipped
1 teaspoon rosewater
150 g (5½ oz/1¼ cups) raspberries, to serve
60 g (2¼ oz/½ cup) chopped raw pistachio nuts, to serve

Bring the milk to the boil in a saucepan with the sugar, orange zest and a pinch of salt. Add the rice, reduce the heat and simmer gently for 30 minutes, stirring occasionally. When the rice has cooked, allow it to cool before folding in the whipped cream and rosewater.

Spoon the rice pudding into serving bowls and top with the raspberries and pistachios. Serves 6

# chocolate marquise

100 g (3½ oz) dark chocolate, chopped
2½ tablespoons unsalted butter, softened
3 tablespoons caster (superfine) sugar
2 tablespoons unsweetened cocoa powder
2 egg yolks
1 teaspoon rosewater
150 ml (5 fl oz) cream
150 g (5½ oz/1¼ cups) raspberries, to serve
6 white nectarines, sliced, to serve
50 g (1¾ oz/½ cup) flaked almonds, toasted, to serve
icing (confectioners') sugar, to serve

Melt the chocolate in a heatproof bowl set over a saucepan of boiling water, making sure the base does not touch the water. Beat the butter with half the sugar in a large bowl until pale and fluffy. Mix in the cocoa. Beat the egg yolks with the remaining sugar in a large bowl until pale and smooth, then add the rosewater. Whip the cream until thick. Mix the melted chocolate into the butter mixture, fold in the egg mixture, then fold in the cream. Spoon into a lined 8 x 22 cm (3¼ x 8½ in) tin and chill for 3 hours, or until set.

Turn out the marquise and cut into thick slices. Serve with raspberries, white nectarines, toasted flaked almonds and a dusting of icing sugar. Serves 4–6

# blood plum and cinnamon jellies

6 blood plums, quartered
225 g (8 oz/1 cup) caster (superfine) sugar
1 cinnamon stick
1 vanilla bean, halved lengthways
juice of 1–2 oranges
6 gelatine leaves
pouring cream, to serve

Put the plums, sugar, cinnamon stick, vanilla bean and 750 ml (26 fl oz/3 cups) water into a saucepan. Bring to the boil, then reduce the heat and simmer for 30 minutes. Remove from the heat and strain the syrup through a very fine sieve or muslin cloth. Pour the syrup into a measuring jug and add enough orange juice to make 600 ml (21 fl oz) plum syrup.

Soak the gelatine leaves in a large bowl of cold water for 10–15 minutes, or until very soft. Return the syrup to the saucepan over low heat, until the syrup is warm. Squeeze any excess liquid from the gelatine, then stir it into the warm syrup. Pour the jelly into six 100 ml (3½ fl oz) moulds and refrigerate for 3 hours or overnight, until set. Serve with a drizzle of cream. Serves 6

baked quinces with orange and cardamom almond bread

winter fruit crumble

# baked quinces

2 large quinces, peeled, cored and quartered
juice of 2 oranges
3 tablespoons sugar
2 tablespoons honey
biscotti or almond bread, dusted with icing (confectioners')
    sugar, to serve
plain yoghurt or thick (double/heavy) cream, to serve

Preheat the oven to 180°C (350°F/Gas 4). Line a baking tray with baking paper and lay the quince pieces on it. Cover them with the orange juice, sugar and honey and another piece of baking paper.

Bake for 1 hour, then reduce the oven temperature to 140°C (275°F/Gas 1) and bake the quinces for a further 2 hours, or until they are soft and have turned a deep ruby red.

Serve the quinces with biscotti or almond bread dusted with icing sugar, with a dollop of yoghurt or thick cream on the side. Serves 4

# winter fruit crumble

500 g (1 lb 2 oz/1 bunch) rhubarb, roughly chopped
juice of 1 orange
6 dried figs, finely sliced
2 green apples, peeled and roughly chopped
3 tablespoons caster (superfine) sugar
60 g (2¼ oz/½ cup) plain (all-purpose) flour
90 g (3¼ oz/½ cup) soft brown sugar
100 g (3½ oz/1 cup) ground almonds
3 tablespoons unsalted butter

Preheat the oven to 180°C (350°F/Gas 4). Toss the rhubarb with the orange juice, figs, apple and caster sugar and put the mixture in an ovenproof dish.

Put the flour, brown sugar and ground almonds in a bowl and then add the butter and rub it into the dry ingredients until the mixture begins to resemble breadcrumbs. Cover the fruit with this mixture and bake for 45 minutes. Serve with cream or vanilla custard. Serves 6

# jaffa mousse

140 g (5 oz) bitter chocolate, chopped
4 tablespoons Grand Marnier
4 egg yolks
4 tablespoons cocoa powder
2 teaspoons grated orange zest
185 ml (6 fl oz/¾ cup) cream, whipped
4 oranges

Melt the chocolate and 2 tablespoons of the Grand Marnier in a bowl set over a saucepan of simmering water. Add the egg yolks, one at a time, stirring each one well into the chocolate mixture before adding the next. The chocolate may begin to stiffen but it will soon become smooth again. When you have added all the yolks, take the chocolate mixture off the heat and cool it a little.

Fold the cocoa and grated orange zest into the whipped cream, then fold the cream into the chocolate. Pour the mixture into a bowl and leave it in the refrigerator for several hours to chill.

Peel the oranges with a sharp knife and cut them into slices. Put the orange slices in a bowl with the remaining Grand Marnier. Divide the oranges among four to six dessert plates and top with a large spoonful of the mousse. Serves 4–6

This jaffa mousse is a long-time favourite but it comes with a warning — it's very rich and very moreish.

jaffa mousse

# glossary

## balsamic vinegar

Balsamic vinegar is a dark, fragrant, sweetish aged vinegar made from grape juice. The production of authentic balsamic vinegar is carefully controlled. Bottles of the real thing are labelled *Aceto Balsamico Tradizionale de Modena*, while commercial varieties simply have *Aceto Balsamico de Modena*.

## betel leaves

This delicate green leaf, also known as wild betel leaf or char plu, is commonly eaten raw in Thai cuisine, where it is often used as a base or a wrapping for the small appetisers known as miang. The leaves are sold in bunches in Thai or Asian speciality shops.

## black sesame seeds

Mainly used in Asian cooking, black sesame seeds add colour, crunch and a distinct nuttiness to whatever dish they garnish. They can be found in most Asian grocery stores. Purchase the seeds regularly, as they can become rancid with age.

## bocconcini cheese

These are small balls of fresh mozzarella, often sold sitting in their own whey. When fresh they are soft and springy to the touch and have a milky taste. They are available from delicatessens.

## brown miso

Brown miso (hatcho miso) is a fermented paste of soya beans, salt and either rice or barley. Miso is used extensively in Japanese cooking, for example, as an ingredient in sauces and pickles, as well as in soups, dressings and stocks. Brown miso has a richer flavour than white miso. It is available from Asian shops and health food stores.

## bulghur wheat

Popular in the Middle East, bulgur is the key ingredient in tabouli and pilaff. Steamed and baked to minimise cooking time, you can buy these wheat kernels either whole or cracked into fine, medium or coarse grains.

## butter puff pastry

This is puff pastry made with butter rather than vegetable fat, which gives it a much more buttery flavour than standard puff. If you can't find any, use ordinary puff pastry and brush it with melted butter to add flavour.

## buttermilk

This low fat dairy product is made from skim milk and milk powder, with a culture similar to yoghurt introduced. It is often used in baking (as a raising agent) and can be found in the refrigerated section of most supermarkets. It has a tart taste.

## cajun spice mix

This is an American spice blend, easily found in ready mixed packages from most supermarkets. The predominant flavours are cumin, cayenne pepper, chilli, mustard and mixed herbs. It is wonderful sprinkled over chicken or lamb, especially when the meats are to be barbecued.

## capers

These are the green buds from a Mediterranean shrub, preserved in brine or salt. Salted capers have a firmer texture and are often smaller than those preserved in brine. Rinse away the brine or salt before using them. Salted capers are available from good delicatessens.

## cardamom

A dried seed pod native to India, cardamom is the third most expensive spice (after saffron and vanilla). The inner seeds when crushed give off a sweet, strong aroma. It is used whole or ground and can be found in the spice section of most supermarkets. Cardamom should be used sparingly, as it has quite a strong flavour.

## chinese black beans

These salted black beans can be found either vacuum-packed or in tins in Asian food stores. Their strong flavour can be used to bring a rich saltiness to stir-fries and sauces for beef dishes.

## chinese black vinegar

This rice vinegar is sharper than white rice varieties and is traditionally used in stir-fries, soups and dipping sauces. The Chinese province of Chekiang has the reputation for producing the best black vinegars.

## chinese five-spice powder

An aromatic mix of ground spices, Chinese five-spice powder is made up from star anise, black pepper, fennel seeds, cassia and cloves. It can be rubbed into the skin of chicken or duck or used sparingly to add an interesting flavour to pork or beef.

## chipotle chillies

Large Jalapeño chillies that have been smoked and dried are known as chipotle chillies. They are available from delicatessens and speciality stores in tins, preserved in a smoky rich sauce or they can be bought in their dried form, but must be reconstituted in warm water prior to use.

## chocolate

Couverture is the best quality chocolate to use. This bittersweet chocolate contains the highest percentage of cocoa butter. Available from good delicatessens and food stores. If you are unable to obtain chocolate of this standard, then it is preferable to use a good quality eating chocolate rather than a cheap cooking chocolate. Cooking chocolates, on the whole, do not have a good flavour and tend to result in an oily rather than buttery texture.

## choy sum

Also known as flowering Chinese cabbage. It has mid-green leaves, tender stems and tiny yellow flowers.

## crème fraîche

A naturally soured cream that is lighter than sour cream, it is available at gourmet food stores and some large supermarkets.

## curry leaves

These are the smallish green aromatic leaves of a tree native to India and Sri Lanka. Curry leaves give a distinctive flavour to south Indian dishes. They are usually either fried and added to the dish or used as a garnish at the end.

## daikon

Daikon, or mooli, is a large white radish. Its flavour varies from mild to surprisingly spicy, depending on the season and variety. Daikon contains an enzyme that aids digestion. It can be freshly grated or slow-cooked in broths, and is available from most large supermarkets or Asian grocery stores. Select firm and shiny vegetables with unscarred skins.

## dried asian fried onions

Crisp-fried shallots or onions are available from most Asian grocery stores and are normally packaged in plastic tubs or bags. They are often used as a flavour enhancer, scattered over rice and savoury dishes.

## dried berries

American dried mixed berries can be found in speciality food stores. All dried berries, and especially cranberries, can bring a wonderful sweet-tart element to cakes and flavoured butters, and when reconstituted can be added to fresh fruit salads. To reconstitute the berries, simply cover with boiling water and allow them to absorb the water until they are completely soft and plump.

## dried green tea noodles

These are dried Japanese wheat-based noodles, which have been flavoured with green tea. They are a beautiful pale green colour, and are perfect for cold noodle salads.

## dried kombu

Actually large sheets of dried kelp, dried kombu is boiled with dried bonito to make dashi. Dried kombu can be bought from speciality Japanese stores or some Asian supermarkets.

## enoki mushrooms

These pale, delicate mushrooms have a long thin stalk and tiny caps. They are very fragile and need only a minimal cooking time. They are bland in flavour but have an interesting texture and appearance, so are ideal for blending with other mushrooms or for using in stir-fries to add an interesting texture.

## feta cheese

Feta is a white cheese made from sheep's milk or goat's milk. The fresh cheese is salted and cut into blocks before being matured in its own whey. It must be kept in the whey or in oil during storage or it will deteriorate quickly. Persian feta is particularly creamy. Feta is available from delicatessens and most supermarkets.

## french beans

This green bean is a very thin variety that is crisp and tender. Also known as string beans, they are sometimes available with yellow, purple or cream pods.

## fresh horseradish

Horseradish is the root of the mustard family — large and white, it has a knobbly brown skin. It is very pungent and has a spicy, hot flavour. It is usually freshly grated as a condiment for roast beef and smoked fish. When commercially produced, horseradish is often blended with cream to give it a smoother texture. Dollop on roast beef or smoked salmon.

## galangal

Although a member of the ginger family, the flavour of galangal is quite different. It is quite perfumed and almost a little like camphor. Its root, though similar to ginger in appearance, is quite fibrous and hard, making it difficult to chop. Galangal is most commonly used in the cuisines of Malaysia and Indonesia and comes into its own in the soups of Thailand. It can be bought fresh or sliced and preserved in brine in bottles from Asian stores.

## goat's curd

This is a soft, fresh cheese made from goat's milk, which has a slightly acidic but mild and creamy flavour.

## gruyère cheese

A firm cow's milk cheese with a smooth texture and natural rind. It has a nutty flavour and melts easily, making it perfect for tarts and gratins.

## haloumi cheese

Haloumi is a semi-firm sheep's milk cheese. It has a rubbery texture which becomes soft and chewy when the cheese is grilled or fried. It is available from delicatessens and most large supermarkets.

## haricot beans

There are many types of beans that belong to the haricot family, including cannellini (kidney-shaped beans) and flageolet (white or pale green beans), and also navy beans, which are famous for their use in baked beans. In Europe and the United States, haricot are also called white beans.

## hijiki

Hijiki is a dried, brown seaweed. Its texture is quite different to that of other seaweeds; rather than being smooth, it is more like slightly thick and chewy twigs. The dried seaweed needs to be soaked before use. It is rich in calcium and is ideal sautéed with deep fried tofu or when used in a Japanese-style salad. It is available from Japanese shops and some supermarkets.

## indian lime pickle

Lime pickle is available from Indian grocery stores or large supermarkets. It is usually served as a side dish in Indian cooking.

## kaffir lime leaves

Also known as makrut, the glossy leaves of this South-East Asian tree impart a wonderful citrusy aroma. Always try and use fresh, rather than dried leaves.

## lavash bread

A Jewish-style bread that is sold fresh as thin unleavened squares or dried in sheets similar to a crispbread.

## marsala

Perhaps Italy's most famous fortified wine, marsala is available in sweet and dry varieties. Often used in desserts such as zabaglione, it is superb with eggs, cream and almonds.

## mascarpone cheese

This heavy, Italian-style set cream is used as a base in many sweet and savoury dishes. It is made from cream rather than milk, so is high in fat. A popular use is in the Italian dessert tiramisu. It is sold at delicatessens and supermarkets.

## mirin

Mirin is a rice wine used in Japanese cooking. It adds sweetness to many sauces and dressings, and is used for marinating and glazing dishes like teriyaki. It is available from Asian grocery stores and most supermarkets.

## miso paste

An important ingredient in Japanese cooking, miso paste is made of fermented soya beans and other flavourings — wheat, rice or barley. It is used as a flavouring and a condiment. *See also* brown miso and white miso.

## mizuna

These tender young salad leaves have a pleasant, peppery flavour.

## mozzarella cheese

Fresh mozzarella can be found in most delicatessens and is identified by its smooth, white appearance and ball-like shape. It is not to be confused with mass-produced mozzarella, which is mostly used as a pizza topping. Mozzarella is usually sold packed in whey.

## mustard seeds

Mustard seeds have a sharp, hot flavour that is tempered by cooking. Both brown and yellow are available, although brown mustard seeds are more common.

## niçoise olives

Niçoise or Ligurian olives are small black olives that are commonly used in salads or scattered over prepared dishes. They are not suitable for stoning and making into pastes.

## nori

Nori is an edible seaweed sold in paper-thin sheets. To concentrate the flavour, lightly roast the shiny side of the sheets over a low flame. Nori sheets are available from most large supermarkets and Asian grocery stores.

## orange flower water

This perfumed distillation of bitter-orange blossoms is mostly used as a flavouring in baked goods and drinks. It is readily available from large supermarkets and delicatessens.

## organic produce

The term organic refers to produce that has been grown within a strictly defined and monitored system of agriculture. It is a system that uses no artificial fertilizers or chemicals and which uses minimal processing or additives during commercial production. The result is food that is much healthier for you and which mostly has a better flavour.

## oyster mushrooms

These beautifully shaped, delicately flaovured mushrooms are commonly a pale greyish brown or white but are also available in pink and yellow colours. They are often referred to as abalone mushrooms. Their flavour is quite sharp when raw and are therefore more suitable to creamy pasta or stir-fried dishes.

## palm sugar

Palm sugar is obtained from the sap of various palm trees and is sold in hard cakes or cylinders and in plastic jars. If it is very hard it will need to be grated. It can be found in Asian grocery stores or large supermarkets. Substitute dark brown sugar when palm sugar is unavailable.

## pancetta

This is the salted belly of pork, somewhat like streaky bacon. It is available from delicatessens and some supermarkets. Pancetta is available either rolled and finely sliced or in large pieces ready to be diced or roughly cut.

## panettone

An aromatic northern Italian yeast bread made with raisins and candied peel, panettone is traditionally eaten at Christmas, when it is found in Italian delicatessens or large supermarkets. They are available in large and small sizes.

## pickled ginger

Japanese pickled ginger is available from most large supermarkets. The thin slivers of young ginger root are pickled in sweet vinegar and turn a distinctive salmon-pink colour in the process. This soft pink colour is often exaggerated to a hot pink colour in commercially produced ginger, which has had food colouring added. The vinegar is an ideal additive to sauces where a sweet, gingery bite is called for.

## pine mushrooms

Also known as matsutake, these Japanese mushrooms are brown in colour and thick and meaty in texture. They are best if cooked simply by sautéeing in butter with a little garlic.

## pink peppercorns

These are not true peppercorns but rather are the aromatic dried red berries from the tree *Schinus molle*. They have an aromatic peppery flavour that is perfect for balancing rich flavours.

## pomegranate molasses

This is a thick syrup made from the reduction of pomegranate juice. It has a bittersweet flavour, which adds a sour bite to many Middle Eastern dishes. It is available from Middle Eastern specialty stores. The closest substitute is sweetened tamarind.

## preserved lemon

These are whole lemons preserved in salt or brine, which turns their rind soft and pliable. Just the rind is used — the pulp should be scraped out and thrown away. It is available from delicatessens.

## prosciutto

Prosciutto is lightly salted, air-dried ham. It is most commonly bought in paper-thin slices, from delicatessens. Parma ham and San Daniele are both types of prosciutto.

## quince paste

Quinces are large, aromatic fruits with a high pectin content. When cooked and reduced, the resulting paste is of a jelly-like consistency and has a rich pink colour. Quince paste can be purchased at most delicatessens.

## raw caster sugar

Also known as superfine sugar, this is a finer form of raw sugar. It's colouring brings a lovely brown tone to the food it is sweetening and a slightly caramel flavour.

## rice paper wrappers

Rice paper wrappers are predominantly used in the cuisines of Vietnam and Thailand. They are made of rice and water paste and come in thin, round or square sheets, which soften when soaked in water. Use to wrap around food. They are available in most large supermarkets or from speciality Asian stores.

## rice wine vinegar

Made from fermented rice, this vinegar comes in clear, red and black versions. If no colour is specified in a recipe, use the clear vinegar. The clear rice wine vinegar is sweeter and milder than its European counterparts or the darker and sharper flavoured Chinese black vinegar.

## ricotta cheese

Ricotta cheese can be bought cut from a wheel or in tubs. The wheel tends to be firmer in consistency and is better for baking. If you only get ricotta in tubs, drain off any excess moisture by letting it sit for a couple of hours in a muslin-lined sieve.

## risoni

Risoni are small rice-shaped pasta. They are ideal for use in soups or salads where their small shape is able to absorb the other flavours of the dish.

## risotto rice

There are three well-known varieties of risotto rice that are widely available today: arborio, a large plump grain that makes a sticky risotto; vialone nano, a shorter grain that produces a loose consistency and maintains more of a bite in the middle; and camaroli, similar in size to vialone nano, but makes a risotto with a good, firm consistency. All varieties are interchangeable, although cooking times may vary by five minutes or so.

## rosewater

The distilled essence of rose petals, rosewater is used in small quantities to impart a perfumed flavour to pastries, fruit salads and sweet puddings. It is available from delicatessens and large supermarkets.

## saffron threads

These are the orange-red stigmas from one species of the crocus plant, and the most expensive spice in the world. Each flower consists of three stigmas, which are hand-picked, then dried — a very labour-intensive process. Saffron should be bought in small quantities and used sparingly — not only due to the cost but as it has a very strong flavour. Beware of inexpensive brands when buying saffron, as cheap, real saffron does not exist!

## sesame oil

Sesame oil is available in two varieties. The darker, more pungent, type is made with roasted sesame seeds and comes from China, while a paler, non-roasted variety is Middle Eastern in origin.

## shiitake mushrooms

These Asian mushrooms have white gills and a brown cap. Meaty in texture, they keep their shape well when cooked. Dried shiitake are often sold as dried Chinese mushrooms.

## shoaxing wine

Shoaxing or shao hsing is a northern provincial town in China, which for centuries has produced a rice wine of the same name. The wine is similar to a fine sherry and is made from glutinous rice. It is often used in braised dishes and sauces.

## sichuan pepper

Made from the dried red berries of the prickly ash tree, which is native to Sichuan in China. The flavour is spicy-hot and leaves a numbing aftertaste, which can linger for some time. Dry-fry and crush the berries for the best flavour. Japanese sancho pepper is a close relative and may be used instead.

## star anise

This is a pretty, star-shaped dried fruit that contains small, oval, brown seeds. Star anise has a flavour similar to that of anise but is more liquorice-like. It is commonly used whole because of its decorative shape.

## sterilizing jars

It's always a good idea to sterilize jars or bottles before filling with food that you may be intending to keep for a while. To do, wash in hot soapy water, boil for 10 minutes in a saucepan large enough to completely submerge the jar, then drain on a clean tea-towel. Dry in 130°C (250°F/Gas 1) oven and then remove and fill while the jars are still hot.

## sumac

Sumac is a peppery, sour spice made from dried and ground sumac berries. The fruit of a shrub found in the northern hemisphere, it is typically used in Middle Eastern cookery. Sumac is available from most large supermarkets and Middle Eastern speciality stores.

## swiss brown mushrooms

These mushrooms have a stronger flavour and texture than the common mushroom. Larger specimens are called portobello mushrooms.

## tahini

This is a thick, creamy paste made from husked and ground white sesame seeds. It is used to give a strong nutty flavour to Middle Eastern salads or sauces. Tahini is available in jars from health food stores and most supermarkets.

## tamarind

Tamarind is the sour pulp of an Asian fruit. It is most commonly available compressed into cakes or refined as tamarind concentrate in jars. Tamarind concentrate is widely available; the pulp can be found in Asian food shops.

## tofu

This white curd is made from soya beans and is a great source of protein. Bland in taste, it takes on the flavour of the other ingredients. Usually sold in blocks, there are several different types of tofu — soft (silken), firm, sheets and deep-fried. Refrigerate fresh tofu covered in water for up to five days, changing the water daily.

## triticale

This grain is a cross between wheat and rye. It is highly nutritious and is often found in mixed breakfast cereals as well as soups and sweet dishes. It can be found in health food stores.

## truffle oil

The truffle is a small fungus that traditionally comes from France and Italy. It is highly prized and quite strong in flavour and aroma. Since they are very expensive and seasonal, another option is to use a few drops of truffle-scented oil, which is often available from delicatessens and speciality food stores.

## umeboshi plums

Despite the name, these are in fact Japanese apricots that have been coloured red and pickled in salt. They have a tangy, salty flavour. They are served with white rice and miso soup as part of the traditional Japanese breakfast, and are also used to flavour sauces and salad dressings. They are available from health food shops and Japanese speciality shops.

## vanilla

The long slim black vanilla bean has a wonderful caramel aroma which synthetic vanillas can never capture. Good quality beans should be soft and not too dry. Store unused vanilla pods in a full jar of caster (superfine) sugar, which will not only help to keep the vanilla fresh but the aroma of the bean will quickly infuse the sugar, making it ideal for use in desserts and baking.

## vine leaves

The large, green leaves of the grapevine are available packed in tins, jars or plastic packs or in brine. They are used in Greek and Middle Eastern cookery to wrap foods for cooking. Vine leaves in brine should be rinsed before use to remove some of the salty flavour. Fresh, young vine leaves can be simmered in water for ten minutes or until soft.

## wakame

Wakame is a seaweed that is most commonly sold in its dried form. It must be soaked in warm water until it softens and is most commonly used in salads and soups. It is available from health food and speciality Japanese stores.

## wasabi

Mostly sold in tubes or in a powdered dried form (mixed to a paste with a little water). It comes from the dark green root of a Japanese aquatic plant and has a very hot flavour. Used to flavour sushi, sashimi or some sauces.

## water chestnuts

The edible tuber of an aquatic plant, the water chestnut is white and adds a delicate, crunchy texture to many South-East Asian dishes. Fresh water chestnuts can be bought at Chinese food stores, or are available whole or sliced in tins.

## white miso

White miso (actually a pale yellow colour) is the fermented paste of soya beans, salt and either rice or barley. It has a sweet, mellow taste and a relatively low salt content. White miso is available from Asian grocery stores and health food stores.

## bibliography

Alexander, Stephanie. *The Cook's Companion*. Penguin Books, 1996.

David, Elizabeth. *Summer Cooking*. Penguin Books, 1955.

Greig, Denise. *The Australian Cook's Dictionary*. New Holland Publishers, 2000.

Grigson, Sophie and Black, William. *Fish*. Headline Book Publishing, 2000.

Hazan, Marcella. *The Essentials of Classic Italian Cooking*. Pan Macmillan Publishers, 1992.

Roden, Claudia. *A New Book of Middle Eastern Food*, Penguin Books, 1986

Roden, Claudia. *Mediterranean Cookery*. BBC Books, 1987.

Sahni, Julie. *Savouring Spices and Herbs*, Morrow, 1996

Solomon, Charmaine. *Encyclopedia of Asian Food*. New Holland Publishers, 2000.

Trang, Corinne. *Authentic Vietnamese Cooking*. Headline Book Publishing, 1999.

Tropp, Barbara. *The Modern Art of Chinese Cooking*, Hearst Books, 1982.

index